# *Illinois*
# CURIOSITIES

Help Us Keep This Guide Up to Date

Every effort has been made by the author and editors to make this guide as accurate and useful as possible. However, many things can change after a guide is published—establishments close, phone numbers change, facilities come under new management, and so on.

We would appreciate hearing from you concerning your experiences with this guide and how you feel it could be improved and kept up to date. While we may not be able to respond to all comments and suggestions, we'll take them to heart, and we'll also make certain to share them with the author. Please send your comments and suggestions to the following address:

GPP
Reader Response/Editorial Department
P.O. Box 480
Guilford, CT 06437

Or you may e-mail us at:
editorial@globepequot.com

Thanks for your input, and happy travels!

Curiosities Series

# *Illinois*
# CURIOSITIES

### Quirky characters, roadside oddities & other offbeat stuff

Richard Moreno

Guilford, Connecticut

The prices, rates, and hours listed in this guidebook were confirmed at press time. We recommend, however, that you call establishments to obtain current information before traveling.

To buy books in quantity for corporate use or incentives, call **(800) 962–0973** or e-mail **premiums@GlobePequot.com.**

Photos by Richard Moreno unless otherwise noted.

Maps by Daniel Lloyd copyright © Morris Book Publishing, LLC
Text design: Bret Kerr
Layout artist: Casey Shain
Project editor: Meredith Dias

Library of Congress Cataloging-in-Publication data

Moreno, Richard.
  Illinois curiosities : quirky characters, roadside oddities, and other offbeat stuff / Richard Moreno.
     p. cm.
  Includes index.
  ISBN 978-0-7627-5861-6
  1. Illinois—Description and travel. 2. Curiosities and wonders—Illinois. 3. Illinois—History, Local. 4. Illinois—Social life and customs. 5. Illinois—Biography. I. Title.
  F541.6.M67 2011
  977.3—dc22

                                                        2010046684

Printed in the United States of America

10 9 8 7 6 5 4 3 2 1

To Pam, who made a great leap of faith
and joined me on this Midwest adventure.

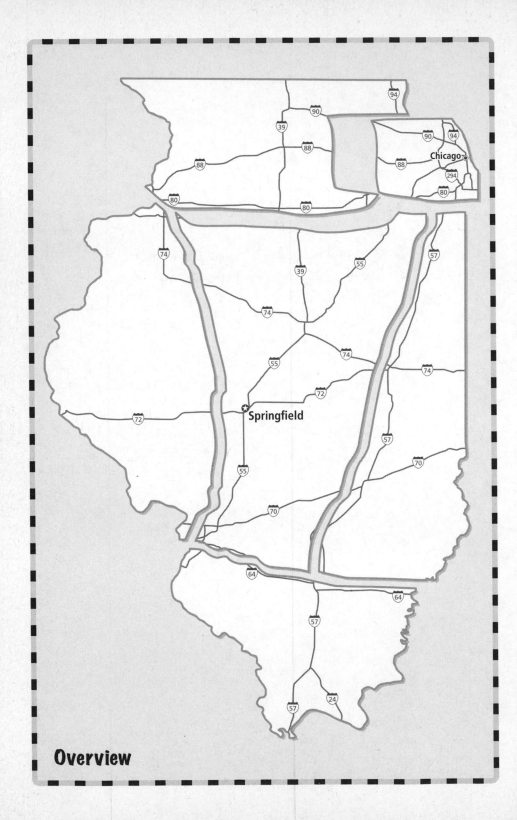

**Overview**

# contents

Introduction    viii

CHAPTER ONE
Chicagoland    1

CHAPTER TWO
Northern    105

CHAPTER THREE
Western    133

CHAPTER FOUR
Central    171

CHAPTER FIVE
Eastern    223

CHAPTER SIX
Southern    253

Index    285

About the Author    293

# introduction

★ ★ ★ ★ ★ ★ ★ ★ ★ ★ ★ ★ ★ ★ ★ ★ ★ ★ ★ ★ ★ ★ ★ ★ ★ ★ ★ ★ ★ ★ ★ ★ ★ ★ ★

**W**hen I relocated from the West to a small college town in rural Illinois a few years ago, I anticipated moving to a place stocked with wholesome people and scenes right out of Norman Rockwell paintings. After all, it was the flag-waving, baseball-loving, apple pie–eating, Chevrolet-driving Midwest. I figured it would have miles of cornfields and soybeans, and perhaps some cows and pigs. In my mind, it was a combination of *Charlotte's Web* (without the talking animals), *Smallville* (without the Boy of Steel and the kryptonite monsters), and *Field of Dreams* (without the dead baseball players). I expected average and ordinary—appropriately, one of Illinois' largest cities is named "Normal"—and predictable and boring.

And while it certainly lived up to some of my preconceptions—there are plenty of cows and pigs and corn and soybeans—I also found it to be far less typical than I expected. I mean Illinois is not only where the corn dog on a stick was invented (in Springfield) but also where the mousetrap was invented (Abingdon). It's the land of both Abe Lincoln and Al Capone. It boasts the first corporate McDonald's franchise restaurant as well as H. H. Holmes's notorious Murder Castle.

In fact, for a state often considered pretty bland and traditional, over the years it has been host to an array of individuals and groups that have embraced religious beliefs and social values that might be considered outside of the mainstream. For example, Erik Jansson, a controversial religious figure in his home country of Sweden, founded the Central Illinois hamlet of Bishop Hill as a utopian, agricultural colony. In 1846, Jansson and several hundred of his followers fled their homeland after repeated clashes with the official Church of Sweden, which did not accept his claims to be a prophet who spoke to God.

Illinois also attracted Mormon Church founder Joseph Smith and his followers, who, in 1839, settled in the remote Western Illinois community of Nauvoo. Smith had tried to put down roots for his Church of Jesus Christ of Latter Day Saints in Ohio and Missouri but was repelled by state and local officials, who viewed his religion as a cult. Similar problems developed in Illinois—particularly in light of the religion's acceptance of polygamy—and, in 1844, Smith was murdered in the town of Carthage.

Almost immediately after the Mormons departed the state for Utah, the Icarians, another religious sect with unconventional ways, moved into Nauvoo and tried to make a go of it. Led by French philosopher Etienne Cabet, the Icarians tried to create a communal society in which no one owned private property and everyone shared equally in what the group produced. Despite numbering more than 500 true believers, the Icarian colony folded after a few years, a victim of infighting between Cabet and his followers.

Even today, there are clusters of Amish and Amish-Mennonites— people who generally eschew modern conveniences like automobiles and electricity—quietly and peacefully existing on communal farms scattered throughout the rural parts of the state.

In the end, I discovered that Illinois isn't quite so run-of-the-mill as I thought but much like the rest of America—ordinary and average, yet strange and weird.

Thank God.

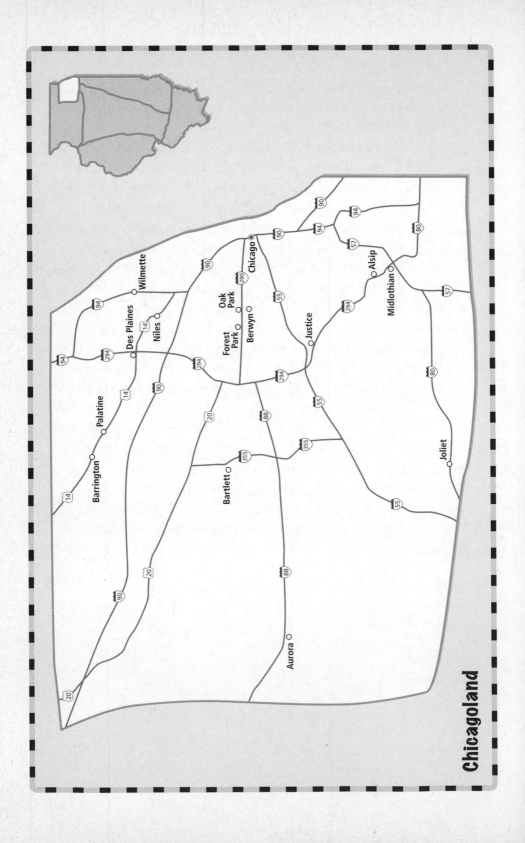

Chicagoland

# 1

# Chicagoland

"It is wonderful to be here in the great state of Chicago."

—Former Vice President Dan Quayle, 1991

**When you get** *down to it, there really are only two places in Illinois: Chicago and all the places that aren't Chicago. People who live outside of the state's largest city, who often feel ignored, sometimes joke that it might be best if Illinois was cut into two states with everything north of I-80 in one state (would it be called Chicagovania?) and everything south in the other (Cornlandia?).*

*Of course, the truth is that Chicago isn't like the rest of the state. It's loud, crowded, ethnic, and urban. Chicago and its neighboring suburbs, often referred to as Chicagoland by the city's media outlets, encompass some three-quarters of the state's population. It's a rarity when any politician not from the Chicago area is elected to statewide office. In fact, disgraced former governor Rod Blagojevich tried so hard to establish his Chicago bona fides that he refused to move from his Chicago home to the Governor's Mansion in Springfield during his stormy tenure in office.*

*Residents of Chicagoland are Windy City–centric. To them, the rest of the state is the hinterlands—a place without good deep-dish pizza or decent Italian beef. Ask a Chicagoan how far it is to Decatur or in what part of the state Charleston is located and you'll likely get a blank stare. Of course a large part of the reason Chicago residents love their city is because of what it has to offer—culture, arts, food, the lake, the Cubs,*

★ ★ ★ ★ ★ ★ ★ ★ ★ ★ ★ ★ ★ ★ ★ ★ ★ ★ ★ ★ ★ ★ ★ ★ ★ ★ ★ ★ ★ ★

da Bears. Ironically, Chicagoans are the first to complain about their city—legendary Chicago newspaper columnist Mike Royko famously wrote: "The subject of criminal rehabilitation was debated recently in City Hall. It's an appropriate place for this kind of discussion because the city has always employed so many ex-cons and future cons." But they are also the first to defend their city when it comes under attack from any outsiders. In 2009, when Chicago unexpectedly lost its bid to host the 2016 Summer Olympics, the Chicago Tribune editorialized: "Chicago would have staged great games and thrown a terrific party for the world. It was not to be. C'est la vie, as they say in Paris, a world-class city that was favored four years ago to win an Olympic Games, but didn't. Paris, by the way, is still a world-class city."

Maybe the best way to think of Chicago is to listen to another native son, writer Nelson Algren, who wrote, "Loving Chicago is like loving a woman with a broken nose."

Yeah, but she's a damned fine woman.

★ ★ ★ ★ ★ ★ ★ ★ ★ ★ ★ ★ ★ ★ ★ ★ ★ ★ ★ ★ ★ ★ ★ ★ ★ ★ ★ ★ ★ ★ ★

## The Sad Tale of the Burr Oak Cemetery
### Alsip

In July 2009, the venerable Burr Oak Cemetery, long one of Chicago-land's most historic predominately black cemeteries, was rocked by a startling discovery—some of its employees were allegedly digging up and dumping bodies from older graves, and then reselling the plots. In some cases the employees were said to be double-stacking the dead, burying the recently deceased atop older bodies.

The story, which National Public Radio described as "a grisly con-spiracy," horrified Chicagoans, many of whom flocked to the cem-etery to find out if the graves of their loved ones had been defiled. Cook County sheriff Tom Dart declared the entire cemetery a crime scene, closed it, and launched an investigation that turned up at least 300 instances where the workers dug up graves, removed the bodies, and resold the plots. By August, four people had been indicted for the scheme, including the former cemetery manager, but no trial date had been set.

The scandal generated considerable interest because of the impor-tance the cemetery has had in Chicago history. Located in the village of Alsip, a half-hour drive south of Chicago, the cemetery was for many years the only place where black Chicagoans could be buried.

Established in 1927, the cemetery's dead include a veritable who's who of prominent black figures, such as former world heavyweight champion Ezzard Charles, as well as famed Chicago blues artists, such as Willie Dixon. Additionally, it is the final resting place of fourteen-year-old Chicagoan Emmett Till, who, in 1955, was kid-napped and murdered in Mississippi after allegedly whistling at a white woman. His death served as an important catalyst for the civil rights movement.

In January 2010, a Cook County Sheriff's study was released that indicated between 140,190 and 147,568 bodies are buried at the 150-acre Burr Oak, while the maximum number it should hold is 138,000. The study also suggested that the practice of stacking

★ ★ ★ ★ ★ ★ ★ ★ ★ ★ ★ ★ ★ ★ ★ ★ ★ ★ ★ ★ ★ ★ ★ ★ ★ ★ ★ ★ ★ ★ ★ ★

caskets on top of each other and discarding remains might have been more common at the cemetery than anyone had suspected. "No one had their arms around how bad this problem was," noted Sheriff Dart.

As a result of the scandal, the company that owns the cemetery, Perpetua, Inc., filed for Chapter 11 bankruptcy. A court-appointed guardian is overseeing the property while it is sold.

Good luck with that.

The Burr Oak Cemetery is located at 4400 127th Street in Alsip. For more information call (773) 233-5676 or go to www.burroakalsip.com.

**The entrance to the notorious Burr Oak Cemetery in the Chicago suburb of Alsip**

★ ★ ★ ★ ★ ★ ★ ★ ★ ★ ★ ★ ★ ★ ★ ★ ★ ★ ★ ★ ★ ★ ★ ★ ★ ★ ★ ★ ★

## Not Just Another Roadside Attraction
Balaji Temple
Aurora

Travelers on I-88, heading east to Chicago, often do a double take when they reach the outskirts of the western suburb of Aurora and see an ornate, multitowered white Hindu temple sitting nearly adjacent to the highway. The elegant temple seems a bit out of place in a landscape dominated by industrial parks, shopping malls, and office buildings.

Known as the Balaji Temple or, by its formal name, Sri Venkateswara Swami Temple of Greater Chicago, the structure is a visually pleasing blend of traditional Indian design with modern American

The $3 million Balaji Temple in Aurora

construction. The facility was constructed in the late 1980s on twenty acres of rural farmland donated by nine Indian families who wanted a Balaji temple for the region. At the time it was built, the Balaji Temple was one of the largest Hindu places of worship in the country.

According to the *Chicago Sun-Times*, the $3 million temple, which is open to visitors, was modeled after one in Tirupati, India, and was the first in the Midwest devoted to Balaji, the modern incarnation of Vishnu, one of the three chief Hindu deities. Prior to the temple's opening, Chicagoans wanting to worship in a shrine to Balaji had to travel 400 miles to Pittsburgh to find anything similar. The *Sun-Times* noted that eighteen artisans were brought over from India to work on the temple's construction, which took several years.

A key aspect in the temple's design, according to the temple website, is that worshipers can easily circulate through its interior, not only around the presiding deity but also around the other eight major shrines erected inside the temple, which can accommodate more than 500 people at a time.

The temple, located at 1145 W. Sullivan Road in Aurora, has seven external towers, ranging in size from 35 to 45 feet. Additionally, several of the outer walls are carved with elaborate designs and bas-reliefs of Hindu symbols, including a ceremonial elephant near the front entrance.

In other words, not your typical suburban sight.

### The Real Road to Perdition?
Barrington

In the daytime, Cuba Road in Barrington doesn't look like much more than a two-lane asphalt road winding through one of the seemingly endless suburbs of Chicago. However, when the shadows begin to lengthen, Cuba Road takes on a very different vibe, particularly in the vicinity of the small but apparently otherworldly White Cemetery.

Over the years, there have been sightings of mysterious glowing white orbs floating over the cemetery's tombstones as well as ghostly

★ ★ ★ ★ ★ ★ ★ ★ ★ ★ ★ ★ ★ ★ ★ ★ ★ ★ ★ ★ ★ ★ ★ ★ ★ ★ ★ ★ ★ ★ ★ ★ ★ ★ ★

The historic White Memorial Cemetery in Barrington, said to be one of Chicagoland's most haunted sites

figures drifting through the graves. Drivers passing the cemetery on Cuba Road have also reported encountering a black vehicle that seemingly appears and disappears. Then there are the tales of an old woman with a lantern who tries to gain the attention of passing cars and of a house that seems to be there and suddenly not there.

No one is certain why there are so many vivid ghost stories associated with Cuba Road and the White Cemetery. In *Haunted Places: The National Directory*, author Dennis Hauck provided no explanation for the phenomena but reported, "eerie glowing globes have been seen hovering in this 1820s cemetery. The lights float near the fence and sometimes over the road surface."

As for the mysterious vanishing house, in her book, *More Chicago Haunts*, author Ursula Bielski ties the disappearing dwelling to the old woman with the lantern: "Cuba Road's so-called ghost house has at least one occupant, according to eyewitnesses who have seen her: an old woman who wanders the road outside the spot where the house has been seen." She also reported sightings of a phantom couple, said to have been sighted strolling hand-in-hand along the roadway before vanishing.

A visit to the cemetery in the safety of daylight reveals a neat, shaded, well-maintained graveyard fronted by a tall, black metal fence. Strolling through the headstones, a visitor will find not only several dating back to the nineteenth century but many that are more contemporary, indicating this is not an abandoned or forgotten cemetery but rather one that remains in use.

But in use by whom or what?

The White Cemetery sits on Cuba Road, west of North Hough Road, in Barrington.

## A Marvel in Marble
Bartlett

When it comes to houses of worship, few are as impressive as the $30 million BAPS Shri Swaminarayan Mandir in the west Chicago suburb of Bartlett. Located on thirty acres, the temple is made of hand-carved Turkish limestone and Italian Carrara marble.

According to the *Daily Herald*, a suburban Chicago newspaper, the temple, which was completed in 2004, was handmade by more than 2,000 craftsmen in India, who worked for more than twenty-two months. The paper noted that the men carving the designs were paid about $1.50 per day while the women, who polished the stone, received $1 per day, standard wages for such work in India.

The finished pieces—there were about 40,000 of them—were shipped and trucked to Bartlett, where they were assembled stone by stone, like a giant 3D jigsaw puzzle, with the help of 1,700 volunteers over sixteen months.

**The $30 million BAPS Shri Swaminarayan Mandir in Bartlett**

The Mandir (which is Sanskrit for a place of worship) isn't quite like anything else in North America. For example, it contains 36,131 cubic feet of limestone for the exterior walls and 31,000 square feet of imported marble for the interior. It has 22,442 square feet of space and stands 78 feet high.

The temple boasts a 22-foot central dome as well as five Shikhars or pinnacles and sixteen smaller domes. The exterior, however, isn't the only thing noteworthy about the building. Inside, ceilings are carved with incredibly intricate, traditional designs. The Pillars of Divinity include

★ ★ ★ ★ ★ ★ ★ ★ ★ ★ ★ ★ ★ ★ ★ ★ ★ ★ ★ ★ ★ ★ ★ ★ ★ ★ ★ ★ ★

more than 150 stone supports covered with detailed carvings of various deities. Amazingly, no iron or steel was used in the construction—in keeping with traditional Indian architecture. Adjacent to the temple is Shri Swaminarayan Haveli, a 16,000-square-foot cultural center that houses a large prayer hall, function hall, dining facilities, and offices.

While the temple is open to the public—remember to remove your shoes upon entering—unfortunately no photography or filming is allowed inside, which means your friends are just going to have to trust you when you describe just how amazing the place is.

BAPS Shri Swaminarayan Mandir can be found at 4N739 IL 59 in Bartlett. For more information, go to www.chicago.baps.org.

## Washing Machine World
Berwyn

There's nothing quiet about the "World's Largest Laundromat" in Berwyn. That hyperbolic claim, "World's Largest Laundromat," is the actual name of the place. The 13,500-square-foot facility, which is open twenty-four hours, has 153 washers and 148 dryers in nearly constant use. There are also fifteen giant, flat screen TVs, a wall of video game consoles and, for good measure, a bird sanctuary filled with chirping miniature doves. This is not a place to catch a nap.

Owner Tom Benson, who has owned the business since 1999, was forced to rebuild the massive launderette in 2005 and 2006 following a fire started by a spark from a dryer. When he plowed his insurance money back into the business, he decided to make the Laundromat more customer-friendly as well as more environmentally sound.

So, not only is it the world's largest Laundromat, but it's also the largest solar-powered one in the country. Benson told *USA Today* that by converting from natural gas to solar power he saves about $25,000 per year in energy costs. The rooftop solar system consists of thirty-six 10-by-4-foot panels that produce more than 2,400 gallons of hot water daily at an average temperature of 120 degrees.

**The World's Largest Laundromat in Berwyn**

Additionally, Benson installed microwave ovens for customer use as well as free wi-fi for computers, banks of vending machines selling everything from snacks to ice cream, and cafeteria-style booth seating. The Laundromat also offers free coffee all day, free doughnuts in the mornings, and free pizza from 5 p.m. to 7 p.m. on Wednesday.

Wandering through the cavernous place, it's difficult not to be overwhelmed by the rows of churning washing machines and spinning dryers. It's remarkably clean for such a busy Laundromat. The online review site, yelp.com, had overwhelmingly positive comments about the business, with one reviewer enthusing: "Pretty much a laundry Disneyland! Take a date!"

You can't get much higher praise than that.

The World's Largest Laundromat is located at 6246 Cermak Road in Berwyn. For more information, go to www.worldslargestlaundry.com.

★ ★ ★ ★ ★ ★ ★ ★ ★ ★ ★ ★ ★ ★ ★ ★ ★ ★ ★ ★ ★ ★ ★ ★ ★ ★ ★ ★ ★

### The Goat's Revenge

Billy Goat Tavern
Chicago

There are certainly more inviting places to eat in Chicago than the legendary Billy Goat Tavern. Tucked into the lower level of Michigan Avenue in downtown Chicago—patrons must climb down a flight of stairs to find it—the Billy Goat Tavern is dingy and dark yet funky and fun.

The business traces its beginnings to 1934, when William "Billy Goat" Sianis purchased the Lincoln Tavern located near Chicago Stadium (now the site of the United Center). According to local lore, Sianis became known as "Billy Goat" when a goat fell off a passing truck and wandered into his bar. He adopted the animal, grew a goatee, and changed the name of his joint to the Billy Goat Tavern.

In 1964, Sianis relocated to the present subterranean locale and in recent years, the company has expanded to other locations on Washington Street, Wells Street, and Madison Street, at Navy Pier and O'Hare Airport, and even in Washington, D.C.

The Billy Goat Tavern owes much of its fame to comedian John Belushi, who famously spoofed it in the 1970s on *Saturday Night Live* with his "Cheezborger! Cheezborger! No Pepsi, Coke!" skit. The bit was inspired by the lively banter between Sianis and Bill Charuchas, a fellow Greek immigrant, who worked at the tavern. The two often prompted customers with "Try the double cheese! It's the best! No

*Trivia*

In 2003, the Illinois General Assembly approved an official state snack food: popcorn.

**Exterior of the Billy Goat Tavern in downtown Chicago**

fries, cheeps!" While Billy Sianis is gone (he passed away in 1970), his nephew, Sam Sianis, continues the tradition.

The Billy Goat is also famous for what Chicago Cubs fans call "the Curse." According to news accounts, Billy Sianis had a pet goat named Murphy that he decided to bring to Game 4 of the 1945 World Series between the Cubs and the Detroit Tigers, which was held at Chicago's Wrigley Field. His plan was to hang a sign around the goat's neck that said, I'VE GOT DETROIT'S GOAT. Sianis bought a ticket for the goat but when he arrived at the ballpark he was told no animals were allowed inside. According to legend, the upset Sianis threw up his hands and declared, "The Cubs ain't gonna win no more! The Cubs will never win a World Series so long as the goat is not allowed in Wrigley Field!"

★ ★ ★ ★ ★ ★ ★ ★ ★ ★ ★ ★ ★ ★ ★ ★ ★ ★ ★ ★ ★ ★ ★ ★ ★ ★ ★ ★ ★ ★ ★ ★

**Trivia**

It's said that on St. Patrick's Day, everyone is Irish. In Chicago, that rampant Hibernian-ism applies to the Chicago River, which, since 1961, has been dyed green to commemorate the Irish saint's holiday.

The curse seemed to stick because the Cubs lost the game that day and were swept at home, losing the series. For the next two decades, the team finished in fifth place or lower. Since 1945, the Cubs haven't appeared in a World Series. In fact, they haven't won since 1908, the longest drought of any major league baseball team.

So the next time you're shopping on Michigan Avenue, head down to the Goat Tavern and grab a "cheezborger."

Just don't ask for fries.

Billy Goat Tavern Original is located at 430 North Michigan Avenue at Lower Level in Chicago. For more information go to www.billygoat tavern.com.

## Millennium Park's Big, Shiny Legume

Chicago

As with anything that is a bit different, the Chicago public sculpture, officially known as *Cloud Gate* and unofficially as "the Millennium Park Bean," was not instantly embraced. Some objected to the price tag, estimated to be $23 million, although all the funding came from private sources. Others thought it looked funny or weird or didn't fit in with the rest of downtown.

But a peculiar thing happened when people finally saw the "Bean." They liked it. In fact, despite creator Anish Kapoor's objections, the sculpture was unofficially unveiled to the public in July 2004, even though it was not finished. The plan was to show it briefly during the grand opening of the surrounding 24.5-acre Millennium Park, then cover it up again and finish polishing its surface to a perfect shine. The public response, however, was so overwhelmingly positive that it was left on display for a while.

In January 2005, the "Bean" was again covered, this time by a large tent. For the next eight months, a twenty-four-person crew from Ironworkers Local 63 polished the seams between the 168 individual stainless steel panels so that the entire surface would be smooth and reflective. The work was formally unveiled in May 2006.

So what is *Cloud Gate*? It's a 66-foot-long, 33-foot-high elliptical-shaped sculpture of seamless, highly polished stainless steel plates

*Cloud Gate*, also known as the Millennium Park Bean, is located in Chicago's Millennium Park.

that was inspired by liquid mercury. The mirror-like surface reflects the Chicago skyline and the clouds passing overhead. A 12-foot-high archway on the bottom of the 110-ton creation leads into a concave chamber where you can touch the surface and catch your reflection.

Kapoor said that he wanted to make something that would interact with the sky and the city skyline. He said that the chamber beneath the gate makes the viewer a participant in the work by reflecting back his or her image in the same way the exterior reflects the surrounding skyline.

*Cloud Gate* can be found in Chicago's Millennium Park. For more information, go to www.millenniumpark.org.

## A Bloody Valentine's Day Present
Chicago

The year was 1929 and trouble was brewing between the Al Capone Italian gang on Chicago's South Side and George "Bugs" Moran's Irish gang from the North Side. For years, the two groups had wrestled for control of Chicago's lucrative bootlegging business and other profitable but illegal activities. Additionally, many believe Moran had been responsible for an earlier, unsuccessful attempt on Capone's life as well as for the murders of several of Capone's close associates.

Moran, on the other hand, probably felt justified in wiping out a few members of Capone's gang because Capone's men had gunned down Dean O'Banion, his mentor and predecessor as boss of the North Side crew.

Several later accounts claim that the plan was to lure Moran and his men into the SMC Cartage garage and warehouse on Clark Street—perhaps with the promise of a shipment of discounted bootleg whiskey—and then ambush them.

On February 14, 1929, five members of Moran's gang, along with a "hanger-on" named Reinhart Schwimmer, entered the garage to wait for the shipment. Already on the scene was John May, a mechanic working on a car. Moran, however, was running late.

**Now a parking lot, this site was where the infamous Valentine's Day Massacre took place in 1929.**

Apparently, lookouts mistook one of the gang members for Moran and gave the sign for the shooters to move in. Two men dressed as cops climbed out of a phony police car carrying shotguns and entered the garage through a rear door. They indicated that all seven men should line up facing a back wall. Moran's men did not appear to resist, perhaps believing they were being rousted by real police.

The faux officers allowed the other two men, both with Thompson submachine guns, into the garage via a front door on Clark Street. Then, the four opened fire on the seven men lined up against the wall. A coroner's report indicated that seventy machine-gun bullets and two shotgun blasts were fired into the men.

★ ★ ★ ★ ★ ★ ★ ★ ★ ★ ★ ★ ★ ★ ★ ★ ★ ★ ★ ★ ★ ★ ★ ★ ★ ★ ★ ★ ★ ★

The SMC Cartage garage stood as a reminder of the heinous crime committed within its bullet-ridden brick walls until 1967, when then–Chicago mayor Richard J. Daley ordered it demolished as part of an effort to clean up his city's reputation by wiping away any places or crime scenes associated with the Mob. The site is now a parking lot for a senior citizen home.

The site of the Valentine's Day Massacre is at 2122 North Clark Street in Chicago.

## So You Want to See Oprah?

Harpo Studios
Chicago

Without a doubt, the biggest star in Chicago is Oprah Winfrey. Host of a wildly popular syndicated talk show, Oprah—most folks refer to her by her first name—is not only one of the richest people in the world with a net worth of more than $2.3 billion, but also among the most influential. Today Oprah's talk show is seen by more than thirty million people a week. She also created the enormously popular "Oprah's Book Club" that has been responsible for boosting the sales of any book mentioned on her show.

Despite her rise to international prominence, Oprah has maintained a residence in Chicago, where she also tapes her programs. Her company, Harpo (her name backward) Studios, is headquartered in Chicago's West Loop neighborhood. Obtaining tickets for her show, however, is not easy.

Her official website notes that demand for tickets far exceeds the supply, so her company has created a reservation lottery system. To have a chance at a ticket you must:

1. Become a member of her official website, Oprah.com.
2. Submit your reservation request during the reservation window period. This means checking the Current Reservation Availability section of the website, which lists the next available time period when tickets will be available (usually at least a month in advance).

(Continued on page 21)

Oprah Winfrey's Harpo Studios in
Chicago's West Loop neighborhood

# The Walls Have Ears ... and Eyes ... and Mouths

There's little doubt that Crown Fountain in downtown Chicago's Millennium Park is one of the coolest things to ever spout water in the Windy City. Completed in 2004, the fountain consists of two 50-foot-high glass-brick towers that bookend a shallow, 232-foot-long black granite reflecting pool. The towers, stationed at opposite ends of the pool, use more than a million light-emitting diodes (LEDs) to display giant digital video images of human faces or scenes. From May to October, a stream of water gushes from the location of the digital mouths of the two towers. The fountain is intended to be interactive—so it's not uncommon to see children as well as adults frolicking in the water, particularly during the hot summer.

Crown Fountain in Chicago's Millennium Park

While some art critics complained about the design and concept of the fountain when it was unveiled, over time Crown Fountain has become a beloved city landmark. The harshest attack on the fountain came in 2006 after the city of Chicago installed surveillance cameras atop the two towers. The action triggered a public outcry and the cameras were quickly removed. Apparently, Chicagoans don't mind a fountain that can keep its eyes on you—just not too much.

The Crown Fountain is located in Chicago's Millennium Park. For more information, go to www.millenniumpark.org.

(Continued from page 18)

3. Submit your request at any time within the reservation window. A random selection process will be used to fill the seats. All requests have the same chance of being selected.

4. Within twenty-four hours after the window has closed, you will receive an e-mail informing you of your request status. If you have been selected, you will need to confirm your reservation within forty-eight hours. If you were not selected, you can try again in the next reservation window.

If you do all of the above, perhaps you'll be in the audience on the day when Oprah gives something else cool away—like maybe a copy of this book. Please note that Oprah's talk show will go off the air in September 2011—so you might want to catch the program before it's too late.

Harpo Studios is at 1058 West Washington in Chicago. For additional information, check out www.oprah.com.

## What's the Big Deal about Chicago-Style Pizza?
Pizzeria Uno
Chicago

In much of the country, pizza is made of dough stretched thin and made round, and then covered with a tomato-based sauce as well as cheese and various chopped up meats and vegetables. Chicago-style pizza, also known as deep-dish pizza, is pretty much the same thing—except for that thin part.

Chicagoans love thick pizza. Unlike the wafer-thin sheets of crispy dough covered with sauce and cheese that define pizza in other parts of the country, Chicago pizza is hearty and filling fare.

It usually has a cornmeal and olive oil crust that stands as much as 3 inches at the edges, then a layer of meats or vegetables (sometimes a whole patty of Italian sausage), which is covered by slices of mozzarella cheese. Atop that is a sauce made of seasoned, crushed or pureed tomatoes, which is garnished with a grated cheese blend.

The pie is served after being baked at a high temperature for about twenty minutes. Deep-dish pizza is generally eaten using a fork and a knife since it's too gooey and thick to pick up with your hands.

There's some disagreement regarding who invented this culinary concoction. While everyone agrees that Italian immigrants brought pizza to Chicago in the late nineteenth century, its evolution from round pies of bread covered with tomato, spices, and cheese to the hefty wedge known as Chicago-style pizza is less certain.

Most historians credit Pizzeria Uno in downtown Chicago as being the birthplace of the original Chicago-style pizza in 1943. But the identity of the actual creator of the dish remains shrouded in controversy. Part of the problem is there is no clear paper trail and conflicting claims of fatherhood. Pizzeria Uno was founded by Richard Novaretti, known as Ric Riccardo, and Ike Sewell, both gifted self-promoters. Another partner in the business was Rudy Malnati Sr., who some claim was instrumental in developing the recipe.

According to historian Tim Samuelson, it is most likely that the concept for deep-dish pizza either developed over time or was a collaboration of several people. He told the *Chicago Tribune* in 2009 that most credit Riccardo with coming up with the idea and Sewell for making it famous.

Regardless of its origins, it is true that deep-dish pizza quickly took off in Chicago. In 1954, the original Gino's Pizza opened on Rush

## Trivia

Chicago is home of the largest Polish community outside of Poland. It's estimated that one out of every ten Chicagoans (a city of about 2.8 million) can claim Polish ancestry.

Above, a slice of Chicago-style deep-dish pepperoni pizza; left, Pizzeria Uno in downtown Chicago, where deep-dish pizza was born

★ ★ ★ ★ ★ ★ ★ ★ ★ ★ ★ ★ ★ ★ ★ ★ ★ ★ ★ ★ ★ ★ ★ ★ ★ ★ ★ ★

Street, followed by Pizzeria Due (also owned by Sewell) a year later. In the 1960s, Gino's East opened at 160 East Superior Street, and, in 1971, Lou Malnati's Pizzeria (owned by the son of Rudy Malnati Sr.) opened in the suburb of Lincolnwood. A few years later, Nancy's Pizza and Giordano's Pizza opened, both of which introduced a variation of deep-dish pizza, the stuffed pizza (an even thicker version). Nearly all of these restaurants have expanded to multiple locations throughout the Chicagoland area.

So, is Chicago-style pizza worthy of all the hype? I'll let you know after just one more bite.

The original Pizzeria Uno is located at 29 East Ohio in Chicago. For reservations or to order a pizza, call (312) 321-1000 or go to www.unos.com.

## Tsavo's Man-eaters
Field Museum
Chicago

There is something strange about the lions in the Kenyan region of Tsavo. For one thing, the fully grown males don't have big, full manes like other African lions. Additionally, for a period of time in 1898, a pair of Tsavo lions acquired a taste for something that most lions tend to shun—human flesh.

The tale of the man-eating Tsavo lions began in March of 1898 when Indian workers erecting a railway bridge over the Tsavo River started being attacked by two lions. The British, who controlled Kenya at the time, had brought the workers to Africa to help build the Kenya-Uganda Railway. During the next nine months, the two big cats killed and ate as many as seventy-two workers—with some claiming nearly double that many were attacked and consumed.

Lt. Col. John Henry Patterson, who supervised the construction, set traps and attempted to ambush the lions—even sitting in a tree all night with his rifle—but the killing continued. Finally, on December 9, 1898, he managed to shoot one of the big cats. In his later published

★ ★ ★ ★ ★ ★ ★ ★ ★ ★ ★ ★ ★ ★ ★ ★ ★ ★ ★ ★ ★ ★ ★ ★ ★ ★ ★ ★ ★ ★ ★

account, which became the basis for the 1996 film, *The Ghost and the Darkness*, Patterson said he initially wounded the lion in the hindquarters but it escaped. He claimed that as he continued to hunt the animal into the night, it, in turn, began stalking him. He shot it several more times but wasn't certain it was dead until he found the body the next morning. It had taken five shots to finish the job.

Three weeks after killing the first lion, he managed to track down the other one. In his account, Patterson said he shot the beast five times and, despite having a shattered leg, it continued to charge him and chased him up a tree. After the animal limped off, he came down from the tree only to have the cat charge him again. He fired two more shots, hitting it in the chest and in the head. The last bullet finally stopped it in its tracks.

Patterson took the remains of the two lions and made them into trophy rugs. In 1924, when he came to lecture at Chicago's Field Museum, Patterson agreed to sell the hides and skeletons to the museum, which reconstructed them as lifelike models and put them on display.

New research has revealed several things about the two Tsavo lions: They didn't eat as many people as claimed by John Patterson (they ate somewhere between thirty-five and seventy-two), and it's thought they may have acquired their taste for people after digging up the bodies of dead or dying slaves dumped by ruthless slave traders on the Tsavo caravan route, or because one of them had a severe tooth abscess, which would have made relatively soft humans an easier thing to eat.

As for the lack of a mane, again researchers have several explanations. One is that Tsavo lions live in an extremely dry climate so they've evolved to have less hair, which keeps them cooler. Another theory is that their manes are torn off by the many thorn-bushes that proliferate in the region.

But regardless of how many they killed, the legend of the man-eating cats remains a compelling one that helps to make them one

★ ★ ★ ★ ★ ★ ★ ★ ★ ★ ★ ★ ★ ★ ★ ★ ★ ★ ★ ★ ★ ★ ★ ★ ★ ★ ★ ★

**Mounted skins of two of the man-eating lions of Tsavo**

of the most popular attractions in the Field Museum. In fact, the two mounted lions don't seem so dangerous when you look at them posed behind a large glass panel. They seem almost friendly, like a pair of big kitties. Just don't get too close.

The Field Museum is located at 1400 South Lake Shore Drive in Chicago. For additional information, go to www.fieldmuseum.org.

# A Whole Meal in a Bun

Another Chicago invention is the Chicago-style hot dog. While it has a lot of similarities with hot dogs found everywhere else—like having a dog and a bun—it's the mountain of toppings that make it different. According to many food historians, the Chicago-style hot dog was invented in 1929 at a food stand on Maxwell Street known as Fluky's. Originally known as the "Depression Sandwich," it sold for a nickel and allegedly was created when the neighborhood's Italian and Greek vendors competed to see who could provide the most sandwich for the money.

While the hot dog, basically a sausage wrapped in bread, was introduced to Chicago during the 1893 World's Columbian Exposition, the Chicago-style dog is an entirely different creature. Generally, it includes a boiled or steamed all-beef frankfurter on a poppy-seed bun that's topped with mustard, green relish, chopped onions, tomato wedges, a pickle spear, hot or sweet sport peppers, and celery salt.

So the next time you're in Chicago and want to try something authentic, head to one of the dozens of hot dog stands in the city and ask for a dog "dragged through the garden."

A Chicago-style hot dog—a frankfurter that's been "dragged through the garden"

# The Joy of Italian Beef

Native Chicagoan Hillary Clinton had it on her fiftieth birthday and comedian Jay Leno eats one whenever he's in Chicago. The culinary delicacy both enjoy so much is the Italian beef sandwich, which was invented in Chicago. A genuine Italian beef sandwich consists of thin slices of beef, Italian spices (which can depend on the vendor but usually include pepper, garlic, and oregano), crusty bread, and sweet or hot peppers. Other options can include a slice of provolone cheese or a cup of dipping gravy.

As to who actually made the first Italian beef sandwich, there's the rub. Most foodies credit Al Ferreri, his sister Frances, and her husband, Chris Pacelli Sr., for inventing the sandwich in 1938, when they began making sandwiches to deliver to local factory workers. But Scala's Original Beef and Sausage Company says its founder, Pasquale Scala, created the spiced beef during the Great Depression to serve at weddings and banquets.

Al's Italian Beef, where some say Chicago's famous Italian beef sandwich was invented in the 1930s

Regardless of who was first, it has become one of Chicago's most famous indigenous foods. In addition to Al's Beef, which has several franchises around the city, other popular Italian beef purveyors include Johnnie's Beef, Roma's Italian Beef, Luke's of Chicago, and Portillo's.

Bon appétit.

### Not So Little House on the Prairie

Robie House
Chicago

Architect Frank Lloyd Wright of Chicago was considered one of twentieth-century America's premier designers of homes and buildings. Born in Wisconsin in 1867, Wright moved to Chicago at the age of twenty to work as an apprentice architect. In 1893, he opened his own firm and began developing what became known as the Prairie School style: horizontal buildings that reflect and emulate the Midwestern landscape.

Perhaps the best example of the Prairie School style is the Robie House, which Wright designed in his Oak Park studio home in 1908. Completed in 1910, the house was a marvel of modern design with its sweeping horizontal lines, low, overhanging roof, and wide-open interior spaces, often with stained glass windows (using patterns designed by Wright).

The house was built for Frederick C. Robie, son of a successful Chicago businessman. The 9,000-square-foot home cost $58,500, a significant sum for the time (in current dollars it would equal about $1.3 million), which included the land, design and construction, and furnishings (many of which were designed by Wright).

Unfortunately, Robie and his family only lived in the house for about fourteen months. Financial problems following the death of his father forced him to sell the place in 1911. The next owner was David Lee Taylor, president of a Chicago advertising agency, who purchased

### Trivia

In 1990, Illinois designated the square dance as the official state dance (don't those politicians have more important things to do?).

**Interior of the Robie House, a masterpiece designed
by master architect Frank Lloyd Wright**

the house and all of the Wright-designed furnishings. He died less
than a year later and the house was sold to Marshall D. Wilber, who
resided in it for the next fourteen years.

In 1926, the home and its contents were sold to the Chicago
Theological Seminary, which converted it into a dormitory and dining hall. In the early 1940s and again in the late 1950s, the Seminary
announced plans to demolish the house and replace it with a larger
student dormitory. The first effort stalled because of the outbreak of
World War II and the second threat was quelled when Wright, then
ninety years old, returned to the house to protest its demolition.

In 1958, William Zeckendorf, a friend of Wright's, and other investors purchased the structure from the Seminary and, in 1963, it was
donated to the nearby University of Chicago. In the late 1990s, super-
vision of the property was turned over to the nonprofit Frank Lloyd
Wright Preservation Trust, which has undertaken a $10 million resto-
ration, and opened it for public tours.

Robie House is located at 5757 South Woodlawn Avenue in Chicago's Hyde Park neighborhood. For more information, go to www.gowright.org.

### The Big Bronze Knob
University of Chicago Campus
Chicago

Most visitors to the University of Chicago campus probably have no idea why there's a large bronze statue of a jellyfish-like thing sitting on a concrete slab on South Ellis Avenue. Called *Nuclear Energy,* the sculpture was erected in 1967 to commemorate the twenty-fifth anniversary of the first self-sustaining controlled nuclear chain reaction, which took place on that spot on December 2, 1942.

In the early 1940s, a group of scientists led by physicists Enrico Fermi and Leo Szilard worked at the University of Chicago to create a controlled, self-sustaining atomic reaction using uranium—the building blocks for developing an atomic bomb. Working in a converted handball court under the grandstands at the university's Stagg Field Stadium, the scientists made history when they successfully started and, more important, stopped a twenty-eight-minute nuclear chain reaction.

The first nuclear reactor was a crude construct consisting of a pile of uranium pellets separated from each other by graphite blocks. The controls were cadmium-coated rods that could absorb the neutrons produced by the uranium. Withdrawing the rods increased the neutron activity and would lead to the chain reaction. Inserting them back into the pile would dampen the reaction and bring it to an end.

Later reflecting on what had been achieved by the effort, which became known as the Manhattan Project, Szilard said, "We turned the switch, saw the flashes, watched for ten minutes, then switched everything off and went home. That night I knew the world was headed for sorrow."

The castle-like building that had housed the project, along with Stagg Field, were demolished in the late 1960s and the university

**This unusual sculpture marks the spot at the
University of Chicago where the first self-sustained,
controlled atomic reaction took place.**

installed on the site the 12-foot sculpture, designed by Henry Moore,
an internationally known abstract sculptor. Despite its rounded,
knobby crown, which many believe represents a mushroom cloud on
top of a human skull, Moore reportedly said he hoped those viewing
it would "go around it, looking out through the open spaces, and
that they may have a feeling of being in a cathedral."

Still looks like a jellyfish to me.

*Nuclear Energy* is located on the 5600 block of South Ellis Avenue
on the University of Chicago campus.

# A Dinosaur Named Sue

While it is kind of fun to hang out with her today, you wouldn't have wanted to meet Sue when she (or he—no one is certain of its sex) was alive. Standing 13 feet high and 42 feet long from head to tail, and with some teeth nearly a foot long, Sue was a terrifying creature deserving of the name of her species, Tyrannosaurus Rex, meaning "tyrant lizard kind."

Sue is the largest, most complete, and best-preserved T-Rex fossil ever discovered and is a featured attraction at Chicago's Field Museum. Her fossilized remains were uncovered in 1990 on the Cheyenne River Sioux Indian Reservation near Faith, South Dakota, and acquired by the museum in 2000. When alive, Sue weighed about

A full-size model of the fossil of the largest T-Rex ever uncovered stands in Chicago's Field Museum.

seven tons and lived in the Late Cretaceous Period about sixty-seven million years ago. The creature was named for its discoverer, fossil hunter Sue Hendrickson.

The skeleton on display is authentic except for the 5-foot-long skull, which is a replica cast from the original. The actual skull was too heavy to be placed on the steel support system that holds the rest of the dinosaur's bones. The real one, however, is displayed on the second floor—and it's no less frightening.

★ ★ ★ ★ ★ ★ ★ ★ ★ ★ ★ ★ ★ ★ ★ ★ ★ ★ ★ ★ ★ ★ ★ ★ ★ ★ ★ ★ ★ ★ ★ ★ ★ ★ ★

*Trivia*

Illinois's official state fossil is the Tully Monster. The soft-bodied mammal resembles an underwater slug with small fins and a weird long snout. It is named after amateur fossil hunter Francis Tully of Lockport, who discovered it in 1958.

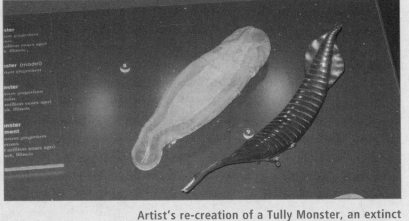

Artist's re-creation of a Tully Monster, an extinct marine mammal only found in Illinois

### Home of the Sacred and the Profane

Hull House
Chicago

Few Chicago landmarks have been as acclaimed and allegedly accursed as the historic Hull House. Built in 1856 by real estate developer Charles J. Hull, the two-story mansion was in a dilapidated state by 1889, when Jane Addams and her friend Ellen Starr rented it to serve as a social settlement house for the poor. The two had been inspired to help the city's downtrodden after visiting similar settlement houses in London.

★ ★ ★ ★ ★ ★ ★ ★ ★ ★ ★ ★ ★ ★ ★ ★ ★ ★ ★ ★ ★ ★ ★ ★ ★ ★ ★

Under Addams's leadership, Hull House became a beacon of hope for many newly arrived immigrants in the city. Over the next two decades, Hull House expanded to encompass thirteen buildings, which included an art gallery, a gymnasium, a swimming pool, a public kitchen, a boarding club for girls, a book bindery, a kindergarten, and day care facilities.

After Addams's death in 1935, Hull House continued her work and even expanded into other parts of the city (today, the Jane Addams Hull House Association is an umbrella agency for a number of social organizations in various Chicago locations).

In 1963, the University of Illinois–Chicago purchased the original complex. It demolished many of the surrounding Hull House buildings for its campus but spared the Hull House and adjacent dining hall. In 1967, the house was restored to its late nineteenth century appearance and became a public museum devoted to Addams and the social settlement movement.

There are also tales of a more supernatural nature involving the house. In her book, *Twenty Years at Hull House*, Addams wrote about a bizarre episode when one day three Italian women burst into the house demanding to be shown the "Devil Baby."

Allegedly, the baby was the cursed offspring of a religious Italian girl married to an atheist. According to their story, the husband ripped a holy picture from the bedroom wall one day and said he would rather have a devil in his house than such imagery. Nine months later, the woman gave birth to an abomination. The horrified father took the baby to Hull House, where it was locked away in the attic.

## Trivia

**Fluorite is the Illinois official state mineral and Illinois is the country's largest producer of the material, which is used in making steel, aluminum, and glass.**

The famous (and allegedly haunted) Hull House, where activist
Jane Addams began a social movement that changed America

Addams said the story quickly swept through the surrounding neighborhoods and, despite her protestations, for more than six weeks a steady stream of visitors came by Hull House to see Satan's spawn.

In the end, the legend finally faded away. Some, however, believe that Hull House once housed a severely disfigured boy who was hidden in a room in the upper floors of the house. Who knew Quasimodo lived in Chicago?

The Jane Addams Hull House Museum is located at 800 South Halsted Street in Chicago. For more information, go to www.uic.edu.

# Where Mrs. O'Leary's Cow Kicked Over the Lantern (Allegedly)

One of the seminal events in Chicago history was the Great Fire of 1871. Folklore attributes the fire to a lantern kicked over by a cow in a barn owned by Patrick and Catherine O'Leary on Chicago's West Side. While the actual cause isn't known, it is believed that the cow probably didn't do it. The previous summer and fall had been dry and at the time Chicago consisted largely of wooden structures. Additionally, firefighters went to the wrong location and when they got to the scene the fire had spread into surrounding neighborhoods. The conflagration continued for two days, consuming an area about 4 miles long and nearly a mile wide. When the fire finally burned itself out, 300 people had lost their lives and nearly 100,000 were homeless.

This flame-like sculpture marks the spot where the Great Chicago Fire of 1871 started.

Ironically, the fire did not destroy the O'Leary's house. It stood until 1956 when it was torn down—no joke—to build the Chicago Fire Academy. Today, an impressionistic bronze sculpture of flames by artist Egon Weiner stands on the site. On most days, you can catch academy employees standing around the statue—having a smoke.

The former site of the O'Leary property is at Dekoven and Jefferson Streets.

# A River in Reverse

From 1880 to 1900, Chicago's population grew from about a half million people to nearly 1.7 million. The sewage from all those people was dumped into the Chicago River, which flowed directly into Lake Michigan, the source of the city's drinking water. Following deadly typhoid, cholera, and dysentery epidemics in the 1880s, city and state officials decided the best way to fix the problem would be to reverse the Chicago River so it flowed away from the lake and toward the Mississippi River and Gulf of Mexico. Between 1892 and 1922, a system of canals was built to change the river's direction. The result was the world's largest municipal earth-moving project and a safe water supply for Chicago.

The Chicago River flowing through the city's downtown

### The Windy City's Iconic Buckingham Fountain
Grant Park
Chicago

One of Chicago's most recognizable landmarks is historic Buckingham Fountain in downtown Grant Park. This multitiered water attraction has appeared in television shows and films: most famously, in the opening credits of the popular '80s and '90s TV show, *Married With Children*.

The fountain, constructed of Georgia pink marble, has been around so long it's easy to take it for granted. It was completed in 1927, a gift to the city from philanthropist Kate Buckingham to honor her late brother, Clarence. Famed Chicago architect Edward H. Bennett, who designed the fountain, said his inspiration was the Latona Basin in Louis XIV's gardens in Versailles.

Bennett said the fountain, which was the largest in the world when completed, represented Lake Michigan, while the four sea horses at the corners, sculpted by Marcel Francois Loyau, represent the four states that touch the lake—Illinois, Wisconsin, Indiana, and Michigan.

Similar to a wedding cake, the fountain consists of a tier of three basins atop a pool that is 280 feet in diameter. The lower basin is 103 feet, the middle one is 60 feet, while the top tray is 24 feet. A total of 134 jets spray water in different configurations including thirty-five that point upward from the top basin and a central jet that produces a 150-foot plume of water.

*Trivia*

The world's largest cookie and cracker factory is the Nabisco plant in Chicago, which produces more than fifteen billion Oreo cookies annually.

★ ★ ★ ★ ★ ★ ★ ★ ★ ★ ★ ★ ★ ★ ★ ★ ★ ★ ★ ★ ★ ★ ★ ★ ★ ★ ★ ★ ★

In addition to paying for the fountain, Mrs. Buckingham established a $300,000 trust fund so that taxpayers wouldn't have to pay for all of the costs needed for future repairs and maintenance. In 1994, the trust fund, which had increased in value to millions of dollars, paid for a $2.8 million restoration of the fountain. In 2008 and 2009, the fund again was tapped for additional renovations and restoration.

The fountain operates from 8 a.m. to 11 p.m. daily from about April to mid-October, depending on the weather. When working, the fountain will produce a twenty-minute water display at the top of every hour. After dusk, computer-synchronized lights and music accent the water shows. In other words, it's pretty cool.

The Buckingham Fountain is located at 500 South Columbus Drive in Chicago. For more information, go to www.cpdit01.com/resources/buckingham_fountain.cfm.

### A Building with Stones
Tribune Tower
Chicago

In 1922, *Chicago Tribune* owner Col. Robert McCormick decided to build a new office building for his thriving media company. The paper had outgrown its seventeen-story offices on the corner of Dearborn and Madison Streets. Rather than simply select an architect, Col. McCormick opted to hold an international competition for what he hoped would be "the most beautiful office building in the world."

After receiving more than 260 entries, no doubt attracted by the $50,000 first prize, the paper announced the winners were New York architects John Mead Howells and Raymond Hood, who submitted plans for a neo-Gothic structure with flying buttresses that would rise 462 feet over Michigan Avenue.

Construction of the $8.5 million, thirty-six-story tower took more than two years but it was completed in 1925. The tower was built using materials and techniques that were state-of-the-art for the time, including a steel frame fireproofed with concrete. The outer

The historic *Chicago Tribune* building is embedded with
stones from landmark structures from around the world.

★ ★ ★ ★ ★ ★ ★ ★ ★ ★ ★ ★ ★ ★ ★ ★ ★ ★ ★ ★ ★ ★ ★ ★ ★ ★ ★ ★

walls are Indiana limestone. A unique feature of the building was the incorporation into its ground level walls of about 150 hunks of brick and stones from historically significant sites in all fifty states and from around the world. Col. McCormick had begun collecting historical artifacts during his own worldwide travels. *Tribune* correspondents augmented this collection with pieces acquired while working on overseas assignments.

As a result, visitors to the building can walk around its exterior spotting stones from the Mosque of Suleiman the Magnificent in Istanbul, Turkey, the Arc de Triomphe in Paris, and the Great Pyramid of Cheops in Egypt. Stones are still being added. According to the *Tribune*, the stones are authenticated before they are considered for inclusion into the building. They must then be stored for at least ten years to ensure they remain historically significant. When the decision is made to place them into the building's walls, masons cut the outline of the object into the limestone and cement it in place.

The interior of the building also has an interesting design touch—in the multistory entrance area, known as the Hall of Inscriptions, the walls have been carved with famous quotations about the ideals and responsibilities of a free press. What you won't find, however, is a

## *Trivia*

Chicago became known as the "Windy City" not because of the ferocious breezes that blow off Lake Michigan but because a catty New York newspaper editor, Charles Dana, gave it the name after growing weary of hearing Chicagoans boast endlessly about their city during the bidding for the 1893 World's Fair, which was awarded to Chicago.

quip made by one of Col. McCormick's political opponents (the Colonel was extremely, extremely conservative): "He is the greatest mind of the fourteenth century."

The Tribune Tower stands at 435 North Michigan Avenue in Chicago. For more information, go to www.chicagotribune.com.

### Gateway to Nowhere
The Stockyards
Chicago

One of poet Carl Sandburg's most famous poems is simply entitled "Chicago," and its opening line is: "HOG Butcher for the world." The poem, written in 1916, echoes the fact that for nearly a century Chicago was the meatpacking center of America. From the mid-nineteenth century to the mid-twentieth century, Chicago was the place where much of the nation's supply of beef and pork was processed.

There were several reasons Chicago evolved into America's main meat processor, including its location as the link between the West, where much of the livestock came from, and the East, where most of the meat was consumed. In 1865, a consortium of nine railroad companies decided to consolidate the city's stockyards, which had previously been scattered throughout the city, and created the Union Stock and Transit Company, also known as The Yards.

They purchased about 320 acres (later expanded to 475 acres) of unused swampland in southwest Chicago and transformed it into a vast complex that eventually included 2,300 individual livestock pens as well as offices for merchants and livestock brokers, hotels, saloons, and restaurants. At its peak, The Yards stretched from 39th Street to 47th Street and from Halsted to Ashland Avenue, an area of about one square mile.

About 50,000 people worked at the stockyards ranging from slaughterhouse workers to meatpackers to the company managers. By 1870, an estimated two million animals were passing through the facility annually, a number that increased to nine million two decades

The Union Stockyard Gate, erected in 1875, is a reminder of the time when Chicago was "HOG Butcher for the World."

later. The Yards became the largest meat packing facility in the world, supplying more than 80 percent of the domestic meat in the country.

The concentration of so many meat processing businesses and stockyards in one place produced, not surprisingly, an obnoxious stench. But, according to local legend, people who lived in the surrounding neighborhoods, most of whom worked in The Yards, said it was actually the smell of money.

In about 1875, John B. Sherman, superintendent of The Yards, commissioned an impressive triple-arched limestone gate to serve as the main entrance to the complex, located on Exchange Avenue at Peoria Street. John Wellborn Root of the prominent Burnham and

Root architectural firm in Chicago designed the imposing gateway, which contains the image of a steer carved in the stone above the central arch.

The Yards remained America's meat market until the 1950s, when it became cheaper to slaughter animals where they were raised and transport them using trucks instead of the railroad. This decentralization of the industry started a decline of the facility, which was closed in 1971 and converted into the Stockyard Industrial Park.

The stone gate, however, was preserved and remains a symbol of the stockyard's longtime prominence as the heart of the nation's meat industry. And that ain't no bull.

The Old Stone Gate of Chicago Union Stockyards remains standing at South Peoria Street and West Exchange Avenue in Chicago. For more information, go to www.cityofchicago.org.

## A Nice Place to Visit But You Wouldn't Want to Work There
James R. Thompson Center
Chicago

It's been called Chicago's worst office building as well as one of its most architecturally interesting. The James R. Thompson Center (formerly the Illinois State Office Building in Chicago), completed in 1985, has been praised for its innovative design and damned for being a lousy place to work.

Costing $89 million, the 1.2 million-square-foot building was designed to consolidate state government agencies with offices in the Windy City into one location. It also includes a large commercial area with shops and a food court as well as a massive collection of contemporary artwork by Chicago natives.

Its unusual, round design by architect Helmut Jahn earned it international attention and it won the 1986 Distinguished Building Award of the Chicago Chapter, American Institute of Architects.

But the building has also earned plenty of scorn for being a crummy working environment. For one thing, the interior of the

★ ★ ★ ★ ★ ★ ★ ★ ★ ★ ★ ★ ★ ★ ★ ★ ★ ★ ★ ★ ★ ★ ★ ★ ★ ★ ★ ★ ★ ★ ★

**The futuristic James R. Thompson Center, considered
by some to be the worst office building in Illinois**

structure is a huge, open glass-lined atrium. Employees say it looks
beautiful but it's noisy because sound carries throughout the atrium,
and it's too warm in the summer months and too cold in the winter.

"Someone also needs to make old Helmut (Jahn) sit on the crap-
per in one of the men's rooms which are all disgusting," wrote one
state employee on the www.yelp.com review website. "There is no
ventilation so you have to suffer through the most horrible . . . smells
known to mankind. Also, who was the dingbat who made all the toilets electronic? When the power goes out, the toilets don't flush."

In August 2009, a piece of decorative granite weighing 600
pounds fell off the building. In response, state officials erected protective scaffolding around the building and announced that about 1,000

★ ★ ★ ★ ★ ★ ★ ★ ★ ★ ★ ★ ★ ★ ★ ★ ★ ★ ★ ★ ★ ★ ★ ★ ★ ★ ★ ★ ★ ★

similar stone panels would have to be removed from the building's exterior at a cost of about $1 million.

At last report, officials were consulting with the architect to figure out the best way to fix the problem, said to have been caused by corrosion behind the panels. It all makes you wonder: What was the second most distinguished building in 1986?

The James R. Thompson Center stands at 100 West Randolph Street in Chicago. For more information, contact (312) 814-6660, www.cms.il.gov.

### These Dollhouses Are Not Playthings
Art Institute of Chicago
Chicago

Established in 1879, the Art Institute of Chicago is one of America's finest art museums. In its collection are some of the world's most noteworthy works of art including Pablo Picasso's *The Old Guitarist*, Georges Seurat's *Sunday Afternoon on the Island of La Grande Jatte*, Grant Wood's *American Gothic*, and Vincent Van Gogh's *Self-Portrait, 1887*.

But tucked into a lower level of the Art Institute are perhaps its most unusual holdings—a room filled with sixty-eight miniature rooms displaying American, European, and Asian architecture and furnishings, but in a scale of 1 inch to 1 foot. Called the Thorne Miniature Rooms, this collection of tiny but extremely detailed and accurate replicas was created by Mrs. James Ward Thorne, a wealthy Chicago socialite.

Married to the son of the founder of Montgomery Ward, Mrs. Thorne had loved dollhouses and miniature furniture as a child. Following a trip to Europe, during which she collected fine miniature furniture and accessories, she decided in 1933 to commission more than two dozen tiny rooms crafted by a special team she assembled for the work.

Mrs. Thorne's initial set of rooms was exhibited in the 1933–34 Chicago's Century of Progress Exhibition. Between 1937 and 1940,

★ ★ ★ ★ ★ ★ ★ ★ ★ ★ ★ ★ ★ ★ ★ ★ ★ ★ ★ ★ ★ ★ ★ ★ ★ ★ ★ ★ ★ ★ ★

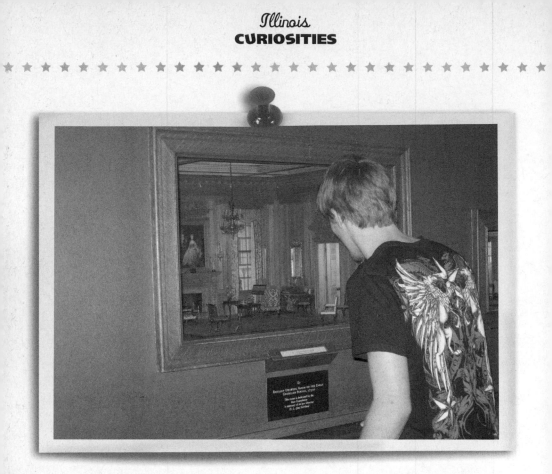

**The Thorne Miniature Rooms Collection at the Art Institute of Chicago**

Mrs. Thorne commissioned dozens of additional room-boxes that duplicated the interiors of elegant European castles and historic homes as well as American settings from the colonial period to Art Deco. Many of these were displayed at the 1939 San Francisco's Golden Gate International Exposition and the 1939 New York World's Fair.

Following the World's Fair, Mrs. Thorne gifted sixty-eight of the rooms to the Art Institute, which put them on display (another twenty of the rooms are owned by the Phoenix Art Museum).

First-time visitors to the collection are often amazed at their incredible detail. Looking through the glass windows that front each room is like gazing into a scene from the past. The exquisite workmanship is

★ ★ ★ ★ ★ ★ ★ ★ ★ ★ ★ ★ ★ ★ ★ ★ ★ ★ ★ ★ ★ ★ ★ ★ ★ ★ ★ ★ ★ ★ ★

evident in the tiny but elegant statues, chairs, tables, sofas, fireplaces, mirrors, and other furnishings. In fact, the only thing big about it might be the fact that it's the world's largest collection of miniatures.

The Art Institute of Chicago is located at 111 South Michigan Avenue in Chicago. For more information, go to www.artic.edu.

## Sometimes the Best Things in Life Are Free

Lincoln Park Zoo
Chicago

Lincoln Park, located on the Chicago lakefront, must be the only public park in the world to boast a free zoo, a mystery mausoleum, and a beautifully restored, historic toilet.

The park started out in the early nineteenth century as a public cemetery where victims of cholera and smallpox were buried in shallow graves, according to the Chicago Park District's records. Because of the public health threat such a burial ground represented, in the 1850s Chicagoans demanded the Chicago City Cemetery be converted into a park. In 1860, the city set aside sixty unused acres of the area for what it named Lake Park. Following the assassination of President Abraham Lincoln, the park's name was changed to honor him.

In the 1870s, the Lincoln Park Commission, created by the state legislature, finally exhumed and relocated the bodies from the cemetery to other locations so the park could be expanded.

A major exception to the cemetery relocation is a stone vault called the Couch Mausoleum, which has the distinction of being one of the few Lincoln Park–area structures to survive the Great Chicago Fire of 1871. Depending on the source, the crypt contains anywhere from zero to thirteen bodies. A sign next to the stone tomb explains that Ira Couch was a wealthy hotelier who died in 1858 and was buried in the tomb, which may or may not contain other family members. As to why the tomb wasn't relocated in the 1870s, the sign merely indicates, "THERE IS NO OFFICIAL ANSWER AS TO WHY THIS TOMB WAS LEFT BEHIND."

★ ★ ★ ★ ★ ★ ★ ★ ★ ★ ★ ★ ★ ★ ★ ★ ★ ★ ★ ★ ★ ★ ★ ★ ★ ★ ★ ★ ★ ★

**Entrance to the Lincoln Park Zoo, the
oldest free public zoo in the US**

The Lincoln Park Zoo was founded in 1868 and is the oldest and
one of the largest free public zoos. Located on forty-nine acres, it is
home to more than 1,100 mammals, birds, reptiles, and amphibians.
It started out with two swans donated from New York's Central Park.

The Lincoln Park Zoo is home to a number of restored historic
structures including the Kovler Lion House, a beautiful 32,700-square-
foot Prairie-style building that was completed in 1912 and renovated
in 2007. In 2008, the zoo completed perhaps its most unusual restoration—refurbishment of Carlson Cottage, a Victorian-era "comfort
station" (restroom). Built in 1888, the elegant stone structure with
a high-pitched shingled roof served as a public commode for many
decades. Sometime in the mid-twentieth century it was closed and

sat empty and forgotten for years. Now that it has been restored it is used as the operations hub for the zoo's dozens of volunteer gardeners. It's just too pretty to be a toilet anymore.

The Lincoln Park Zoo is located at 2001 North Clark Street in Chicago. For more information, go to www.lpzoo.org.

## Stairway to Heaven
Willis Tower
Chicago

It sounds strange to call venerable Sears Tower in Chicago by its new name, Willis Tower. Big, iconic skyscrapers like the 110-story Willis Tower (that just sounds so wrong) are not supposed to change their names. It's like the Chrysler Building in New York suddenly becoming the Smith Building. But that's what happened in 2009, when a British insurance company, Willis Group Holdings, Ltd., leased a portion of the building and obtained its naming rights.

Regardless of its name, the tower remains an impressive achievement. It weighs 440 million pounds and stands 1,450 feet high. It has more than 3.5 million square feet of office and retail space. Its 104 elevators move at speeds of up to 1,600 feet per minute. It also boasts 992 toilets, including one on the 103rd floor that is the second highest in the world (look out below).

The tower traces its beginning to the late 1960s when Sears, Roebuck and Company, at the time the world's largest retailer, decided to consolidate its thousands of Chicago area employees into one building. Sears hired the Chicago architectural firm of Skidmore, Owings and Merrill to design a structure that would be one of the world's largest office buildings.

Skidmore, Owings and Merrill created what has been described as a "bundled-tube" construction, which was essentially building nine separate 75-foot-by-75-foot square, steel-frame buildings, and then binding them together so that the three-by-three square formed one massive larger structure.

View of Willis Tower (formerly Sears Tower), the tallest
building in the world from 1974 to 1998

★ ★ ★ ★ ★ ★ ★ ★ ★ ★ ★ ★ ★ ★ ★ ★ ★ ★ ★ ★ ★ ★ ★ ★ ★ ★ ★

Work on the tower began in August 1970 and was completed in May 1973. The complete structure, which had the distinction of being the world's tallest building from 1974 to 1998, contains enough concrete to build an eight-lane, 5-mile-long highway.

Of course, the coolest part about Willis Tower is the public observation floor or Skydeck, located on the 103rd floor. It offers stunning views of the entire city as well as four surrounding states. The $14.95 admission charge includes a nine-minute movie, *Reach for the Sky*, that explains the history of Chicago and the tower.

A recent addition is the Skydeck Ledge, a couple of clear, Plexiglas chambers attached to the 103rd floor that offer unobstructed views from 1,354 feet up—in other words, an acrophobia sufferer's worst nightmare.

The Willis Tower Skydeck is located at 233 South Wacker Drive in Chicago. For more information, go to www.the-skydeck.com.

## Home of the Loveable Losers

Wrigley Field
Chicago

In the world of baseball stadiums, Chicago's Wrigley Field is a shrine. Built in 1914, it is the second oldest ballpark in the country after Boston's Fenway Park, which was opened two years earlier. The park was originally known as Weeghman Park, after Charles H. Weeghman, who owned the Chicago Federals/Whales baseball team, part of the Federal League, a short-lived independent professional baseball league.

In 1916, Weeghman purchased the Cincinnati Cubs in the National League and moved them to Chicago. Four years later, the Wrigley family, which owned the Wrigley Gum Company, acquired the team and park. The park was renamed Cubs Park and, after 1926, Wrigley Field in honor of William Wrigley Jr., the club's primary owner. The park has been expanded over the years, so that today it seats more than 41,000 fans.

★ ★ ★ ★ ★ ★ ★ ★ ★ ★ ★ ★ ★ ★ ★ ★ ★ ★ ★ ★ ★ ★ ★ ★ ★ ★ ★ ★ ★ ★ ★ ★ ★

**Front entrance to famous Wrigley Field in Chicago,
home of the Chicago Cubs baseball team**

Many historic baseball events have been associated with the park, colloquially known as "the friendly confines." For example, it was the site of Babe Ruth's famous "called shot," when the legendary hitter allegedly pointed to a spot in center field during the third game of the 1932 World Series and then hit the next pitch over the fence at that spot.

Tradition is a big thing at Wrigley so the park retains its original 1937 scoreboard; the score and pitcher's number must still be changed by hand. That was also the same year that the team planted

Boston ivy and Japanese bittersweet plants on the park's outfield walls, which give the stadium its distinctive look.

Additionally, Wrigley was one of the last professional baseball stadiums to get lights for night games—not until 1988. Prior to that, the team played 5,687 consecutive day games. For decades it's also been tradition for fans to toss back onto the field any home run balls hit by the opposing team (although it's rumored that some hardcore fans always carry a "throw back ball" to toss back while pocketing the real one).

Following each game, a white flag printed with a giant blue "W" is flown from the center-field flagpole to signify a Cubs win while a blue flag marked with a big "L" is raised after a loss.

For Cubs fans, perhaps the most interesting statistic related to Wrigley is the fact that the team has never won a World Series title since moving into the park nearly a century ago. The team's last championship came in 1908, six years before Wrigley was built. The Cubs have been in six World Series in the intervening years, and come close on a couple of occasions, but have never won (see "The Goat's Revenge" for a possible explanation).

The address for Wrigley Field is 1060 West Addison Street in Chicago. For more information, go to www.cubs.com.

## Chicago's Fascist Tribute
Burnham Park
Chicago

Chicago loves its statues, fountains, busts, and other public monuments. Scattered throughout the city are tributes to famous people, noteworthy events, spiritual ideals, like freedom and democracy—and a Mussolini-era fascist named Italo Balbo.

The Balbo Monument was a gift from Italian dictator Benito Mussolini to the people of Chicago that was erected in front of the Italian pavilion for the 1933–34 Chicago World's Fair. It is basically a centuries-old marble column mounted atop a large stone pedestal on which is inscribed, in Italian, a description of the column (it came

★ ★ ★ ★ ★ ★ ★ ★ ★ ★ ★ ★ ★ ★ ★ ★ ★ ★ ★ ★ ★ ★ ★ ★ ★ ★ ★ ★ ★ ★

from a 2,000-year-old Roman settlement) and a message of thanks from Mussolini.

The Italian strongman shipped a rare and ancient piece of Roman architecture to the Windy City in gratitude for the city of Chicago naming a street in honor of Balbo, who was one of Mussolini's closest advisers and marshal of the Air Force. In June 1933, two dozen seaplanes departed from Italy under the command of Balbo and, after stops in Ireland, Iceland, and Canada, dramatically landed in formation on Lake Michigan during the fair.

The appearance—clearly done for propaganda points—greatly impressed many Chicagoans (who were not yet completely aware of the fascist agenda) including Mayor Ed Kelly. In Balbo's honor, and in a blatant attempt to capture the votes of the city's growing Italian-American population, Kelly renamed a three-block stretch of 7th Street along the lakefront after the dashing Italian aviator. The street renaming clearly touched Il Duce; hence his decision to give the monument to the city.

Balbo triumphantly returned to Italy, but only after receiving numerous honors including a ticker-tape parade in New York and lunch with President Roosevelt (Chicagoans are not the only ones who failed to foresee the dangers of the burgeoning fascist movement). In 1940, he was killed when his plane was accidentally shot down over Northern Africa by Italian anti-aircraft fire.

There was an attempt to change the street's name following World War II, but Mayor Kelly was fearful of alienating his Italian-American voters and squashed the effort. Additional attempts were made to change the street's name in the 1980s and 1990s but they, too, failed for various reasons.

Today, visitors to Chicago's museum campus area (home of the Field Museum and the Shedd Aquarium) can cruise on Balbo Drive and see the Balbo Monument at South Lake Shore Drive near Soldier Field. And maybe wonder why.

★ ★ ★ ★ ★ ★ ★ ★ ★ ★ ★ ★ ★ ★ ★ ★ ★ ★ ★ ★ ★ ★ ★ ★ ★ ★ ★ ★ ★ ★ ★

## The Real "Das Boot"

Museum of Science and Industry
Chicago

It was like something out of a World War II movie. On June 4, 1944, the German submarine, U-505, was cruising off the coast of West Africa, searching for American and Allied ships to attack. During the previous several years, the U-505 had conducted nearly a dozen patrols, sinking eight ships.

Allied forces, however, were aware that several U-boats were stationed near Cape Verde in Africa. An anti-submarine task force that included an aircraft carrier and five destroyers was sent to the area to conduct high-frequency detection sweeps. That morning, one of the destroyers reported a possible sonar contact. The ship laid down a pattern of depth charges and Hedgehog bombs, which damaged the underwater vessel, the U-505, and caused it to surface.

After the destroyers collected the surrendering U-boat crew of fifty-eight, a nine-man boarding party was sent into the submarine to salvage the boat. Wary of any booby traps or ambushes, and not sure of how much damage the sub had suffered, the sailors slowly searched the craft. The U-boat crew, in fact, had set time bombs to sink the boat but the boarding party was able to disable all of them.

Once the U-boat was secured, the U.S. Navy decided to secretly haul it to a base in Bermuda so it could be studied. The U-505 proved to be a gold mine of military information, yielding two M4 Enigma coding machines and 900 pounds of codebooks and publications—all of which proved useful in the Allied wartime code-breaking efforts.

To keep the Germans from discovering that the U-550 had been captured, the Navy transported the prisoners to a POW camp in Ruston, Louisiana, where they were treated well but isolated from the rest of the population and not allowed to send out letters. The prisoners responded by making unsuccessful attempts to tell others of their capture, including making balloons out of cellophane bags filled with

★ ★ ★ ★ ★ ★ ★ ★ ★ ★ ★ ★ ★ ★ ★ ★ ★ ★ ★ ★ ★ ★ ★ ★ ★ ★ ★

hydrogen gas made from cleaning supplies, which were painted with Iron Crosses and the words, "U-505 lives!"

Immediately following the war, the prisoners were sent back to Germany and the U-505 was donated to the Museum of Science and Industry in Chicago, where it was put on display, becoming the only German submarine in the United States In the late 1990s, it became apparent that the ship, which had been parked outside for more than fifty years, was being destroyed by the elements. In 2004 and 2005, the boat underwent extensive renovations and was moved into a climate-controlled environment inside the museum where it is open to the public.

The U-505 is located inside the Museum of Science and Industry at 57th Street and Lake Shore Drive. For more information, go to www.msichicago.org.

### The Ancient Mariner
Shedd Aquarium
Chicago

Granddad the Australian Lungfish has seen it all. Since 1933, he's been a resident of Chicago's Shedd Aquarium—the longest-living fish in any aquarium in the world. The twenty-five-pound, gray-spotted, brown fish arrived in the Windy City from Sydney, Australia for an appearance at the 1933 Chicago's World's Fair. Scientists believe he was about five years old at the time, making him more than three-quarters of a century old today.

The year Granddad arrived in Chicago, Franklin Roosevelt had just become president, the original *King Kong* had just premiered in New York, the first issue of *Newsweek* magazine had recently been published, and the first Major League Baseball All-Star Game was played at Chicago's Comiskey Park (then-home of the White Sox).

According to news accounts, Granddad journeyed to Chicago via steamship and train to appear at the World's Fair. After his fair run, he was turned over to the Shedd Aquarium, which had opened in

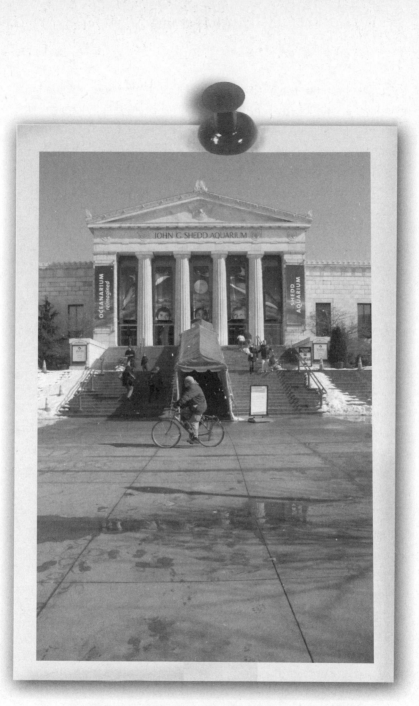

The Shedd Aquarium in Chicago is home of "Granddad"
the Australian Lungfish, the oldest living fish in any
aquarium in the world.

1930. At the time, the Shedd offered the greatest variety of sea life exhibited in one location. It had six galleries of aquatic animals that branched out from a central rotunda, which housed a 40-foot tropical swamp (replaced in the '70s by a tropical reef display).

In the 1990s, the Shedd nearly doubled in size when it added the 170,000-square-foot Oceanarium, which included large, open pools and displays for beluga whales, dolphins, and penguins. In 2003, it added Wild Reef, featuring a 400,000-gallon floor-to-ceiling shark habitat. The Shedd is the world's largest indoor aquarium with 422,000 square feet housing more than 8,000 freshwater and salt-water aquatic animals.

Granddad lives in one of the original gallery sections in a 6,000-gallon, temperature-controlled tank with four other Australian lungfish, a couple of turtles, and a few smaller fish. He's fed three to four times a week, usually a potpourri of smelt, small frozen fish, and shrimp, as well as romaine lettuce and, his favorite food, sweet potatoes.

Shedd scientists say they don't know how long a lungfish can live. Members of the species are not particularly active. In their natural setting, they spend much of their time camouflaged and waiting for prey to snap up when they swim by. The fish are noteworthy because they have both gills and primitive lungs, meaning they can breathe air. The lung apparently provides the lungfish with the ability to survive in Australia during dry periods when the streams become stagnant or when water quality changes.

Physically, lungfish are usually olive-green to brown on the back and sides with scattered dark blotches. They have a long, heavy body with large scales and paddlelike pectoral fins and pelvic fins. They grow to about 4 feet long and live in a handful of river systems in Australia. Fossil records indicate they've been around for more than 380 million years—a record of longevity that even Granddad can't beat.

John G. Shedd Aquarium is located at 1200 South Lake Shore Drive in Chicago. For more information, go to www.sheddaquarium.org.

# America's First Indoor Solar System

In the early 1920s, the Carl Zeiss Jena Company in Germany, famous for its microscope and camera lenses, developed an optical projection device that would create the illusion of the night sky. Meanwhile, Chicago businessman and philanthropist Max Adler was looking to invest in a public facility that would benefit future generations of his community. In 1928, he learned of the Zeiss projector and became so impressed that he donated the funds to construct the first modern planetarium in the United States. In May 1930, the Adler Planetarium opened adjacent to the Shedd Aquarium and the Field Museum of Natural History.

The Adler Planetarium can be found at 1300 South Lake Shore Drive in Chicago. For more information, go to www.adler planetarium.org.

The Adler Planetarium in Chicago, the oldest planetarium in America

### Artwork That's Full of It

East Village
Chicago

You have to admire Chicago sculptor Jerzy S. Kenar's conviction. In 2005, the internationally acclaimed artist grew tired of people not cleaning up after their dogs. So he decided to make something that would draw attention to the issue.

He created a bronze sculpture that resembles a big, coiled pile of dog poop on a concrete pedestal and placed it in front of his studio-home in Chicago's East Village.

Fed up with his neighbors not picking up after their dogs, artist Jerzy S. Kenar created this fountain shaped like a pile of dog poo, which he placed outside of his studio.

# Where America's Friendly Neighborhood Drugstore Began

We can thank the city of Chicago for all those Walgreen's drugstores that have cropped up on nearly every street corner in nearly every community in America. When Charles C. Walgreen opened a drugstore on Chicago's South Side in 1901, he sought to make his establishment different from his competitors, so he sold hot and cold sandwiches and something called a malt milkshake, which was invented by one of his employees. According to some accounts, Walgreen was the first pharmacist to take full advantage of the relatively newfangled invention called a telephone. When a customer phoned in an order, it's said Walgreen would loudly repeat it to his employees, then pleasantly chat with the customer long enough for the order to be delivered to the customer while he or she was still on the phone with him. In 1997, the Walgreen's chain pioneered the drive-through window for prescriptions—proving once again the company was a step ahead of the competition.

"This (work) is dedicated to all the dogs in the neighborhood," he told *Time Out Chicago* magazine. Kenar, who owns a pit bull, said his intention was not to start a fight with anyone but rather to show some irony and humor.

His work has generated some objections as well as plenty of chuckles. One neighbor told *Time Out Chicago* that "we're trying to make this neighborhood beautiful and he puts up a sh-t fountain?" But, the neighbor added that she did laugh when she first saw it.

★ ★ ★ ★ ★ ★ ★ ★ ★ ★ ★ ★ ★ ★ ★ ★ ★ ★ ★ ★ ★ ★ ★ ★ ★ ★ ★ ★ ★

Ironically, the Polish-born Kenar is primarily known for his religious sculpture, such as the holy water font at Loyola University's Madonna della Strada Chapel. In 1995, the city of Chicago opened a permanent gallery of Kenar's sculptures at the O'Hare International Airport and three years later his work, *Together United*, was installed at the Harold Washington Library in Chicago. More recently, in 2006, the Chicago Public Art Commission placed his *Black History Fountain*, an interactive granite and live-water sculpture, in front of the Renaissance Park Community Center.

As for his dog feces fountain, it's become a bit of a tourist draw. Photos can be found all over the Internet depicting visitors squatting over it, pretending to lick it, dining on top of it (usually hot dogs), and performing other semi-profane acts. No word on what he might do for an encore.

Jerzy S. Kenar's studio is located at 1001 North Wolcott Avenue, Chicago. For more information about the artist and his work, check out www.jerzykenar.com.

## The Original House of Blues

South Michigan Avenue
Chicago

The little storefront on South Michigan is usually pretty quiet. Few of those who pass by pay much attention to the nondescript two-story building. But between 1957 and about 1966, it was the home of Chess Records, the legendary music company that recorded artists like Muddy Waters, Howlin' Wolf, Chuck Berry, and Willie Dixon.

Brothers Leonard and Phil Chess founded Chess Records in 1950. The two originally began recording acts performing at a Chicago nightclub they owned and then began making records full time. The brothers specialized in recording black blues musicians, most originally from the South, who had come to Chicago during the "great migration" of the early- to mid-twentieth century (when many Southern blacks moved to Chicago for better economic opportunities).

★ ★ ★ ★ ★ ★ ★ ★ ★ ★ ★ ★ ★ ★ ★ ★ ★ ★ ★ ★ ★ ★ ★ ★ ★ ★ ★ ★ ★ ★ ★

**Former site of the legendary Chess Records recording studio in Chicago**

The Chess brothers' first studio was located at 4750 Cottage Grove but, in 1957, they moved into the Michigan Avenue locale. During the decade Chess operated in the building, the company produced hit songs by Little Milton, Etta James, the Dells, Koko Taylor, and the Yardbirds.

A fictionalized version of the rise of Chess Records was told in the 2008 film, *Cadillac Records*, starring Adrien Brody (as Leonard Chess) and Beyoncé (as Etta James) as well as in *Who Do You Love*, also released that year.

In 1964, the Rolling Stones famously made a pilgrimage to the Michigan Avenue location to record more than twenty tracks, including a tribute song entitled "2120 South Michigan Avenue." Those songs were released on an album called *The Chess Sessions*.

★ ★ ★ ★ ★ ★ ★ ★ ★ ★ ★ ★ ★ ★ ★ ★ ★ ★ ★ ★ ★ ★ ★ ★ ★ ★ ★ ★ ★ ★ ★ ★

Chess Records ceased to exist as an independent label after 1969, when Leonard Chess died and his son, Marshall, sold the label. By 1975, the company was gone. In 1990, the Michigan Avenue building, originally built in 1911, was designated a Chicago landmark. A few years later, Marie Dixon, widow of Willie Dixon, who had produced and recorded so many memorable songs at the site, purchased the building and restored it as an educational foundation for young black artists.

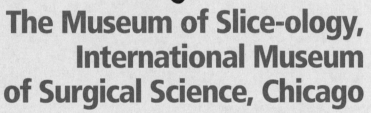

# The Museum of Slice-ology, International Museum of Surgical Science, Chicago

In 1935, Dr. Max Thorek established the International College of Surgeons to promote the exchange of knowledge and understanding among surgeons throughout the world. About fifteen years later, he started a museum to display objects and artwork related to the history and development of the surgical sciences. Over the years, the museum, housed in a historic Chicago lakeside mansion, has grown to include not only historic artifacts but also exhibits about cutting edge surgical developments, such as "Surgicogenomics" (genes and stem cells in surgery).

Wandering the museum's four floors, visitors can find everything from the crude, such as sixteenth century amputation saws, to the sophisticated, like a collection of manmade heart valves. Who would have thought that blades and bones could be so interesting?

The International Museum of Surgical Science is located at 1524 North Lake Shore Drive. For more information, go to www.imss.org.

Willie Dixon's Blues Heaven Foundation is located at 2120 South Michigan Avenue, Chicago, (312) 808-1286, www.bluesheaven.com.

### Even the Ceiling Is a Work of Art
Chicago Cultural Center
Chicago

They just don't build libraries like the old Chicago Public Library (now the Chicago Cultural Center) anymore. The Classical Revival–style structure was erected in 1897 to serve as the city's first permanent public library and as the Grand Army of the Republic Museum. It consisted of a four-story north wing and a five-story south wing.

Designed to be an impressive civic building, the structure cost nearly $2 million and featured an interior extensively decorated with marble and bronze as well as an intricate stained glass dome and mosaics designed by the Tiffany Glass and Decorating Company.

The dome, which sits atop of Preston Bradley Hall, is 38 feet in diameter and is believed to be the largest Tiffany dome in the world. The visually striking ceiling is made of 2,848 faceted glass jewels of rippled and streaky opalescent glass that are cut into a fish-scale pattern. In the middle of the dome is a glass rosette encircled by the signs of the zodiac. In addition to the dome, the Tiffany Company also created 10,000 square feet of glass and mother-of-pearl mosaics to highlight the marble upper walls.

On the walls of the building are a number of inspirational inscriptions. For example, there is John Milton's quote, "A good book is the precious life blood of a master spirit embalmed and treasured up on purpose to a life beyond life," as well as one from Isaac Barrow, "He who loveth a book will never want a faithful friend, a wholesome counsellor, a cheerful companion, or an effectual comforter." There are also inscriptions about books and reading in foreign languages including quotes from Omar Khayyam, Confucius, Voltaire, and Goethe.

**The stained glass ceiling of the Chicago Cultural Center, designed by Tiffany Glass Company**

By the 1970s, it had become obvious that the elegant building had become too small for the library's books and periodicals collections. After briefly exploring the possibility of demolishing the building, the city decided to erect a new, larger facility on another site (the Harold Washington Library Center that opened in 1989) and to convert the old structure into the nation's first free municipal cultural center.

In 1994, the renovated library was reopened as the Chicago Cultural Center, which included an art gallery, meeting rooms, a studio theater, dance studio, cafe, and the Museum of Broadcast Communications. Each year, more than 1,000 programs and exhibitions are held in the building, informally known as "the People's Palace."

The Chicago Cultural Center is at 78 East Washington Street in Chicago. For more information, go to www.chicagoculturalcenter.org.

## Where the Ghosts and the Spirits Play

Excalibur Nightclub
Chicago

It's said the Excalibur Nightclub in downtown Chicago is the most
haunted building in the city. Looking at it from the outside, it's easy
to believe the claim. With its thick, rough-cut granite walls, the place
is gothic, dark, and creepy—and certainly looks out of place amid the
sleek, more modern high rises and office buildings that surround it.

But besides its gloomy, Addams Family–friendly appearance, there
are a number of explanations given for why the Excalibur is said to
be haunted. Some say that during the Great Chicago Fire of 1871,
several women took refuge in a building previously located on that
site. Unfortunately, the fire also burned down that structure and the
women perished. Allegedly, the restless spirits of those unfortunate
women roam the building.

In 1915 a steamer ship named the *Eastland* capsized while tied to
a dock in the Chicago River. Some 844 passengers and crew died in
the disaster, which is considered the worst single shipping accident
to ever occur on the Great Lakes. According to another legend, the
Excalibur building was converted into a makeshift morgue following the event. Some believe ghosts of Eastland victims now reside in
the building. Regardless of why specters have taken residence in the
Excalibur, numerous books, articles, and cable TV documentaries have
alleged the place is haunted.

As for the actual history of the building, it was constructed in 1892
to house the Chicago Historical Society. Architect Henry Ives Cobb
incorporated a Romanesque Revival style, popular at the time, in the
design and sheathed it in heavy granite because the organization
needed a fireproof building to protect its historic papers and artifacts.

In the early 1930s, the society relocated to Lincoln Park and the
building served as the Institute of Design and, in the '50s and '60s, as
recording studios for blues and rock 'n' roll performers.

**Entrance to the Excalibur club, a classic neo-Gothic
building that is rumored to be haunted**

By the 1980s, it had become a popular nightclub called Limelight,
and that's when employees began reporting strange occurrences,
such as glasses falling and breaking for no apparent reason and
alarms inexplicably being triggered. In 1989, its name was changed
to Excalibur. More recently, the northern portion of the building was
converted into a second nightclub known as Vision.

To capitalize on the building's spooky reputation, the club created
Supernatural Chicago, a ninety-minute show every Friday night that
highlights the city's most well known paranormal episodes. Host Neil
Tobin, a self-described "Necromancer," uses mindreading, magic, and
other tricks to involve the audience. Scoff if you dare.

The haunted Excalibur nightclub sits at 632 North Dearborn Street in Chicago. For information about hours call (312) 266-1944 or go to www.excaliburchicago.com.

## He Probably Should Have Stayed In That Night
Biograph Theater
Chicago

On July 22, 1934, notorious bank robber John Dillinger wanted to catch a movie. Bad idea. A fugitive from the FBI and other law enforcement officials—J. Edgar Hoover had declared him Public Enemy Number One—Dillinger was confident he'd not be spotted since he'd recently had his appearance altered using plastic surgery.

Dillinger had been hiding out with a girlfriend, Polly Hamilton. One of Hamilton's friends was a madame named Anna Sage. According to FBI records, Sage, who was from Romania, was about to be deported as an undesirable alien because of her profession so she approached the agency to cut a deal—she would finger Dillinger if the feds would help her stay in the country.

Once she had an understanding with the FBI, Sage told the agents that she, Hamilton, and Dillinger were probably going to the movies the next night. She said she would call them with the name of the theater and would wear an orange dress so they could identify her (in popular legend, she is said to be the "woman in red").

That evening at about 8:30 p.m., Sage, Hamilton, and Dillinger walked to the nearby Biograph Theater to see *Manhattan Melodrama*, starring Clark Gable. When the film ended two hours later, the trio exited the theater and turned left. FBI special agent Melvin Purvis, who had been hunting Dillinger for some time, was standing in a doorway when Dillinger walked past. He lit a cigar, which was the signal to other FBI agents to move in.

"Dillinger quickly realized what was happening and acted by instinct," said the official FBI account. "He grabbed a pistol from his right trouser pocket as he ran toward the alley. Five shots were fired

★ ★ ★ ★ ★ ★ ★ ★ ★ ★ ★ ★ ★ ★ ★ ★ ★ ★ ★ ★ ★ ★ ★ ★ ★ ★ ★ ★ ★ ★

The Biograph Theater, where outlaw John Dillinger was gunned down in 1934

from guns of three FBI agents. Three of the shots hit Dillinger and he fell face down on the pavement."

The agents rushed the mortally wounded criminal to a nearby hospital where he died a few minutes later.

Unlike many locations associated with notorious events, such as the garage where the Valentine's Day Massacre occurred, the Biograph Theater is still around. Considered one of Chicago's oldest neighborhood movie houses, the Biograph was built in 1914 and restored in 2004. It still boasts its original overhanging canopy marquee and a freestanding ticket booth, both of which are characteristics of movie theaters of the time.

As for Anna Sage, the woman who betrayed Dillinger, despite her deal with the FBI, she ended up being deported to Romania in 1936. She died eleven years later from liver disease.

The Biograph Theater stands at 2433 North Lincoln Avenue in Chicago. For more information, go to www.victorygardens.org.

## The Strange Case of H. H. Holmes's Murder Castle
Chicago

Chicago can claim a lot of "firsts," such as being the home of the first Ferris Wheel and the first skyscraper. Sadly, it was also where America's first known serial killer committed his evil deeds. The story of Dr. Henry H. Holmes and his Murder Castle began in the summer of 1886 when Holmes, whose real name was Herman Mudgett, went to work in a drugstore owned by Dr. E. S. Holton, in Englewood, a suburb of Chicago that is now part of the city.

After Dr. Holton died of natural causes, Holmes took over the drugstore claiming he had purchased it from Mrs. Holton, whom he claimed had moved to California. It's believed Mrs. Holton, however, was one of his first victims since she was never heard from again.

In addition to being a killer, Holmes was also a bigamist and a philanderer. In 1878, he had married Clara Lovering in New Hampshire but later abandoned her. Nine years later, he married Myrtle Belnap in Minneapolis, despite still being married to his first wife. That marriage ended in 1889 but a year later he was having an affair with Julia Conner, the wife of one of his employees. By 1893, he had tired of Conner and began a relationship with Minnie Williams. Shortly after, Conner and her daughter disappeared. A year later, he married Georgianna Yoke and shortly after that Williams and her sister, whom Holmes had seduced, also disappeared.

But the murders of those women only hinted at the horrors that would be attributed to Holmes. In 1889, he purchased a large lot across the street from the drugstore and started building a three-story, block-long hotel, which the media later dubbed the Murder Castle.

The Englewood Post Office sits on the site of the
infamous "Murder Castle" built by serial killer
H. H. Holmes in the late nineteenth century.

During the hotel's construction, Holmes repeatedly changed builders so only he completely understood the design of the structure. While
the ground floor housed his relocated drugstore and several shops, the
upper two floors contained a maze of more than seventy rooms along
with secret passages, trap doors, soundproof rooms, stairs that led
nowhere, and doors that could only be opened from the outside.

Even more bizarre were the special elements he incorporated, such
as a hot burning, gas-fueled kiln in the basement and vault rooms
with mysterious gas lines controlled from his office. In 1892, Holmes's
lodging house was completed and he began advertising rooms for
rent, specifically targeting out-of-town visitors coming to Chicago for
the upcoming World's Fair.

# Ferris's Folly?

When Chicago was selected to host the World's Columbian Exposition in 1893, organizers gathered the city's top architects and engineers and challenged them to create a project that could rival past marvels like the Eiffel Tower, built for the 1889 Paris International Exposition. Among those in the audience was George Washington Gale Ferris Jr., a promising thirty-two-year-old Chicago engineer, who had been born in Galesburg, Illinois. Ferris came up with an idea for a giant 250-foot, rotating wheel with thirty-six passenger cars. The fair's board of directors, however, believed the fifty-six-ton sphere would likely collapse under its own weight. It finally approved the project, but told Ferris he had to find his own funding. After spending $25,000 of his own money on plans and specs, the engineer attracted enough investors to complete the attraction and, on June 21, 1893, the Ferris Wheel was officially opened for business. It easily repaid its $250,000 cost and made about $726,000 during the fair's nineteen-week run.

No one knows how many people Holmes killed, although he later said twenty-seven, and some sources have claimed he murdered as many as 200. But it wasn't Holmes's murders that brought him to the attention of police. In 1895, he was arrested in Philadelphia for trying to defraud an insurance company. Chicago police searched the abandoned hotel and discovered in the basement a vat of acid with a human skull and parts of eight ribs not quite dissolved, mounds of quicklime, the kiln, a dissection table, surgical tools, and more bones.

★ ★ ★ ★ ★ ★ ★ ★ ★ ★ ★ ★ ★ ★ ★ ★ ★ ★ ★ ★ ★ ★ ★ ★ ★ ★ ★ ★ ★ ★ ★ ★

In August 1895, a portion of the Murder Castle was mysteriously destroyed by fire. A month later, Holmes was convicted in Philadelphia of murder and sentenced to death. On May 7, 1896, Holmes was hanged and buried, according to his wishes, in a coffin filled with cement that was covered with even more cement (he was concerned about his body being dug up by grave robbers). He is buried in the Holy Cross Cemetery, located south of Philadelphia.

As for the Murder Castle, in 1937, the aging structure was sold to the U.S. government, which demolished it for a new post office. Today, the post office is still there. There are no plaques or signs memorializing the heinous crimes once committed on the site. It's as if it was all a bad dream.

The former site of H. H. Holmes's Murder Castle is on the corner of South Wallace and 63rd Streets in Chicago (now the Englewood Post Office).

## House of Shards
Navy Pier
Chicago

The last place you'd expect to find the world's largest stained glass museum is at downtown Chicago's Navy Pier, a tourist area more known for its 150-foot-high Ferris Wheel and acres of shops and restaurants than for something quite so scholarly. But in 2000, about 150 historic and culturally significant stained glass panels were installed in an 800-foot-long series of galleries along the lower level terraces of the Pier's Festival Hall.

Officially known as the Smith Museum of Stained Glass Windows, it is the first museum in the United States devoted entirely to stained glass windows. The collection has windows dating from 1870 to the present and includes both religious as well as secular designs. The works are divided into four categories: Victorian, Prairie, Modern, and Contemporary.

One of the historic stained glass panels on display in the Smith Museum of Stained Glass Windows at Chicago's Navy Pier.

The impetus for the museum is to recognize the role Chicago played in the commercial stained glass universe. Prominent local artists and companies designed and created many of the windows and nearly all were originally installed in local buildings.

The museum notes that part of the reason Chicago developed such a thriving stained glass industry is that there was a demand for it when the city was forced to rebuild following the Great Chicago Fire of 1871. The business began to decline during the Great Depression and faded away during World War II, when most of the city's building construction was halted.

Among those represented in the collection are internationally famous artists like Frank Lloyd Wright and Louis Sullivan of Chicago and Louis Comfort Tiffany of New York. In fact, the museum boasts thirteen glass panels created in Tiffany's legendary studio. Among the newer pieces are mosaic-like portraits of Dr. Martin Luther King Jr. (entitled *I Have a Dream*) and basketball great Michael Jordan, both created by Seymour Adelman, a Chicago-based stained glass artist.

All of the windows are protected by bulletproof glass so, unlike most museums, visitors are encouraged to look at the works close-up and aren't told how to dress, not to take photos, not to chew gum, eat or drink, or not to speak too loudly. You really couldn't find a more perfect museum for its setting.

The Smith Museum of Stained Glass Windows can be found at Chicago's Navy Pier. For more information, go to www.navypier.com /things2do/rides_attract/smith_museum.html.

### Hugh Hefner's Original Party Pad

Gold Coast Neighborhood
Chicago

Long before *Playboy* magazine founder Hugh Hefner lived in his mansion with his warren of scantily clad bunnies in the tony Holmby Hills area of Los Angeles (made famous in reality shows such as *The Girls Next Door*), he toiled away in Chicago. Hef, in fact, was born in

This stately brick and limestone condo complex in Chicago's Gold Coast neighborhood was once the original Playboy Mansion.

Chicago in 1926. It was also in Chicago that he created the publication that would make him very wealthy and famous.

The story of how Hefner established *Playboy* is well known: In 1953, he was a twenty-seven-year-old freelance cartoonist who borrowed $8,000, including $1,000 from his mother, to publish a magazine that would promote a hedonistic lifestyle, feature well written stories and articles, and contain photos of nude women. He pasted up the first issue, which featured a cover image of then-unknown Marilyn Monroe (as well as a nude centerfold of her), on the kitchen table of his apartment. The rest, as they say, was history.

★ ★ ★ ★ ★ ★ ★ ★ ★ ★ ★ ★ ★ ★ ★ ★ ★ ★ ★ ★ ★ ★ ★ ★ ★ ★ ★ ★ ★ ★

By 1959, Hefner was a big success and began looking for a suitable location to serve not only as his home and office but as a showcase for the "swinging" lifestyle promoted in his magazine. He purchased a stately seventy-two-room mansion in Chicago's elegant Gold Coast neighborhood and renamed it the Playboy Mansion. The brick and limestone house, built in 1899 for Dr. George Isham, soon became the site of regular, lavish parties where *Playboy* centerfold models and other beautiful women (called "Bunnies" in the magazine) mingled with famous actors, athletes, and other celebrities. Hefner hung a brass plate on the mansion door inscribed, "Si Non Oscillas, Noli Tininnare," which was Latin for, "If you don't swing, don't ring."

In 1971, Hefner purchased the 21,987-square-foot Gothic Tudor Playboy Mansion West in Holmby Hills, California. Over the years, he has expanded and renovated the twenty-nine-room house, originally built in 1927.

During the early 1970s, Hefner split his time between the two Playboy Mansions. However, in 1974, he decided to move full-time to the California home. In the early 1980s, his company donated the original Playboy Mansion to the School of the Art Institute of Chicago for dormitories. In 1993, the building was sold to a development company, which gutted the mansion and converted it into upscale condominiums.

Now if only those walls could talk.

The location of the former Chicago Playboy Mansion is 1340 North State Parkway in Chicago.

*Trivia*

The world's first skyscraper (steel-frame building) was built in 1885 in Chicago. Called the Home Insurance Building, it was an amazing ten stories high.

★ ★ ★ ★ ★ ★ ★ ★ ★ ★ ★ ★ ★ ★ ★ ★ ★ ★ ★ ★ ★ ★ ★ ★ ★ ★ ★ ★ ★ ★ ★

## Would You Like Fries with That Funeral?

Gatling's Chapel
Chicago

Gatling's Chapel on Chicago's South Side offers something not found at too many other funeral businesses: a drive-up viewing service.

Visitors drive up to a speakerphone and push a button. A voice asks for the name of the deceased. After signing a conveniently located guest book, the bereaved is told to proceed to a viewing area. There, on a 25-inch television monitor inside a white canopy, the visitor can view a headshot of the deceased. The image only lasts three seconds but the visitor can push a button to see the image as many times as he or she wants.

Owner Lafayette Gatling, a former construction worker, said he came up with the idea in the late 1980s because when he was a laborer he would feel uncomfortable paying his respects while wearing dirty work clothing. "The working person doesn't have time to come in," he told the *New York Times* in 1989.

Gatling also told the *Times* that the video system provides a measure of decorum for some otherwise sticky situations. For example, he said it is invaluable when the deceased has a wife and a girlfriend, both of whom want to pay their respects.

"This way the girlfriend can go through the drive-through and pay her respects in whatever name she chooses, while the wife is inside with the deceased," he said. "It happens all the time."

If you say so.

The Gatling Chapel drive-through, located at 10133 South Halsted Street, is open twenty-four hours a day. For more information, go to www.gatlingchapelinc.com.

## Birthplace of the Golden Arches

Des Plaines

When you visit the lovingly re-created replica of the first official McDonald's fast food restaurant in Des Plaines, you would think it's

# Pulaski Street's Giant Indian, South Side Chicago

If you look at the northwest corner of 63rd and Pulaski Streets, you'll see a pharmacy, an eye care center, a tobacco shop, and, on top of the building, a 45-foot-tall fiberglass statue of a bespectacled Indian. In 1966, the building's owner, an avid collector of Indian paraphernalia, bought the oversized figure, known as Geronimo, from an Indian reservation in Arizona.

Once he was installed, Geronimo faced a problem—vandals peppered his body with real arrows. Initially, the arrows were removed but after a while a few were left sticking to his body because they attracted attention to the businesses. In fact, the chief made a brief cameo appearance in the 1992 movie, Wayne's World.

The giant Indian originally promoted the tobacco shop—a nod to the wooden cigar store Indian statues of yesterday. Longtime neighborhood residents remember a placard on his chest advertising White

Owl cigars. More recently he's been repainted, de-arrowed, and adopted by the eye clinic, which fitted him with a pair of black-frame glasses and installed a new sign on his chest with the bizarre message, Eye Can See Now.

You can't miss Pulaski Street's Giant Indian at 6258 South Pulaski Street in Chicago.

A giant statue of a Native American improbably sells eyeglasses on Chicago's Pulaski Street.

**The first franchised McDonald's restaurant has
been lovingly replicated in Des Plaines.**

where the company was founded. But you'd only be partly correct.
The Des Plaines location was the first franchise opened by Ray Kroc,
who later owned the company, but it was actually the ninth McDonald's restaurant in the chain.

The McDonald's company was actually started in 1940 in San Ber-
nardino, California, by two brothers, Dick and Mac McDonald. The
original food stand offered some two dozen items, mostly barbecue.
However, in 1948, the brothers took notice of the fact that most of
their business was in hamburgers and devised the "Speedee Service
System," which streamlined the menu to a handful of items, namely
hamburgers.

By 1954, the brothers had expanded to eight other locations
in Southern California and Arizona by franchising their successful
formula to other operators. That year, Ray Kroc, a milkshake-mixer

salesman, became fascinated with their hyper-efficient restaurant concept and persuaded the brothers to partner with him in expanding the
restaurants outside of their existing base in California and Arizona.

On April 15, 1955, he opened his first franchise in Des Plaines, a
Chicago suburb. During the next few years, the entrepreneurial Kroc
rapidly expanded the McDonald's brand throughout the country and
within four years there were one hundred McDonald's restaurants
(today, there are about 31,000).

In 1961, Kroc bought out the McDonald brothers for $2.7 million.
The parting, however, wasn't amicable; Kroc thought he had paid too
much and the brothers later believed he squelched on several aspects
of the deal, which was originally sealed with a handshake.

In 1984, the year Kroc died, the McDonald's Corporation knocked
down the aging Des Plaines store where it all began (at least according to company lore) and replaced it with a gleaming, new replica
of the original. Today, the restaurant no longer serves any food but
stands as a frozen-in-time icon. Mannequins dressed in 1955 uniforms
eerily stand inside the building, which is open seasonally (Memorial
Day to Labor Day). In addition to boasting original equipment and
furnishings, in the basement there is a small display of historic photos,
old advertisements, and a video on the company history.

And, after that, if you're just salivating for a Big Mac or a McRib
sandwich—there is an operational McDonald's restaurant right across
the street.

McDonald's #1 Store Museum can be found at 400 North Lee
Street in Des Plaines. Go to www.aboutmcdonalds.com/mcd/our
_company/museums/first_store_museum.html for more information.

## The Greatest Show beneath the Earth
Forest Park

Anyone wandering through the Woodlawn Cemetery in Forest Park
can't help but notice an unusual collection of five stone elephant statues surrounding a large plot of graves. A granite marker indicates the

★ ★ ★ ★ ★ ★ ★ ★ ★ ★ ★ ★ ★ ★ ★ ★ ★ ★ ★ ★ ★ ★ ★ ★ ★ ★ ★ ★ ★ ★

**This elephant statue marks the site of Showmen's Rest, where fifty-six circus performers and workers were buried following a tragic train accident in 1918.**

name of the site is Showmen's Rest and it is a 750-plot section of the cemetery that is maintained by the Showmen's League of America in memory of departed show people.

Showmen's Rest, in fact, traces its beginning to 1917, when the Showmen's League of America purchased a section of the Woodlawn Cemetery to serve as a burial ground for its members. The league had been formed five years earlier to promote friendship and fellowship among show people.

On June 22, 1918, eighty-six members of the Hagenback-Wallace Circus were killed in a tragic train accident near Hammond, Indiana. The circus, which had 400 performers and roustabouts (temporary help

★ ★ ★ ★ ★ ★ ★ ★ ★ ★ ★ ★ ★ ★ ★ ★ ★ ★ ★ ★ ★ ★ ★ ★ ★ ★ ★ ★ ★ ★ ★ ★ ★

hired to set up and tear down the tents), was traveling to Hammond for a performance when its train was struck by an empty troop train.

According to a later inquiry, the troop train's operator fell asleep and missed several warnings to stop. Meanwhile, the circus train had stopped to cool an overheated wheel bearing. At about 4 a.m., the troop train slammed into the back of the stationary circus train. A fire broke out, which burned many of the crash survivors who were trapped beneath the wreckage.

Five days after the disaster, fifty-six of the dead were buried in Woodlawn Cemetery. Because many of the victims' real names were not known, many headstones were merely labeled UNKNOWN MALE. a few indicate descriptions or nicknames, such as baldy and 4 horse driver.

To commemorate the dead, the five elephant statues erected around the perimeter of the mass of graves have one foot raised and perched on a ball and trunks down. An elephant with a raised trunk is said to represent joy and excitement while a lowered trunk symbolizes mourning. The largest of the elephants stands in the center on a stone pedestal carved with the words, SHOWMEN'S LEAGUE OF AMERICA. the bases of the four smaller elephants contain the words SHOWMEN'S REST.

At night, you can sometimes hear the faint sound of trumpeting elephants—which sounds kind of spooky until you realize the cemetery is only about a mile away from the Brookfield Zoo.

Showmen's Rest is tucked inside the Woodlawn Cemetery at 7750 West Cermak Road in Forest Park.

## The Queen of Joliet
Joliet

In the category of great Illinois inventions, it's hard to find anything quite as amazing as soft serve vanilla ice cream. The tasty dessert traces its roots to 1938, when John F. McCullough and his son Alex, who owned an ice cream business, began experimenting with a soft frozen dairy product in their company in Green River (located in the Quad Cities area).

This Joliet storefront, now home to a Spanish-language church, was once the first Dairy Queen shop.

★ ★ ★ ★ ★ ★ ★ ★ ★ ★ ★ ★ ★ ★ ★ ★ ★ ★ ★ ★ ★ ★ ★ ★ ★ ★ ★ ★

After perfecting a formula that was soft and flavorful yet could hold its shape, the two contacted Sherb Noble, a friend and customer, who agreed to sell the frozen treat on an all-you-can-eat basis at his ice cream stand in Kankakee. In the first two hours, they were astounded when he served more than 1,600 dishes of soft serve ice cream to customers paying 10 cents apiece.

Convinced they were onto something special, the McCulloughs bought the rights to a commercial device they found that could make large quantities of their soft serve ice cream. John McCullough named their dessert, "Dairy Queen," because he said it would be the queen of the dairy industry.

In 1940, the McCulloughs and Noble opened their first soft serve ice cream shop, which they named Dairy Queen, after their ice cream, in a brick building in the town of Joliet, located about 40 miles south of Chicago.

The business was a huge success and Noble began opening additional shops in the Midwest. Additionally, the McCulloughs began franchising the company name, ice cream machines, and mixes to other owners. By 1947, there were one hundred DQs and by 1950, there were 1,446. Today, there are more than 5,900 Dairy Queen restaurants around the world.

Of course, along the way the company added items to the menu. A company timeline shows that the company added milkshakes and malts in 1949, banana splits in 1951, Dilly Bars (round frozen vanilla bars dipped in chocolate) in 1955, and broilers for hamburgers and hot dogs in 1958. In 1998, the company was purchased by Warren Buffett's Berkshire Hathaway Inc., which continues to own it.

As for that first Dairy Queen store in Joliet, unfortunately it closed a number of years ago. More recently, the building was converted into a small storefront church. You might say it has gone from serving ice cream to serving a higher authority.

The site of the first Dairy Queen is at 501 North Chicago Street.

# The Little Burger Joint That Could, Choo-Choo Restaurant, Des Plaines

While McDonald's may be the big name in dining usually associated with Des Plaines, there's another hamburger joint in town that's been around even longer. In 1951, the Choo-Choo Restaurant opened in downtown Des Plaines. The concept was unique—serve hamburgers in baskets placed on a Lionel model train that ran around the counter and stopped in front of the customers.

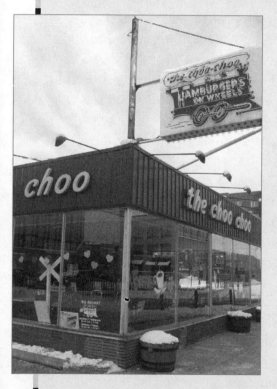

The historic Choo-Choo Restaurant, where burgers are served from a model train

Two brothers, Roy and James Ballowe, are credited with the idea. Roy is said to have thought of it while sitting in a foxhole in the Philippines during World War II. The Des Plaines Choo-Choo opened in May 1951 and quickly became a local icon.

Stopping for a meal at the Choo-Choo is like stepping into the past. Little of the interior has changed. It still has its original Formica counter surfaces, terrazzo floors, faux wood paneling, and Naugahyde chairs.

The Choo-Choo Restaurant is located at 600 N. Lee Street in Des Plaines. For more information call (847) 391-9815 or go to www.thechoochoo.com.

## The Blues Brothers' Home Away from Home

Old Joliet Prison
Joliet

Even though it no longer has any inmates, the Old Joliet Prison still looks like the kind of place where you wouldn't want to spend much time. Opened in 1858, the seventy-two-acre, Gothic Revival–style prison was built on a solid limestone base to prevent prisoners from building escape tunnels. On three sides, it had imposing 25-foot-high limestone walls with turret-like guard towers (the fourth side was the location of the main administration building, which looks like a castle). At the time it was completed, the facility was large enough for 761 inmates, making it the largest prison in the country. By 1872, the prison population had reached more than 1,200, as the 4-foot-by-7-foot cells originally designed for one inmate were used to house two.

Because of its generally harsh and crowded conditions, life in Joliet in the nineteenth century wasn't easy. According to the informational signs posted by the Joliet Area Historical Museum, "inmates were initially treated with little respect and strict rules. Transported daily through a routine of lockstep marching, inmates would wake, eat, work and sleep on a defined and repetitive basis."

Additionally, prison cells had no windows or little ventilation and didn't have running water or toilets until 1956. Prior to that renovation, inmates utilized sewage buckets in their cells and a communal washroom. The twentieth century brought modest reforms such as schooling, music programs, and sports teams for the inmates as well as the electric chair, brought to the prison in 1928 (it was the location of the state's first execution by electrocution).

Among the more famous inmates to be housed in Joliet were Nathan Leopold and Richard Loeb, two brilliant University of Chicago students, who, in 1924, kidnapped and murdered Robert Franks just to see if they could get away with it (obviously, they didn't).

In 2002, state officials ordered the then-144-year-old prison to be closed because of its unsafe conditions. More recently, the city of Joliet has converted the former prison parking lot near the entrance

The castle-like entrance to the historic Joliet Prison,
made famous in the film *The Blues Brothers*

into the Old Joliet Prison Park with information kiosks explaining the place's history. Additionally, the city is trying to interest investors in redeveloping the historic prison—although it's tough to imagine such an ominous place succeeding as a prison-themed multiplex theater or shopping mall. No doubt shoplifting would be virtually nonexistent.

Over the years, the prison has been a popular location for television and movie projects, most famously in the beginning of the 1980 comedy, The Blues Brothers, when one of the main characters, "Joliet" Jake Blues (John Belushi), is released from the prison. Additionally, the facility has appeared in several episodes of the Fox TV drama *Prison Break*.

The Old Joliet Prison can still be seen at 1125 Collins Street in Joliet. For more information, go to www.visitjoliet.com/prison.html.

★ ★ ★ ★ ★ ★ ★ ★ ★ ★ ★ ★ ★ ★ ★ ★ ★ ★ ★ ★ ★ ★ ★ ★ ★ ★ ★ ★ ★ ★

### The Legend of Resurrection Mary
Justice

Few ghost stories about the Chicago area are as well known as those involving Resurrection Mary, a phantom hitchhiker who several drivers claim to have picked up at various locations on Archer Avenue in the Chicago suburb of Justice, and then dropped off at the Resurrection Cemetery.

Tales about Mary, said to be an attractive, blond, blue-eyed young woman dressed in a white party gown, started cropping up in the 1930s. According to the Ghost Research Society (yes, such a group exists), the earliest eyewitness account came from a South Side Chicago man who said that late one night he picked up a young woman of that description, actually went dancing with her (she was, he said, cold to the touch) and then dropped her off at the cemetery, where she mysteriously disappeared.

A 1992 *Chicago Tribune* story described Mary as "the ghost of a woman who was killed in a car crash in the 1930s and buried, in her dancing dress and shoes, in Resurrection Cemetery." The article continued, "shortly after her death, travelers, mostly men, reported seeing her apparition on the roads around Resurrection Cemetery, and others encountered her in ballrooms and dance clubs nearby. They have danced with her, talked with her and driven her home, only to have her disappear from their presence."

A cab driver's sensational account of a late night encounter with Mary appeared in 1979 in the *Chicago Tribune's Suburban Trib* publication. In this version, a cabbie identified as Ralph said he had spotted a young woman walking beside the road who was wearing no coat despite blizzard conditions. He offered her a ride and she allegedly jumped into his car.

"She had on this fancy kind of white dress, like she'd just been to a wedding or something, and those new kind of disco-type shoes, with straps and that," he told the newspaper. "I asked her where she was going and she said she had to get home . . . a couple miles

Entrance to Resurrection Cemetery in Justice, said to be
one of Chicagoland's most haunted sites

up Archer there, she jumped with a start like a horse and said 'Here! Here!' I hit the brakes. I looked around and didn't see no kind of house. 'Where?' I said. And then she sticks out her arm and points across the road to my left and says 'There!'

"And that's when it happened. I looked to my left, like this, at this little shack. And when I turned she was gone. Vanished! And the car door never opened. May the good Lord strike me dead, it never opened."

Some believe that Mary is actually Mary Bregovy, a young Polish-American woman who died in a car accident in 1934, and who is buried in Resurrection Cemetery. According to them, she wanders around the area because her grave was disrupted. Allegedly, during the 1920s and '30s, many graves were purchased with twenty-five-year leases. When the lease ended, the family members were offered a chance to repurchase the site or, if they didn't, the deceased was disinterred and the plot resold.

Is Mary real? A recent drive on Archer Avenue, past the Resurrection Cemetery, revealed a vast burial ground that paralleled the road for what seemed like at least a half mile. The Catholic cemetery, which has been around since 1907, was big but ordinary. There were no pretty female hitchhikers in white dresses beside the road.

Of course, it was also the middle of the day—when it was safe to check such things out.

The Resurrection Catholic Cemetery & Mausoleums (708-458-4770) is at 7201 Archer Avenue in Justice. Please note, however, that the cemetery's managers—spoilsports that they are—dismiss any ghost stories related to the area.

## Bachelor's Grove Cemetery
Midlothian

It's no wonder the ghosts said to roam Bachelor's Grove Cemetery in the south Chicago hamlet of Midlothian might be a bit ticked off. For one thing, the tiny, one-acre cemetery has been virtually abandoned for the past half century, so it's overgrown with tall grass and weeds.

Additionally, in the 1960s, the main access road was closed, which made it even more isolated and a perfect target for vandals.

According to some sources, the cemetery once had as many as one hundred tombstones but only about twenty remain today—most either destroyed or carted off. Graves have also been dug up, with bones scattered about on the grounds. Headstones too heavy to remove have been knocked over or covered with spray-painted graffiti.

The result is a cemetery that has been called one of the most paranormally active in the Midwest. Ghost hunters claim more than one hundred documented reports of such things as glowing balls of light and ghostly apparitions. There have also been stories of a vanishing farm house, disappearing car lights on the nearby Midlothian Turnpike, and sightings of a young boy and a mysterious woman who, when there is a full moon, wanders the cemetery holding a baby.

The cemetery, which sits in the Rubio Woods Forest Preserve, was founded in the 1830s and was originally known as Everden, after a nearby property owner who donated the land. The name, Bachelor's Grove, can be traced to the early 1800s, when German immigrants established a small settlement in the woods there. The hamlet, which had a post office, was named Batchelor's Grove after a pioneer family. Over the years, the spelling has been Americanized to Bachelor's Grove.

According to historians, when the Rock Island and Pacific Railroad was built through the area in 1853, most of the residents of Bachelor's Grove relocated to the nearest rail station, leaving the cemetery to fend for itself.

The ghost stories associated with Bachelor's Grove first popped up in the 1950s, when local teenagers discovered the abandoned cemetery and began hanging out there, often picnicking among the graves (when they weren't destroying them). Soon, there were tales of pale blue lights and spectral figures.

Today, the cemetery is no longer visited as much as it once was because there's not much of it remaining. Still, there is a feeling that

★ ★ ★ ★ ★ ★ ★ ★ ★ ★ ★ ★ ★ ★ ★ ★ ★ ★ ★ ★ ★ ★ ★ ★ ★ ★ ★ ★

comes over visitors who stroll down the dirt road leading to the cemetery. It's not exactly fear or fright. Okay, maybe it is fear and fright.

Bachelor's Grove Cemetery is located at 143rd Street and the Midlothian Turnpike in Midlothian. A good source of information can be found at www.bachelorsgrove.com.

## Ernest Hemingway's Gingerbread House Birthplace
Oak Park

Famed writer Ernest Hemingway's delicate Queen Anne–style birthplace home in Oak Park is hard to reconcile with his macho reputation.

With its turret, wrap-around porch and Victorian trim, the Hemingway Birthplace, as it is known, is graceful and elegant. The house was built in 1890 by the famed writer's maternal grandfather, Ernest Hall. Hemingway was born in a second floor bedroom on July 21, 1899, the second child of Dr. Clarence and Grace Hall Hemingway.

Hemingway only resided in the home for the first six years of his life. In addition to his older sister, those living in the 5,500-square-foot house when he was born included his parents, grandfather, an uncle (Tyley), and a maid. He would later gain three more sisters and a brother.

The house's design reflected its era, having a large entry hall, a parlour/living room, a formal library, a large dining room, and a kitchen on the first floor. On the second floor, the family had a nursery, five bedrooms, and a bathroom. The attic was filled with Hemingway's father's collection of wildlife specimens.

Following the death of his grandfather in 1905, the family moved to a more modern, Prairie-style house at 600 North Kenilworth Avenue, located a few blocks away. The latter house, which remains a private residence, is where Hemingway lived for the next thirteen years (and, tragically, where his father committed suicide).

Hemingway left Oak Park in 1919 and, of course, went on to great acclaim as a writer, penning classic novels such as *The Sun Also Rises*, *For Whom the Bell Tolls*, and *The Old Man and the Sea*.

Ernest Hemingway's birthplace in the
Chicago suburb of Oak Park

★ ★ ★ ★ ★ ★ ★ ★ ★ ★ ★ ★ ★ ★ ★ ★ ★ ★ ★ ★ ★ ★ ★ ★ ★ ★ ★ ★

As for the Birthplace, after the Hemingway family sold the house, it went through a succession of owners and was substantially modified over time. The Ernest Hemingway Foundation of Oak Park acquired the house in 1992 and raised more than $1 million to restore it to its original appearance. Today, the Birthplace is open daily to the public for regularly scheduled tours.

At the time Hemingway lived in the house, Oak Park was a conservative, upper middle class suburb of Chicago favored by bankers and physicians. The writer would later refer to his hometown as a place of "wide lawns and narrow minds."

To visit the Ernest Hemingway Birthplace, head to 339 North Oak Park Avenue in Oak Park. Call (708) 848-2222 or go to www.ehfop .org for more information.

## A Funeral Home Where You Can Putt Around

Ahlgrim's Funeral Home
Palatine

It sounds like a joke but it's real—there's a funeral home in the Chicago suburb of Palatine that has a nine-hole miniature golf course in the basement. Known as Ahlgrim Acres, the golf course even has a tongue-in-cheek horror-theme with holes that feature a coffin, skulls, a bloody scythe, a hangman's noose, headstones, a mummy, and a tiny crypt. Screams and spooky music permeate the air.

The golf course was the idea of the funeral home's owner, Roger Ahlgrim, who, in 1964, moved into the building and found it had a large basement that he didn't need. Since he loved playing miniature golf, he decided to build an indoor, nine-hole course in the space.

For the next several decades, the attraction was something only enjoyed by a selected few, basically family and staff. As his children grew up, he added a full size shuffleboard course, a ping-pong table, bumper pool, and a foosball table, along with a variety of video and pinball games. Word of the bizarre

Tucked in the basement of Ahlgrim's Funeral Home in the Chicago suburb of Palatine is Ahlgrim Acres—a nine-hole miniature golf course, open by appointment.

miniature-golf-course-in-the-funeral-home began to spread and Ahlgrim started welcoming local church and civic groups to meet in the basement.

In recent years, Ahlgrim Acres has been open to the public by appointment (847-358-7411) although never when there is a funeral in progress (there should be some decorum). Ahlgrim Acres Miniature Golf is located at 201 North Northwest Highway in Palatine. For more information, go to www.ahlgrimffs.com/golfcourse.htm.

## Baha'i in the Sky

Wilmette

You can see the Baha'i House of Worship from miles away. Located at 100 Linden Avenue in Wilmette, about 18 miles north of Chicago, the domed, nine-sided temple stands 160 feet high, rising above the surrounding residential neighborhood and overlooking the shores of nearby Lake Michigan. But what makes the structure so striking is its elegant, lace-like exterior ornamentation. No wonder it was selected one of the state of Illinois's official "Seven Wonders of Illinois."

The Baha'i facility in Wilmette is one of only seven Baha'i Houses of Worship in the world. The cornerstone for the building was laid in 1912, but work did not begin in earnest until 1920 and it wasn't completed until 1953. A French-Canadian architect, Louis Bourgeois, who had joined the religion in the early twentieth century, designed the temple, including full-scale drawings of the building's intricate ornamentation.

Bourgeois's plans called for a concrete and steel superstructure on which thin, white 100-foot-square molded concrete panels would be attached. At the time it was being built, the use of architectural concrete was in its infancy so many of the techniques and materials were being used for the first time in the construction of the temple.

According to *Structure* magazine, creating brilliantly white concrete was one of the main challenges. The company responsible tried several mixes before finding a concrete blend that incorporated white opaque quartz from South Carolina with clear translucent quartz from Virginia to achieve the extremely white look Bourgeois wanted. In the end, 743 tons of quartz were used to create the panels.

The temple's interior is equally impressive with tall, sweeping windows and walls covered with intricate patterns. The interior of the dome is a tight mass of interwoven concrete and stained glass. The temple originally cost more than $2.6 million, paid out as it was raised, which explains why it took so long to complete.

Wilmette's elegant Baha'i House of Worship is one of the official "Seven Wonders of Illinois."

# The Leaning Tower of Niles

Industrialist and inventor Robert Ilg Sr. wanted to do something special for the employees of his Ilg Hot Air Ventilation Company. So, in 1934, he built them a twenty-two-acre recreational park in the Chicago suburb of Niles, complete with two large spring-fed swimming pools with cabanas and a wooden toboggan run. To store water needed for the pools, he erected a large tower. However, he didn't want the usual tank-on-a-tripod design of most water towers and constructed a half-size replica of Italy's famous Leaning Tower of Pisa to hide the water tower.

The Niles Leaning Tower is about 95 feet high (the original is 177 feet) and leans at about half the tilt of the original. In 1960, Ilg donated part of the park to the local YMCA to build a high-rise residential complex. Four years later, when he died, he left the tower to the YMCA with the condition that it remain standing until 2059. The YMCA, in turn, leased the tower to the village of Niles for $1 per year.

The Leaning Tower of Niles is located at 6300 Touhy Avenue.

The suburb of Niles contains a half-size replica of the famous Leaning Tower of Pisa.

The Baha'i faith was founded in 1863 in Persia and was introduced to Americans during the 1893 World's Columbian Exposition in Chicago. A few years after the exposition, members began discussing the need to have a Baha'i temple built in North America. One of the American church's leaders was Corrine True of Chicago, who succeeded in having it located in the Chicago area. In 1996, the temple underwent a $6 million restoration, which ensured it would continue to remain a wonder.

The impressive Baha'i Temple is located at 100 Linden Avenue in Wilmette. For hours and other information, go to www.bahai.us /bahai-temple.

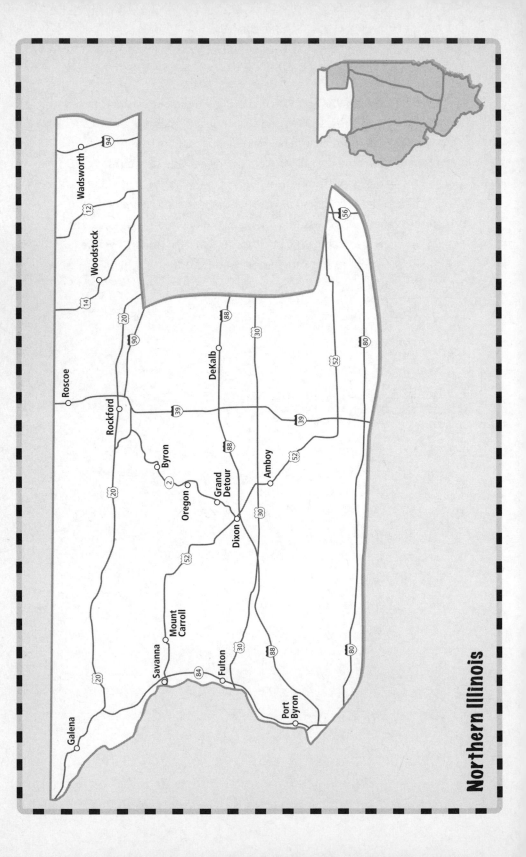

**Northern Illinois**

# 2

# Northern Illinois

"Ditches along prairie roads of Northern Illinois
Filled the arch of night with young bullfrog songs."

—Carl Sandburg, "Young Bullfrogs," 1918

**Perhaps the most** *amazing thing about Northern Illinois is how rural and bucolic it is while still being in the shadow of the uber-urbanized Chicago region. Like much of the rest of the state, it's got acres of corn and soybeans, but it also boasts the second-largest city in the state, Rockford (population 157,000) as well as several scenic river corridors including the Great River Road along the east side of the Mississippi and the magnificent Rock River, which meanders westward from the Wisconsin border down to the Mississippi River at Rock Island.*

*The official Illinois state slogan is the "Land of Lincoln," but the northern part of the state, which includes the area west of Chicagoland, north of I-80, south of Wisconsin, and east of the Mississippi River, could just as easily be known as the "Realm of Reagan." The fortieth president was born in Tampico, Illinois, a tiny village of about 800 people, but spent much of his childhood and teen years in nearby Dixon. "It was in Dixon that I really found myself," Reagan later wrote. "We arrived there in 1920 when I was nine years old, and to me it was heaven."*

*In his memoirs, Reagan praised growing up in Northern Illinois, noting, "As I look back on those days in Dixon, I think my life was as sweet* and idyllic as it could be, as close as I could imagine for a young boy to the world created by Mark Twain in The Adventures of Tom Sawyer."

This is also where, in 1843, Margaret Fuller wrote one of her most famous poems, "Ganymede to His Eagle," while standing on a cliff overlooking the Rock River near Oregon, Illinois. Fuller, a prominent early nineteenth century journalist, editor, critic, and women's rights advocate, spent that summer traveling around the upper Midwest and New England states, interacting with several Native American tribes. Inspired by her surroundings, Fuller wrote:

Upon the rocky mountain stood the boy,
A goblet of pure water in his hand,
His face and form spoke him one made for job,
A willing servant to sweet love's command.

Of course, not everyone who hails from the northern quadrant of the state has waxed so poetic about the area. Supermodel Cindy Crawford is from DeKalb, where she was co-valedictorian of her high school class, but she's not on record saying too much about her hometown. Ditto for Ally McBeal actress Calista Flockhart from Freeport. On the other hand, 1970s rock band Cheap Trick, which was founded in Rockford, once named an album after their hometown (and two members continue to live there).

Additionally, Illinois's northern territory is home to not only Pretzel City U.S.A. (Freeport) but also the Barbed Wire Capital of the World (DeKalb), the Plow Capital of the World (Moline), and the Melon Capital of the World (Thomson).

What more could anyone ask for?

## Wood for Thought
Amboy

When a summer storm slammed into the city park in the small farming community of Amboy in 1999, it tore up chain link fences and
some five dozen mature trees. Surveying the tangle of damaged trees,
then-mayor Hank Gerdes recalled someone had told him about a
pair of chainsaw artists, originally from Amboy, who could transform
tree trunks into works of art. He had a crazy thought: Why not hire
the artists, Bob and Marie Boyer, to carve any salvageable wood into
sculptures for the park?

A few of the more than two dozen carved wooden
figures found in the Amboy City Park

Other city officials embraced the plan, agreed to hire the Boyers, known as "The Chainsaw Two," and Amboy gained a new attraction. During the past decade or so, the Boyers have created about thirty carved wooden images ranging from a giant cross, to a 6-foot lion, to former U.S. presidents Ulysses S. Grant, Abraham Lincoln, and Ronald Reagan (all from Illinois). Each image represents some aspect of Amboy life or history.

# Quite a Pair—Turkey Testicle Festivals in Byron and Huntley

Who even knew that turkeys had nuts (apparently they're in a chest cavity rather than between their legs)? Obviously, the good people of Byron and Huntley are not only aware of turkey anatomical parts but have capitalized on those two particular glands with their annual Turkey Testicle Festivals. The Byron event, started in 1979, is held the second Saturday in October while Huntley's, which began in 1984, is conducted on the weekend before Thanksgiving. Proceeds from both are donated to various local charities.

Of course, the big question—what do they taste like? According to veteran testicle tasters, they have a soft, fatty consistency with a flavor similar to that of chicken organs such as liver or gizzards. It's recommended that first timers dip them in ketchup or Tabasco sauce. Lots of ketchup or Tabasco sauce.

Byron's Turkey Testicle Festival is held at the Union Street Station bar and restaurant in Byron, which is located 12 miles southwest of Rockford. Huntley's event is held in the Parkside Pub in Huntley, which is 43 miles east of Rockford.

The shiny, varnished rustic statues are scattered throughout shady Amboy Green River City Park, which has recovered nicely since the big storm. One of the first wooden icons was a 6-foot-tall baseball player, stationed, naturally, near the park's baseball diamonds. The player has the number 4 on his jersey, which was Baseball Hall of Famer Lou Gehrig's number, because Marie Boyer is related to him. The Boyers also created images of a football player, a bear, eagles, a squirrel, and an owl. Local citizens and businesses sponsored other carvings including a 7-foot farmer, who actually resembles a prominent local farmer, and a large representation of a steam engine with a coal car, boxcar, flatcar, and caboose, because the Illinois Central Railroad was important to the creation of the community in 1854.

Clearly, it beats having to turn all those dead trees into toothpicks or garden mulch.

Amboy Green River City Park is located on East Main Street in Amboy. The town is 13 miles southeast of Dixon via IL 52.

## A Couple of Sharp Guys
DeKalb

It's said that the invention of barbed wire tamed the American West. It also made Joseph Glidden and Isaac Ellwood of DeKalb very, very rich. The first patent for barbed wire was granted in 1867 to Lucien Smith of Kent, Ohio, but it was Glidden who improved the design and made it workable (and was granted his own patent in 1874). The problem with earlier barbed wire was that the barbs slid along the wire. Glidden concocted a way to crimp the barbs to keep them in place.

Later, Glidden partnered with Ellwood, a DeKalb hardware store owner and entrepreneur, to begin selling his invention. The two were immediately successful, as western ranchers found it was a cheap and easy way to install fencing that could restrain cattle. Within a few short years, DeKalb—and, bizarrely, not some place like Texas or Arizona—became the center of the barbed wire manufacturing industry in the United States.

**Thirty-room mansion built by DeKalb's barbed wire baron Isaac Ellwood in 1879**

Like nearly every wealthy nineteenth century industrialist, Ellwood soon decided to build an oversized mansion as a monument to his success. Ellwood's house, now a museum, was ostentatious to say the least—a three-story, thirty-room, brick Gothic Victorian showcase with six baths and two wine cellars built in 1879.

Glidden, however, continued to live in a more modest house that he built in 1861. The two-story structure, made of locally fired bricks, incorporated a French Colonial architectural style and included a raised basement and a full-length porch. Glidden is said to have worked on his barbed wire innovations in the basement kitchen of the house. Of course, that's not to say Glidden didn't spend his money. At the time of his death in 1906, he was one of the wealthiest men in America. In 1898, he donated sixty-three acres of his DeKalb property for the site of Northern Illinois Normal School, which evolved into Northern Illinois University.

Since 1908, the violet has been the official state flower of Illinois. The white oak is the official state tree.

Today, the Ellwood House (509 North First Street) sits in a small, shaded park in the center of DeKalb, which has grown up to engulf the site of the former estate. A visitor center has been built to the rear of the house, which contains the Barbed Wire History Gallery (more strands of the stuff than you can imagine). The opulent home, which contains its original furnishings, is open for regular tours. Go to www.ellwoodhouse.org for more information.

As for Glidden's abode, it, too, is an historic landmark. Known as the Joseph F. Glidden Homestead and Historical Center, it has been restored and is open for public tours. The homestead is located at 921 West Lincoln Highway (IL 38), south of the Northern Illinois University campus in DeKalb. For more information, go to www.glidden homestead.org.

## The Unofficial Official Ronald Reagan Boyhood Home
Dixon

Just looking at President Ronald Reagan's boyhood home in Dixon explains a lot about the man. It's a simple, two-story Queen Anne–style wood frame home in a quiet, shaded residential neighborhood. Very Norman Rockwell. When the nonprofit Ronald Reagan Boyhood Home Foundation purchased the house in 1980, it carefully restored the structure to its appearance when the former president lived there (for three years, from 1920 to 1923). Reagan later joked that if the house had looked so good when he lived in it he might never have left. Reagan always claimed Dixon, a sleepy, pretty typical small

President Ronald Reagan grew up in this
modest home in Dixon in the 1920s.

Midwestern town on the banks of the Rock River, helped to shape his
worldview.

While Reagan's boyhood home is listed on the National Register of
Historic Places and open for public tours, it's not an official national
historic site. In 2002, federal legislation was approved authorizing the
Department of the Interior to purchase the property and establish an
official historic site under the National Park Service, but the government and the foundation couldn't agree on a fair price—reportedly
the two sides were several millions of dollars apart. As a result, the
foundation continues to operate the house as well as an adjacent
home (the home of the Reagan family's former landlord), which has
been converted into a visitor center and gift shop.

## Trivia

In 1974, a third grader from Decatur began a campaign to designate the regal monarch butterfly as the Illinois official state insect. The General Assembly agreed a year later.

Ronald Reagan's Boyhood Home is located at 816 South Hennepin Avenue in Dixon. For more information, go to www.ronald reaganhome.com. Just don't ask the National Park Service.

# Dixon's Other Favorite Son

While he was born on a farm outside of Galesburg, the founder of the ubiquitous Walgreen's drugstore chain grew up in Dixon. Born in 1873, young Charles Walgreen and his family moved to Dixon in 1887. He attended Dixon High School and the Dixon Business College before taking a job as a bookkeeper at a local general store. After working briefly in a shoe factory, where the top of his middle finger was cut off in an accident, he began working as an apprentice at a Dixon drugstore. In 1893, Walgreen headed to Chicago where he became a registered pharmacist and worked at several pharmacies. In 1901, he purchased his first pharmacy and, over the next quarter century, expanded his holdings to include more than 110 Walgreen stores. Today, there are more than 7,500 Walgreen's across the nation—including one in Dixon.

# Ode to a Plow Maker, Grand Detour

In 1837, John Deere (1804–1886) invented a plow. It was a darned good plow made of polished steel, but it was a plow. However, based on the reverence afforded him at the John Deere Historic Site in Grand Detour, you might think he had invented a cure for the common cold or at least Starbucks coffee. The place is a shrine to the man who helped make it infinitely easier to dig through the Midwest's cakey prairie soil.

A statue of John Deere stands on the grounds of his longtime home and blacksmith shop, now a national historic site.

The attraction boasts an enclosed archaeological dig site preserved as if it had yielded the priceless fossils of million-year-old dinosaurs or the tomb of an Egyptian pharaoh. There's also a life-sized bronze statue of Deere, in full blacksmith regalia, hammering away on an anvil. Today, the Deere company, headquartered in Moline, is one of the largest manufacturers of agricultural equipment in the world with annual revenues of more than $11 billion.

Okay, maybe it was a pretty special plow.

The John Deere Historic Site is located at 8334 South Clinton Street in Grand Detour, which is 6 miles northeast of Dixon via IL 2. For more information, go to www.JohnDeereHistoricSite.com.

## The Dutch Connection
Fulton

At first glance, the big Dutch-style wooden windmill in the center of the Mississippi River town of Fulton seems odd. But it all makes sense once you delve into the town's history. It turns out that Fulton, named in honor of the man who invented the steamboat (Robert Fulton), was settled by a number of immigrants including a large contingent originally from the Netherlands. The first Dutch settler arrived when the town was established in 1835 and by the late 1880s there were several hundred families. In 1974, Fulton decided to celebrate its Dutch heritage with an authentic Dutch Dinner, which grew into the annual Dutch Days Festival, held the first weekend in May.

**Authentic Dutch-style windmill in downtown Fulton**

★ ★ ★ ★ ★ ★ ★ ★ ★ ★ ★ ★ ★ ★ ★ ★ ★ ★ ★ ★ ★ ★ ★ ★ ★ ★ ★ ★ ★ ★ ★ ★

In 1998, the community decided to build a full-size Dutch windmill on a flood-control dike near the center of the town. To ensure its authenticity, the town contracted with a company in the Netherlands to construct a working mill that would be largely preassembled and shipped in sections to Fulton, where the larger parts would be fitted together. Work on the windmill, named De Immigrant, began in 1999 and was completed in 2001. The result is like something out of a Van Gogh painting—a 100-foot-high windmill with four massive wooden sail-arms connected to a half-dome cap. The most surreal part is that it overlooks the Mississippi rather than fields of bright tulips.

Fulton is also home of the new Windmill Cultural Center, which contains displays of twenty-one different European windmills (some up to 6 feet tall). The center also has exhibits describing the Dutch history of the community and the story of Fulton's windmill. Both the windmill and the cultural center are located at 10th Avenue and First Street in downtown Fulton, which sits on the Great River Road (IL 84) that runs parallel to the Mississippi.

Now if I could just remember where I put those verdomd wooden shoes . . .

## The Eternal Indian
Lowden State Park
Oregon

When it comes to Illinois artists, Lorado Taft is considered a giant. Born in 1860 in the Central Illinois town of Elmwood, he graduated from the University of Illinois and taught at the University of Chicago and the Art Institute of Chicago for several decades. Over the years, he produced a number of noteworthy public artworks including the *Fountain of Time* on Chicago's Midway and *Fountain of the Great Lakes* at the Art Institute of Chicago.

In 1898, he and several Chicago artists, architects, and writers founded the Eagle's Nest Art Colony on a bluff overlooking the Rock River. The group would spend several weeks each summer in rustic

Lorado Taft's famous *The Eternal Indian*
statue at Lowden State Park

★ ★ ★ ★ ★ ★ ★ ★ ★ ★ ★ ★ ★ ★ ★ ★ ★ ★ ★ ★ ★ ★ ★ ★ ★ ★ ★ ★ ★ ★

accommodations at the colony. In 1908, Taft began work on a giant statue overlooking the river. The work, officially known as *The Eternal Indian*, is a 48-foot-high concrete image of a robed Native American figure with his arms crossed. At the time of its completion in 1911, it was the largest freestanding concrete statue ever made. Later, the work became known as the *Black Hawk Statue* and was said to represent the famous Sauk war leader who defied the U.S. government's attempts to relocate his people and set off the Black Hawk War of 1832. Some scholars have argued that the statue was never meant to literally honor Indians—Taft's human model for it was his non-Indian brother-in-law—and looks nothing like the real Chief Black Hawk, so its true purpose was to symbolically honor the beautiful surroundings.

Whatever the case, the statue is impressive. Taft couldn't have selected a more perfect setting, as the giant sculpture stands in a clearing more than 100 feet above the Rock River. Perhaps Taft was on to something when he spoke at the statue's dedication and said, "It grew out of the ground."

*The Eternal Indian* stands adjacent to a paved road that winds through Lowden State Park, which is located 2 miles northeast of Oregon via IL 64 (across the Rock River) and North River Road. The park is at 1411 North River Road.

*Trivia*

The Illinois General Assembly named the Bluegill as Illinois's official state fish in 1986.

# President Grant Slept Here (really, he did)

Most folks know that Illinois has been home to presidents Abraham Lincoln, Ronald Reagan, and Barack Obama. But less well known is the fact that the eighteenth president, Ulysses S. Grant, also came from the state. While born in Ohio, Grant moved to Galena, Illinois, in 1860 to work as a clerk for his father, who owned a leather goods store. After the outbreak of the Civil War in 1861, Grant, who had served in the Mexican-American War of 1846–48, became an officer in the Union Army. After assuming command of the Union Army, Grant defeated the Confederate Army and accepted its surrender at Appomattox, Virginia. Following the war, Galena residents gave Grant a two-story brick home in the town as a thank you for his military service. He and his family lived in the elegant Italianate-style home until he was elected president in 1868. After serving two terms in Washington, Grant continued

Ulysses S. Grant home in the historic town of Galena

to make periodic trips to the area, staying in his home during his visits. Today, the Ulysses S. Grant Home is an historic site that is open for public tours. The house is located at 500 Bouthillier Street in Galena.

★ ★ ★ ★ ★ ★ ★ ★ ★ ★ ★ ★ ★ ★ ★ ★ ★ ★ ★ ★ ★ ★ ★ ★ ★ ★ ★ ★ ★ ★ ★

### Bones, Moans, and Groans at Raven's Grin Inn
Mount Carroll

Living next door to Raven's Grin Inn in Mount Carroll is probably like being neighbors of the Addams Family—it's creepy and it's kooky, mysterious and spooky. The three-story Italianate mansion is over-grown with bushes and leafy vines, and there are a number of—shall we say—peculiar things protruding from the house walls and foliage, including a giant hand, a 10-foot skull, the front grill of a police (pronounced "Poe-lease" in honor of the famous horror writer) car, the back end of a taxi, and a variety of other objects not usually associated with well-manicured landscaping.

In the late 1980s, its owner, Jim Warfield, transformed the historic 5,000-square-foot house, built in the 1870s, into a year-round haunted house open to the public. Warfield, whose family has lived in Mount Carroll for several generations, is a former plumber who decided to hang up his pipe wrench and have some fun. The result is a combination haunted house–fun house that channels the manic spirit of old *Mad* magazines through a badly cracked lens.

Visitors to Raven's Grin quickly discover that this is no slam-bam, Six Flags–style amusement ride; Warfield wants everyone to get his or her money's worth. Tours can run more than an hour. Most of the time, Warfield hosts the tour, tailoring his presentation to the particular groups.

But if the exterior seems a bit bizarre—one writer described it as "Frankenstein's junkyard"—it only hints at what's inside. The mansion is crammed with horror-themed posters, objects, stuff (for lack of a better word), visual puns, and the usual assortment of skeletons and coffins. But it also features a host of cleverly designed but scare-inducing tricks like disembodied voices, spectral images, and collapsing walls. A 60-foot slide leads from the house's top floor to a large wine cellar in the basement, which is said to be the most (actually) haunted room in the place.

Front of the eclectic and eccentric Raven's Grin Inn
haunted house attraction in Mount Carroll

Not surprisingly, the busiest time of year is around Halloween, when visitors line up outside. Warfield recommends calling ahead for reservations (815-244-4746).

Raven's Grin Inn is located at 411 North Carroll Street in Mount Carroll (it's at the end of—appropriately enough—a dead end street, near a cemetery). Mount Carroll is 120 miles west of Chicago via US 64. The haunted manor is open every evening from 7 p.m. to midnight, and 2 p.m. to 5 p.m. on Saturday and Sunday. Tours are also available by appointment. For more information, go to www.haunted ravensgrin.com.

Check it out if you dare.

# Getting Yanked Around in Port Byron

They sure know how to have a good time in the Mississippi River town of Port Byron. Every August, eleven twenty-member teams grab a 2,400-foot, 680-pound rope that stretches across the river, between the communities of Port Byron and LeClaire, Iowa, and they pull with all their might. The event, called the Great River Tug Fest, has been going on since 1987 and attracts crowds of more than 35,000 spectators (it's also been televised on the Discovery Channel).

The event was started by Scott Verbeckmoes of Port Byron, who had seen a similar but much smaller event in Michigan. Despite some skepticism, he persuaded folks in both Port Byron and its sister city across the Mississippi to give it a try. He got the Port Byron State Bank to pay for the rope, made of four coils of 600-foot rope purchased from the local hardware store that were spliced together. The tug-of-war usually lasts about two hours. During that period, all river traffic is stopped. As of 2010, Port Byron's tug teams held a 13 to 10 margin of victory over their Iowa competitors.

Who says we Midwesterners don't know how to have fun?

Site of the annual Great River Tug Fest in Port Byron

### Sock Monkey City
Rockford

Who would have anticipated that when the Nelson Knitting Company of Rockford began making Rockford Red Heel work socks in 1932 it would inadvertently spark a national craze? It turned out that the socks, in addition to being durable and affordable, were also perfect for sewing into a stuffed toy monkey (the red heel made an excellent mouth). And since the socks appeared during the depths of the Great Depression, when money was tight, homemade sock monkey dolls quickly became a popular toy for many children.

No one knows who actually made the first sock monkey doll. It is known that sometime in the early 1900s, industrious mothers began fashioning knitted socks into dolls for their children to play with. The familiar red-mouthed sock monkey, however, couldn't have been created until after the appearance of the Rockford Red Heel sock. By the 1940s, homemade sock monkeys had become fairly well known around the country and starting in the early 1950s, the Nelson Knitting Company included a sock monkey doll pattern with each pair of socks.

The Nelson Knitting Company was founded in Rockford by John Nelson, a Swedish immigrant who invented a parallel-row knitting machine that could automatically close the heel and toe of a sock. After focusing on manufacturing the machines for several years, Nelson began making his own brand of socks in 1880. The distinctive

## Trivia

In 1865, Illinois became the first state to ratify the Thirteenth Amendment to the Constitution, which abolished slavery.

ANSWER: A famous sock, called a "Rockford," made on special machines invented here and used in the city's knitting factories for over 100 years.
Today the machines are all silent but the sock with the red heel, knit by the Nelson Knitting Company of Rockford, is still famous. The socks are used to make monkey dolls. These dolls are well-known around the world. They are the last visible symbol of Rockford's knitting industry. The socks are now made in Iowa.
The Missing Link: Socks, Monkeys and Rockford's Industrial Past shows the connection between a machine made in the 1870s and the sock monkey doll of today. It looks at the life of Rockford's knitting industry, the people that worked in the factories, and the popularity of the little doll created from the socks they made.
John Nelson invented a knitting machine in 1873. The machine made socks without seams in the toe or heel. Because there were no seams, the socks were very comfortable and quickly became popular across the country. He helped start the Nelson Knitting Company and made Rockford a leader in sock knitting. Socks knit here were everywhere known simply as "rockfords."

"Nelson," the world's largest sock monkey

red heel was added in 1932, after one of the company's advertising executives, Howard Monk, suggested doing so to distinguish the company's socks from competitors.

While the distinctive heather and white, red-heeled socks are no longer made in Rockford—Nelson Knitting was sold to Fox River Mills of Iowa in 1992—sock monkeys have continued to be popular. In fact, the closing of Nelson Knitting in Rockford hasn't stopped the community from capitalizing on its role in sock monkey lore. In 2005, the Midway Village and Museum Center in Rockford, a local historic museum, started the annual Sock Monkey Madness Festival.

Additionally, Midway Village boasts the world's largest sock monkey, a 7-foot-tall stuffed and knitted simian named Nelson made using forty-four Rockford Red Heel socks, as well as one of the oldest, a handmade doll from 1951, which Nelson Knitting was able to use as proof for its patent claim on the sock monkey design. There are also a number of 6-foot fiberglass sock monkeys scattered around Rockford, each decorated by a local artist. One on display at Midway Village has a guitar and is plastered with Cheap Trick memorabilia—thereby combining two of Rockford's most famous icons.

Midway Village and Museum Center is located at 6799 Guilford Road in Rockford. For more information, go to www.MidwayVillage.com.

## Trivia

The highest natural point in Illinois is Charles Mound, located near the Wisconsin-Illinois border. The gentle, sloping hill rises to 1,235 feet high.

★ ★ ★ ★ ★ ★ ★ ★ ★ ★ ★ ★ ★ ★ ★ ★ ★ ★ ★ ★ ★ ★ ★ ★ ★ ★ ★ ★ ★ ★

### From Bonnie & Clyde to Batman
Historic Auto Attractions
Roscoe

The village of Roscoe, population 10,000, sleepy suburb of Rockford, seems like the last place in the world to find the "Ecto-1" ambulance from *Ghostbusters*, George Sanford's junk truck, the Wagon Queen Family Truckster from *National Lampoon's Vacation*, Barney Fife's

The Batmobile from the film *Batman Returns* is one of the many unique vehicles displayed in the Historic Auto Attractions museum in Roscoe.

police car from the *Andy Griffith Show*, and a host of historic vehicles such as a 1932 Studebaker Commander used by John Dillinger in a bank robbery, Adolph Hitler's parade car, Al Capone's beer delivery truck, and Elvis Presley's 1972 Lincoln Mark IV. But they're there, tucked inside an easy-to-overlook private collection/museum with the decidedly un-sexy name, Historic Auto Attractions.

The collection, which is open to the public, is an eclectic treasure trove of historically important vehicles, celebrity wheels, motion picture memorabilia, political paraphernalia, and just plain interesting stuff. Owner Wayne Lensing is an ex–auto assembly line worker who became wealthy building racing car chassis (his company is Lefthander Chassis). In the 1990s, he purchased a limo once owned by reclusive billionaire Howard Hughes and discovered that other people were as interested in its notoriety as he was. So, he began collecting celebrated, unusual, and/or noteworthy vehicles, particularly those related to entertainers, popular culture, and political figures. In 2001, he opened Historic Auto Attractions, which now contains more than seventy of these unique automobiles. He placed his world-class collection of historic and celebrity cars and memorabilia in an industrial neighborhood in Roscoe because it's adjacent to his business.

Not surprisingly, the Movieland and TV Land rooms are particularly popular, containing such objects as one of the Superman costumes worn by actor Christopher Reeve in the 1978 film of that name; the 1986 DeLorean time machine car used in the *Back to the Future* films; a fiberglass, stone-age-style, foot-propelled vehicle used in the 1994 *Flintstones* movie; and vehicles from the 1960s *Batman* TV show and the 1990s films.

Who would have thought Roscoe would be the center of the cool car universe?

Historic Auto Attractions is located at 13825 Metric Drive in Roscoe (which is about 12 miles north of Rockford via IL 251). It's open Tuesday through Saturday 10 a.m. to 5 p.m., Sunday from 11 a.m. to 4 p.m. For more information, go to www.historicautoattractions.com.

# Where Mascots are Hatched, Savanna

Ever wonder where those fuzzy mascot costumes worn at nearly every high school or college football game come from? It turns out the world's largest manufacturer of mascot attire is a small company in the Mississippi River town of Savanna. Called Facemakers, Inc., the company was founded in 1972 by Alan St. George, who continues to serve as its president. St. George, who lives in a renovated 1899 Victorian castle (Havencrest) in Savanna, attended the Chicago Academy of Fine Arts and stumbled onto his future career after making a werewolf costume to wear at the opening of a horror show, *Tales from the Crypt.* His appearance was so striking that he was hired to make a frog costume to promote another horror film, *Frogs,* and quickly realized that's what he wanted to do for a living. These days, his company, which relocated to Savanna from Chicago in 1976, manufactures a wide variety of fiberglass and felt or fur costumes ranging from Smokey Bear to Tony the Tiger for Kellogg's Frosted Flakes.

Front entrance to Facemakers, Inc., the world's largest manufacturer of mascot costumes

### Fit for a Pharaoh
The Golden Pyramid House
Wadsworth

First time travelers on the Tri-State Tollway (I-94), north of Gurnee
Mills, often wonder about the enormous gold-colored pyramid adjacent to the highway. Known as the Golden Pyramid House, the place
is a 55-foot-tall, 17,000-square-foot private residence that was built in
the late 1970s by a wealthy Armenian-American businessman named
Jim Onan.

According to a 1984 Associated Press story, Onan said he and his
wife built the unusual abode "just to be different." They specifically
selected a pyramid after reading a study that suggested pyramids
produce positive energy. He said he and his four sons built the home
over a six-year period.

In addition to the giant pyramid, the estate includes a 64-foot-
high statue of Ramses and a cluster of three, smaller pyramids that
constitute a multiple-car garage. Inside, the home is furnished with
Middle Eastern antiques and artifacts and has a reproduction of King
Tutankhamen's throne as well as Egyptian-influenced masks, chairs,
and wall designs. Some eighty miniature Sphinxes line the driveway to
the pyramid.

The exterior of the house, which is surrounded by a moat fed by
a natural spring, is made of stainless-steel plates electroplated with
twenty-four-carat gold, making it the world's largest gold-plated
object.

## Trivia

**The official state motto for Illinois is "State Sovereignty, National
Union." Wouldn't that look pretty sweet on the front of a t-shirt?**

★ ★ ★ ★ ★ ★ ★ ★ ★ ★ ★ ★ ★ ★ ★ ★ ★ ★ ★ ★ ★ ★ ★ ★ ★ ★ ★ ★ ★ ★ ★

# The Reel Groundhog Day Town, Woodstock

In a case of life imitating art, the town of Woodstock, located 65 miles northwest of Chicago, has become one of the nation's best-known places to celebrate Groundhog Day. Ironically, Woodstockers (as they're known) didn't really commemorate the day until after the town was used as a shooting location for the 1993 hit film, *Groundhog Day*, starring Bill Murray. In the movie, the town is a stand-in for Punxsutawney, Pennsylvania, the actual place where every February 2 citizens watch to see if a groundhog (called Punxsutawney Phil) will spot his own shadow. But it turned out that picturesque Woodstock made a better-looking Punxsutawney than the real deal. Since then, the city of about 25,000 has held an annual Groundhog Day celebration with free showings of the film, a dinner dance, and a walking tour of the dozen locations that appeared in the film. The town even has its own groundhog, Woodstock Willie, who gives his own prediction about the number of days until spring.

In the 1980s, Onan permitted regular tours of the house, with the proceeds benefiting his church, but discontinued the practice a few years later. More recently, he has opened it up for tours to raise money for a local military memorial and on several other occasions. In 1993, Onan offered his home as a means to pay down the national debt. In a statement, Onan said: "My wife and myself offer today, free and clear, with no tax deduction or credit, the Gold Pyramid

★ ★ ★ ★ ★ ★ ★ ★ ★ ★ ★ ★ ★ ★ ★ ★ ★ ★ ★ ★ ★ ★ ★ ★ ★ ★ ★

House! We make this offer in the hope that the federal government will use the Pyramid House as a successful fundraiser, in much the same way as the state of California uses the Hearst Castle."

The government never took him up on his offer, so for now you can view the big triangular house from the road—it's located at 37921 Dilleys Road in Wadsworth—but don't trespass; Onan has some pretty big dogs.

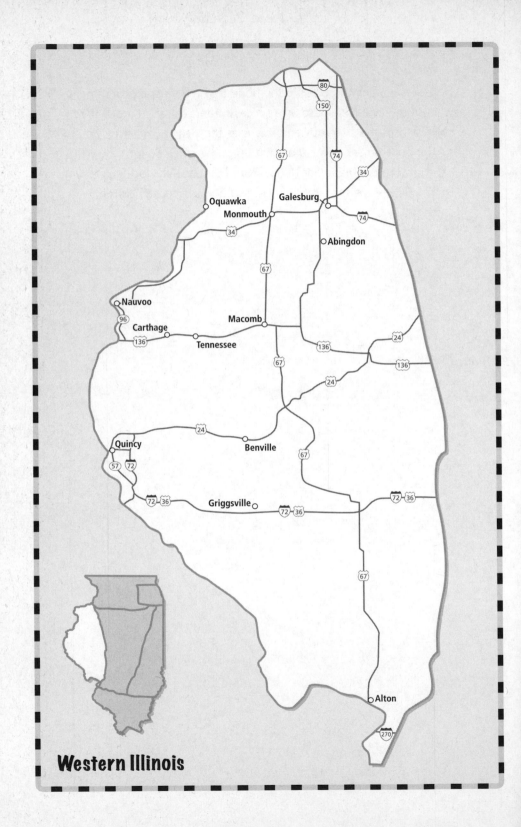

**Western Illinois**

# 3

# Western Illinois

"You have entered the Republic of Forgottonia, Region of Little Return on Tax Dollars. Have Your Visas Ready."

—Billboards posted on Western Illinois roads in 1973

**Corn and soybeans.** *If there are two words that can summarize both the perception and the reality about Western Illinois, it would be those two. The section of the state that borders Iowa and Northern Missouri is largely farm country and boasts some of the best yielding cornfields in the nation. Its relative remoteness from any major metropolitan area—it's more than three hours to Chicago and about the same to St. Louis—has made it a sort of sleepy backwater part of the state that's easy to overlook.*

*Of course, that's not to say there's nothing interesting about this part of the state. After all, it's where the 1950s TV Superman, George Reeves, grew up (Galesburg); where Marcus Dunstan, the screenwriter of the not-so-classic horror films* Saw IV, Saw V, *and* Saw VI, *was born and went to school (Macomb); and where Chris Ward, the author of political comic books on President Barack Obama and former Secretary of State Condoleezza Rice, hails from (Rushville). It's also the birthplace of the world's tallest man, Robert Pershing Wadlow of Alton (8 feet, 11.1 inches), as well as the former world's heaviest man, Robert Earl Hughes of Benville (1,069 pounds).*

*See—there's a lot more to Western Illinois than corn and soybeans. Sort of.*

# Welcome to the Republic of Forgottonia

In the late 1960s, Western Illinois was feeling neglected. Regular passenger train service to Chicago had been cut. A proposal to build a superhighway from Chicago to Kansas City through the area had failed in Congress on two occasions. Carthage College, which had been in the Western Illinois city of the same name since 1870, was abruptly relocated to Kenosha, Wisconsin.

The obvious answer, according to one group of Western Illinois University residents, was to declare independence and secede from the state of Illinois.

Thus, the new republic of Forgottonia (also spelled Forgotonia) was born. In Forgottonia, Springfield was no longer the capital, but rather it was a small settlement south of Colchester named Fandon. The governor was no longer Illinois chief executive, Daniel Walker, but twenty-five-year-old Western Illinois University senior Neal Gamm.

A few true believers overprinted the name of their new state on U.S. postage stamps, and there were even billboards along a few highways announcing when drivers were leaving Illinois and entering Forgottonia. Additionally, Forgottonia supporters designated the "forget-me-not" as the official state flower and the albatross as the state bird.

The new state encompassed sixteen Western Illinois counties. Much like a similar independence movement that began in the 1940s in Northern California and Southern Oregon to create a new state called Jefferson, Forgottonia was birthed out of the frustration that rural Western Illinoisans felt regarding the Chicago-dominated state government.

While Forgottonia's founding fathers and mothers clearly had their tongues firmly planted in their cheeks when they proclaimed their intention to carve out an independent republic, they succeeded in focusing attention on serious public policy issues. The state's political figures began to take notice of the region's inadequate roads, limited rail passenger service, and other shortcomings when it came to infrastructure.

Starting in 1971, the state of Illinois began establishing the "Illinois Service" initiative, which partnered with the then–newly established federal train system, Amtrak, to provide state-subsidized rail service between Chicago and downstate communities. As a result, regular passenger service became available between the state's largest city and Forgottonian cities such as Kewanee, Galesburg, Macomb, and Quincy.

Similarly, Forgottonia's roads were gradually improved. In addition to more regular resurfacing of existing roads, IL 67 between Macomb

Former Forgottonia governor Neal Gamm poses with a toll sign for the short-lived republic in this photo from the late 1970s. PHOTO COURTESY OF WESTERN ILLINOIS UNIVERSITY SPECIAL COLLECTIONS

and Monmouth was widened to four lanes in the early twenty-first century, as were the highways between Quincy and Macomb.

In the end, it turned out that Forgottonia wasn't forgotten—maybe just lost for a while.

# On the Track of the Illinois Military Tract

Following the War of 1812, about five million acres of land between the Mississippi and Illinois Rivers in what became the state of Illinois (granted in 1818) were set aside as "bounty" for soldiers who had fought in the conflict. Known as the Military Tract of 1812, the acreage included present-day Adams, Brown, Calhoun, Fulton, Hancock, Henderson, Knox, McDonough, Mercer, Peoria, Pike, Schuyler, Stark, and Warren as well as parts of Henry, Bureau, Marshall, and Putnam Counties. Each soldier received 160 acres, although many never took possession of their land and sold it to speculators.

### The Big Daddy Totem Pole
Abingdon

Native Americans didn't build it, but the massive totem pole standing in the small town of Abingdon, known as "Big Daddy," is an impressive sight nonetheless. Billed as the tallest totem pole "east of the Rockies," the 83-foot wooden monumental sculpture was carved by artist Steve Greenquist in 1969. When the project was conceived, town fathers believed that it would be the tallest totem pole in the world and were confident it would attract tourists to the out-of-the-way community, located 12 miles south of Galesburg.

Unfortunately, just a few years later a Canadian town snatched away the town's claim to fame. Today, there are at least a half dozen totems taller than the Abingdon pole including a 173-foot one in Alert Bay, British Columbia; a 140-foot pole in Kalama, Washington; and a 137.5-foot monument in Kake, Alaska.

Despite that, the Abingdon totem remains a popular roadside attraction. The pole, carved of red cedar, stands in the center of a landscaped median on the town's Main Street, adjacent to a city park. At the top are the words, "Abingdon, Illinois," painted on a representation of wings. Carved into the length of the pole are various images of objects, people, and animals, including portraits of Abraham Lincoln and Stephen Douglas, ears of corn, and the state flower (a violet). Near the base, the pole has another wide set of wings in the shape of the state of Illinois covered with a variety of designs.

Greenquist, who was sponsored by the Abingdon Development Council, was only eighteen years old and a student at Illinois State University when he conceived and created the work. Since 1998, he has been a high school art teacher in Ankeny, Iowa.

**An 83-foot totem pole stands in the farming community of Abingdon.**

★ ★ ★ ★ ★ ★ ★ ★ ★ ★ ★ ★ ★ ★ ★ ★ ★ ★ ★ ★ ★ ★ ★ ★ ★ ★ ★ ★ ★ ★

### Trivia

**William C. Hooker of Abingdon invented the now-familiar spring-loaded mousetrap. In 1894, he received U.S. patent 528671 for his simple but deadly design.**

There is a certain "fish-out-of-water" aspect to the pole. Totems are monumental sculptures carved by the indigenous people of the Pacific Northwest coastal region (British Columbia, northern Washington, Alaska). While no one is certain of their purpose, it is generally believed the carvings recounted local legends, familial ties, and important tribal events. The native Illini people had no tradition for building totem poles and probably wouldn't have a clue as to why it's in Abingdon.

Just like everyone else.

To spot the Tallest Totem Pole East of the Rockies, head down Abingdon's North Main Street and look up.

### Beware the Piasa Bird
Alton

You wouldn't want to meet a Piasa (pronounced "pie-a-saw") bird in real life. Described as sporting a mouth full of large, sharp teeth, antlers like a deer, giant talons, and a long spiked tail, the creature was said to have lived for thousands of years near the confluence of the Illinois and Mississippi Rivers. The native people greatly feared the monster because it had a taste for human flesh.

What makes the legend of the Piasa more intriguing is that it dates to 1673, when explorers Louis Jolliet and Pere Jacques Marquette discovered pictograph representations of the creature painted on cliffs above the Mississippi River, close to the present day town of Alton.

A few years later, French mapmaker Jean-Batiste Louis Franquelin drew a fantastic picture of the monster based on Marquette's description. This image depicts a vaguely cat-like creature with long claws, a long tail that ends with fish-like fins, a human head, scales, and deer antlers. His creation, like Marquette's description, however, did not have a name or wings.

So how did Marquette's monster become a giant man-eating bird? It turns out the wings, moniker, and other details were concocted in 1836 by John Russell, a professor at Alton Seminary, who published a new description of the beast as well as an entire creation mythology. According to Russell, the monster's name was Piasa, which in the Illini tongue means, "The Bird That Devours Men."

Painting of the ferocious man-eating Piasa Bird on a cliff outside of Alton.

★ ★ ★ ★ ★ ★ ★ ★ ★ ★ ★ ★ ★ ★ ★ ★ ★ ★ ★ ★ ★ ★ ★ ★ ★ ★ ★ ★ ★ ★ ★ ★

Russell wrote that over the years the bird snatched and ate hundreds of the Illini. It was finally killed when a great chief, Ouatogá, prayed to the Great Spirit for help and was told in a dream how to destroy the creature using poisoned arrows.

While the original pictograph of the weird creature is believed to have been destroyed when the cliff was quarried in the late 1840s, it wasn't until the early twentieth century that a version similar to what is seen today was created. In 1924, Herbert Forcade, an eighteen-year-old Boy Scout, decided to paint a winged rendition of the monster on a cliff just north of Alton, which he and his troop presented as a gift to the city. In the 1960s, that cliff was blasted away to widen the Great River Road and a painted metal replica of the terrible bird was hung at Norman's Landing near Godfrey. In 1995, the metal Piasa was taken down when the surrounding property was sold.

In 2000, the current version of the Piasa, partly based on nineteenth century versions (with wings), was painted on a limestone cliff that is several hundred yards from where the original was believed to have been located. Measuring 48 feet by 22 feet, the full-color image is located about a mile north of Alton on the Great River Road (IL 100).

## Walking Tall
Alton

It's no exaggeration to say that Robert Pershing Wadlow was heads above everyone else. At 8 feet, 11.1 inches tall, Wadlow was nearly 2 feet taller than contemporary basketball player Shaquille O'Neal (who is a mere 7 feet, 1 inch tall), when he died in 1940. Wadlow was born in Alton on February 22, 1918. While normal size at birth (he weighed eight pounds, six ounces), he soon began to grow at an extraordinary rate as a result of an out-of-control pituitary gland. By the time he was five years old, he was 5 feet, 4 inches tall and weighed 105 pounds. At eight, he had sprouted to more than 6 feet tall, and by the time he was twelve, he was 6 feet, 11 inches tall.

Life-size statue of Robert Pershing Wadlow of Alton, who still holds the record for being the world's tallest man.

★ ★ ★ ★ ★ ★ ★ ★ ★ ★ ★ ★ ★ ★ ★ ★ ★ ★ ★ ★ ★ ★ ★ ★ ★ ★ ★ ★ ★ ★

As he continued to grow in adulthood, Wadlow's enormous size earned him international attention. His greatest measured weight was 490 pounds—he consumed, on average, 8,000 calories per day—and his shoe size was 37AA. His hands measured 12¾ inches from the tip of his middle finger to his wrist. Not surprisingly, the *Guinness Book of Records* has proclaimed him the tallest person to have ever lived. Unfortunately, as he continued to grow, his bones became more brittle and it became difficult for him to walk without the aid of leg braces and a cane. While making an appearance in Michigan, Wadlow's foot became infected as a result of a blister caused by an improperly fitted leg brace. Despite emergency surgery and blood transfusions, the infection spread and Wadlow died in his sleep on July 15, 1940. He was only twenty-two years old.

Wadlow was buried in the Upper Alton Cemetery in a specially designed 1,000-pound casket that was placed in a 12-foot-long reinforced concrete tomb. In 1985, a life-size bronze statue of Wadlow was erected in front of the Southern Illinois University, Edwardsville Dental School in Alton, just a long stone's throw from his gravesite.

The Upper Alton Cemetery is located at 2090 Oakwood Avenue in Alton, while the Wadlow statue is located in a small park in the 2800 block of College Avenue.

## Toast to a Fragrant Ghost

Mineral Springs Hotel
Alton

The Mineral Springs Hotel in Alton might be the world's most haunted boutique mall. It's not because it's haunted by the ghost of a nineteenth century shopaholic, but rather because the mall is located inside a grand old hotel that was once one of the most spectacular lodging houses in the region.

The hotel was built in 1914 by August and Herman Luer, who originally planned to erect an ice storage plant on the land. While digging a well for the facility, workmen discovered a natural spring that, due

**The Mineral Springs Hotel, said to be one of the most haunted sites in the town of Alton**

to its high mineral content, was thought to have restorative and curative powers. The Luer brothers changed their plans and built a health spa on the site that included a hotel as well as a water-bottling plant and two mineral pools in the lower levels.

The hotel thrived for many decades but closed in the early 1970s. In 1978, it was renovated and reopened as an antique mall with shops, offices, and restaurants. It was following this restoration that people began reporting sightings of ghostly figures in various rooms throughout the hotel. Not surprisingly, the basement swimming pool, now empty, is connected with some of the stories. In his book, *Haunted Alton*, author Troy Taylor noted, "I had the chance to spend the night in the swimming pool a few years ago and maintain that it

143

is one of the creepiest places that I have ever visited . . . this is a very haunted spot."

Perhaps the most famous ghost in the hotel is the so-called "Jasmine Lady." Since the 1980s, hotel visitors have reported seeing a woman fall down the staircase located adjacent to the former hotel lobby, but when they ran to help her she was gone. They also said they could smell a strong jasmine-scented perfume. According to legend, the woman was once a guest in the hotel and her husband caught her in a room having an affair with another guest. She apparently ran out of the room and fell down the stairs, breaking her neck. While there are no news accounts supporting the story, Taylor wrote that even one of the hotel's former owners—a ghost story skeptic— admitted that one day he smelled "a strong, almost putrid, jasmine scent" in the lobby and was puzzled about the source.

Not surprisingly, the hotel has capitalized on its haunted reputation—it offers regular tours of the property and an overnight campout in the swimming pool led by a ghost historian and a psychic. It's just what you might expect from a haunted mall.

For more information about the hotel, go to www.mineralsprings mall-alton.com and www.mineralspringshauntedtours.com.

## Trivia

Illinois has more units of government (city, county, township, etc.) than any other state—more than 6,000.

## Tipping the Scales
Benville

Robert Earl Hughes was one big dude. By the time he was six years old, he weighed an incredible 203 pounds—and, over the years, he just kept getting bigger. Hughes was born in 1926, the son of Abe and Georgia Hughes, in the tiny farm hamlet of Fishhook, located about 20 miles northwest of Quincy. Weighing a hefty but not abnormal eleven pounds, four ounces at birth, Hughes was a fairly average-size baby until he contracted whooping cough when he was about five months old. The ailment permanently threw his pituitary gland into hyper-drive and he began rapidly gaining weight. By age ten, he weighed 378 pounds, and three years later he was a whopping 546 pounds.

In spite of the challenges of being so enormous, by all accounts Hughes was a friendly, gentle soul, who tried to live as normal a life as possible, including doing chores around the family farm and walking to school each day.

At the age of sixteen, Hughes had grown to more than 600 pounds. Two years later, by which time he had gained another one hundred pounds, he had to register for the draft (it was 1944). His parents informed the draft board there was no way they could get him to the registration in Mount Sterling, which was 12 miles away, so the board came to him. The story about the unusual nature of his predicament titillated the local newspapers, which wrote about Hughes, calling him the largest man to ever register for the draft.

The attention brought fame to Hughes, who began making public appearances at local festivals and selling photos of himself. While his mother objected to him being treated like a freak, Hughes apparently enjoyed the attention.

By late 1956, the 5-foot, 9-inch Hughes had reached 1,041 pounds and officially became the heaviest man ever (the previous record holder, 7-footer Miles Darden, weighed 1,020 pounds when he died in 1857).

★ ★ ★ ★ ★ ★ ★ ★ ★ ★ ★ ★ ★ ★ ★ ★ ★ ★ ★ ★ ★ ★ ★ ★ ★ ★ ★ ★ ★ ★ ★

**Benville grave of Robert Earl Hughes,
one-time world's heaviest man**

Two years later, while touring Indiana with the carnival, Hughes developed a skin rash as well as dark blue fingernails. A doctor diagnosed him with measles, which were making his kidney malfunction. On July 8, 1958, Hughes slipped into a coma and died two days later of congestive heart failure.

At the time of his death, his weight was estimated to be 1,069 pounds. While his weight record has since been broken, Hughes still holds the record for largest chest measurement ever recorded: 124 inches.

Hughes was buried in the small Benville Cemetery behind a tiny church in the town of Benville on County Road 6, located 10 miles north of Fishhook. On his hefty tombstone is carved: "Robert Earl Hughes: June 1, 1926–July 10, 1958; World's Heaviest Man—Weight 1,041 pounds."

## Where Joseph Smith Died
Carthage

In the Church of Latter Day Saints (Mormons), there are few places as significant as the simple, two-story stone jail near the center of Carthage, Illinois. The Carthage Jail is the Calvary of the Mormon faith. It is the place where on June 27, 1844, the church's founder, Joseph Smith, and his brother Hyrum, were shot and killed by an angry mob.

According to accounts of the day, the Smith brothers had been incarcerated for their involvement in the destruction of the printing press of a local newspaper that had published negative articles about Smith.

At the time, Smith was not only the head of the Mormon religion but mayor of the city of Nauvoo, located about 20 miles northwest of Carthage. In his role as mayor, Smith declared the paper a public nuisance and ordered the paper's printing press to be destroyed.

Non-Mormons in Western Illinois pushed for action against Smith. Illinois governor Thomas Ford asked Smith and the other city council members to turn themselves in to Carthage authorities for a trial.

Upon arriving in Carthage, the group was arrested and confined to the Carthage Jail, a rough-looking stone structure with two upstairs cells. While waiting in the jail, one of Smith's followers secretly gave Smith a small pistol for his protection. That night, several armed men, faces painted black to obscure their identities, crept into the jail to kill Smith and the others.

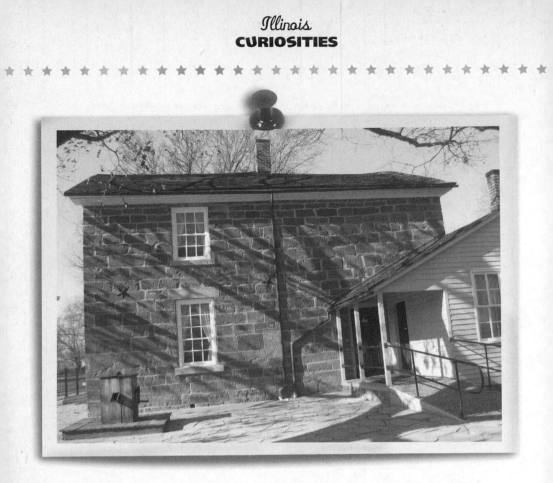

Carthage Jail, where religious leader Joseph Smith was killed

Before the vigilantes could come upstairs, they were spotted. Hyrum Smith and another man used their bodies to barricade the door. The mob rushed the door but the two men held the door shut. A shot struck Hyrum Smith in the face, killing him. According to accounts, upon seeing his brother had been killed, Joseph Smith opened the door slightly and fired several shots at his assailants. Allegedly three men were wounded before the mob rushed into the room and fatally shot Smith.

In 1846, continued harassment of the church by Illinois authorities forced Smith's followers to head to the Valley of the Great Salt Lake in Utah, where they established a more permanent home for the church.

The word, *Illinois*, is derived from the Algonquin word meaning "tribe of superior men."

As for the Carthage Jail, it was converted into a private home, which it remained until 1903, when it was purchased by the Church of Jesus Christ of Latter Day Saints. It was restored to its original appearance in 1938 and assumed its role as one of the church's most important shrines. These days, smiling and super-friendly young representatives of the church offer free tours of the historic building, located at 307 Walnut Street in Carthage. For more information, go to www.lds.org/placestovisit/location/0,10634,1844-1-1-1,00.html.

## Where It Began and Ended for Carl Sandburg

Galesburg

The Carl Sandburg Historic Birthplace is where the life of the famed twentieth century poet, writer, and lecturer comes full circle. It's where he was born in 1878 and where he and his wife had their ashes buried following their deaths, respectively, in 1967 and 1977.

While not as well known today as he was during his lifetime, Sandburg remains pretty big stuff in his hometown of Galesburg. The local community college is named after him, as is the town's biggest shopping mall, which is ironic since Sandburg was a socialist who decried the excesses of capitalism.

The small cottage in which he was born is modest and common—a reflection of Sandburg's working class roots. The simple, wooden three-room home has no running water and is heated by a single wood stove. There's a two-hole outhouse in back. In fact,

★ ★ ★ ★ ★ ★ ★ ★ ★ ★ ★ ★ ★ ★ ★ ★ ★ ★ ★ ★ ★ ★ ★ ★ ★ ★ ★

**House where poet and writer Carl Sandburg
was born in Galesburg in 1878**

the two-story visitor center, housed in a neighboring house built in 1858, is far more impressive looking than the famed author's actual birthplace.

Even today, the neighborhood around the cottage remains decidedly lower middle class. Down the street is the Galesburg Rescue Mission and Women's Shelter, housed in a former school, and nearby is Tom's Gun Shoppe.

Sandburg, who won three Pulitzer Prizes—for his multi-volume biography of Abraham Lincoln in 1940 and for his poetry in 1919 and 1951—only lived in the cottage for the first year of his life. His father August Sandburg was a Swedish immigrant, who worked as a blacksmith's helper for the Chicago Burlington and Quincy Railroad. In 1879, August Sandburg sold the cottage and purchased a larger home in Galesburg for his growing family (Carl was the second of seven children).

While Sandburg lived in North Carolina in his later years, he requested in his will that his remains be returned to the place of his birth. His ashes (as well as those of his wife) were buried in a small park behind his birth home, beneath a giant red granite boulder, called "Remembrance Rock," after the title of his only novel.

The Sandburg Historic Site is open Thursday through Sunday from 9 a.m. to 5 p.m. (9 a.m. to 4 p.m. in the winter months).

The Carl Sandburg Birthplace is located at 331 East 3rd Street in Galesburg. For more information, go to www.sandburg.org.

# When the Man of Steel Blew through Town

Actor George Reeves (birth name: George Keefer Brewer, later changed to George Bessolo, after his stepfather), who played the title role in the 1950s TV show, *Superman*, briefly lived in Galesburg. Born in 1914, in Woolstock, Iowa, Reeves's mother, Helen, separated from his father and returned to her hometown of Galesburg shortly after his birth. A few years later, Reeves and his mother relocated to Pasadena, California, where he attended grammar school, high school, and junior college. In the 2006 film, *Hollywoodland*, about Reeves's alleged suicide in 1959, actor Ben Affleck, portraying Reeves, remarks after an ungraceful fall during a flying scene: "I'd like to thank the Academy and all the good people of Galesburg, Illinois, for making me who I am today."

★ ★ ★ ★ ★ ★ ★ ★ ★ ★ ★ ★ ★ ★ ★ ★ ★ ★ ★ ★ ★ ★ ★ ★ ★ ★ ★ ★ ★ ★ ★

### The Purple Martin Capital of the Universe
Griggsville

The folks in the town of Griggsville really love purple martins. They like the birds so much that more than 5,000 birdhouses line the city streets, and in the town center they erected a 562-unit avian high-rise, which serves as home to hundreds of the blue-black birds (members of the swallow family) that are valued for their ability to allegedly consume 2,000 mosquitoes per day (although some dispute that claim). The town is so proud of the birds that it has proclaimed itself the Purple Martin Capital of the Nation (a claim that even appears on the town's water tower).

Griggsville's purple martin mania can be traced to 1962, when the local Jaycees were trying to combat a persistent mosquito problem—in the summer months Griggsville is a magnet for the bloodsuckers because it's near both the Illinois and Mississippi Rivers—but hesitant to use increasing amounts of chemical pesticides. A local man, J. L. Wade, suggested that purple martins might be the answer because they eat nothing but tons of flying insects and, at the time, were an endangered species. Also, he knew that the birds don't build their own nests but like to inhabit manmade structures.

Wade and the Jaycees consulted with ornithologists and developed a two-story, aluminum bird abode, which became known as the M-12K house. The design was so successful that Wade, who previously manufactured TV antennas, began commercially building the structures; his company is now known as Nature House Inc.

Later that year, the Jaycees installed more than two dozen of the distinctive green and white houses, attached to tall aluminum poles at 100-foot intervals along the community's main road. However, the service club's crowning achievement was erecting a tower of martin manors rising 70 feet high and featuring those 562 apartments. The giant avian condo attracted hundreds of the little birds and thrust Griggsville into the forefront as the country's most purple martin–friendly town.

Of course, 5,000 birdhouses and a comparable number of birds beg the question—do those aluminum houses come with restrooms?

Griggsville's avian high-rise for purple martins

### The Macomb Firestarter

Macomb

Wonet McNeil either was one of the cleverest twelve-year-olds who ever lived—or one of the most powerful.

In 1948, McNeil was at the center of a literal firestorm of controversy. On Saturday, August 7, fire erupted in the kitchen of the Charles Willey farmhouse, located 12 miles south of Macomb. The flames mysteriously appeared behind a wood stove, burning the wallpaper. While the fire was quickly extinguished, what happened next has perplexed investigators ever since. Between August 7 and August 13, an estimated 200 fires mysteriously broke out in the Willey house.

According to the August 13 *Macomb Daily Journal*, "a series of fires which have beset the Charles Willey family, Macomb Route Four, since last Saturday ended this morning when the house burned to the ground." The article said that some suspected the fire was caused by faulty wiring, but added, "the house does not have electricity." It noted that in addition to Charles Willey and his wife, Lou, residents of the house included Mrs. Willey's brother, Arthur McNeil, and his two children, Arthur Jr. and Wonet.

The bizarre sequence of fires generated numerous conspiracy theories. Some speculated that sparks from a faulty chimney caused the fires while others insisted they were the result of ignited furniture polish or fly spray. Air Force officials at Wright Field in Dayton, Ohio, said the fires could have been the work of foreign agents using "radio-ignited sabotage materials."

*Trivia*

Illinois is bordered by five states: Wisconsin, Iowa, Missouri, Kentucky, and Indiana.

Two days later, the *Macomb Daily Journal* announced that authorities had discovered the source of all the fires. "Wonet McNeil, whose thirteenth birthday will be tomorrow, confessed today that she set all of the numerous fires that have plagued the family of Charles Willey, her uncle, since August 7," the *Macomb Daily Journal* reported. "She set the fires, Wonet said, because she wanted to go live with her mother."

Despite the confession, some have questioned whether authorities really did solve the mystery. For one thing, witnesses claimed the fires started in rooms where Wonet was not present and brown spots would spontaneously appear on the walls, which then burst into blue flames. Additionally, the fire marshal's report said "blazes burned at temperatures exceeding 400 degrees, unusual for that type of fire."

Following Wonet's confession, the *Macomb Daily Journal* noted "no one was able to fully explain how the girl, using no more than a match, could have ignited the walls in a manner that mystified members of the family and all of the neighbors."

In the end, a psychiatrist described Wonet as "a victim of a family mix-up and divorce"—and she was sent to live with her maternal grandparents in Marseilles, Illinois. A 1998 *Macomb Journal* story marking the fiftieth anniversary of the events noted that Wonet died in 1948—and took the secret of what did or did not occur on the Willey farm to her grave.

## Where Wyatt Earp Lived Before He Became THE Wyatt Earp
Monmouth

One of Illinois's most well-known native sons is a man not usually associated with the Land of Lincoln. Legendary western lawman Wyatt Earp was born in Monmouth on March 19, 1848. The fourth of six children of Nicholas Porter Earp and Virginia Ann Earp, Wyatt Earp was born in a two-story, pioneer Greek Revival–style house on 3rd Street (although a local Monmouth College history professor has argued he was born in a different house).

Regardless of whether he was actually born in that house, which is officially known as the Wyatt Earp Birthplace and Museum, he certainly didn't initially spend a whole lot of time there or in any other home in Monmouth. Less than two years after his birth, his father announced plans to move to California but made it as far as Pella, Iowa (about 150 miles west of Monmouth).

By 1856, the Earp clan was back in Monmouth, this time residing in a house at either 409 or 411 South B Street (historians aren't sure about this, either), before returning to Pella in 1859. The peripatetic Earps apparently finally headed out to California by wagon train in 1864. About five years later, Earp cropped up in Lamar, Missouri, where he took a position as the town constable, his first stint as a lawman (ironically, about two years later he fled amid charges he had stolen money from the community and was a horse thief).

Earp's ties to Illinois, however, weren't completely severed. By 1872, he was living in the Peoria area, apparently operating a brothel

**Monmouth house where Wyatt Earp was born in 1848**

# Beware the Fighting Teachers

In 1926, ex-Marine Ray "Rock" Hanson, a much decorated war hero (World War I), was hired as the football coach and athletic director at Western Illinois State Teachers College (now known as Western Illinois University). As a coach, Hanson brought a tough, Marine-style work ethic to the football program and believed the team's official name, the Fighting Teachers, was a little less than intimidating. So he successfully lobbied Congress and the Secretary of the Navy to allow the school to use the nickname of the Marine Corps—the Fighting Leathernecks—as well as the Marine's seal and the phrase, "Semper fidelis." In 1927, the team became known as the Fighting Leathernecks. It was the first and only time the U.S. Marine Corps has allowed its nickname to be appropriated by a college team.

with his brother, Morgan. A few months later authorities broke up the operation and it is believed that the Earp brothers soon left the area for good.

Of course, after that Earp went on to become one of the West's most renowned lawmen. His later exploits as a deputy marshal in the lawless town of Dodge City, Kansas, and his role in the infamous shootout at the OK Corral in Tombstone, Arizona, in 1881 made him famous. He died in Los Angeles in 1929 at the age of eighty.

As for the Earp Birthplace and Museum, in 2007 its owners, Robert and Melba Matson, who have fought long and hard to persuade the world that their house is the real deal, put the popular attraction up for sale (they've retired in Arizona). So far no one has met the minimum asking price of $100,000 but the owners remain optimistic. In

★ ★ ★ ★ ★ ★ ★ ★ ★ ★ ★ ★ ★ ★ ★ ★ ★ ★ ★ ★ ★ ★ ★ ★ ★ ★ ★ ★ ★ ★

the meantime, the museum is open daily between Memorial Day and Labor Day from 2 p.m. to 4 p.m. and by appointment. Additionally, the museum hosts an annual Wyatt Earp Day in late July.

The Wyatt Earp Birthplace and Museum is located at 406 3rd Street in Monmouth. For more information, go to www.earpmorgan.com /wyattearpbirthplacewebsite.html.

## The Legend of Cry Baby Bridge
Monmouth

A few miles north of Monmouth is a small, graffiti-covered bridge. It's said that if you park your car in neutral and wait, *something* or *someone* will slowly push the vehicle across the bridge. Known as "Cry Baby Bridge," the span is allegedly haunted by the ghosts of a mother and her baby.

According to one version of the legend, many years ago the woman and the child were traveling across the bridge in a carriage one night when something spooked their horse. Apparently, the carriage overturned and the woman and baby were thrown into the river below and drowned. Some believe that if you park your car on the bridge late at night, put your keys on the hood, and loudly shout, "I killed your baby!" your car doors will mysteriously lock, the car engine will refuse to start, and you will hear a baby crying.

Of course, like most ghost stories there are other versions of the story. Another tale is that the woman was walking across the bridge and tossed her baby in the river, then jumped in afterward. Yet another variation is that there was no woman or baby but rather a bus filled with small children that flipped off the bridge. Some claim it was a group of teens that drowned (but then why isn't it called "Dead Teen Bridge?").

Regardless of which tale you accept, all of the stories agree that the ghost (or ghosts) will push a vehicle across the bridge. Additionally, it's said that if you put baby powder on your bumper you'll find tiny handprints after your car has been shoved from one side to the other. There are also reports of strange lights in the surrounding woods as well as the sound of a crying baby and other noises.

Of course, skeptics argue that it's all a bunch of hogwash. In his book, *Weird Illinois*, author Troy Taylor recounts investigating the bridge with a group of students from nearby Knox College in Galesburg. The group went out to the bridge to figure out why vehicles seemed to move of their own accord. After watching their vehicle seem to move across the bridge, the students used a carpenter's level to see if the bridge was level. It turns out it's not and gravity was the culprit.

The debunkers, however, didn't put baby powder on their bumper, so at least part of the legend is still up for grabs.

## Mormon Holy Land

Nauvoo

When you think about Mormons, or members of the Church of Jesus Christ of Latter Day Saints (LDS), you usually associate them with Utah. After all, the church's headquarters are located in Salt Lake City, Utah, and more than 60 percent of the state is Mormon. But before the Mormons settled in the Valley of the Great Salt Lake in 1847, they tried to establish a permanent home in the Western Illinois community of Nauvoo.

In 1839, the church's founder, Joseph Smith, and his followers purchased a large parcel of swampy land overlooking the Mississippi River, about 45 miles north of Quincy. They established a settlement, which Smith named "Nauvoo," Hebrew for "beautiful place."

Smith had established the Mormon religion in the late 1820s, after claiming that an angel had given him golden plates inscribed with a sacred text he called the *Book of Mormon.* Initially, Smith and his followers tried to settle in Ohio, and then Missouri, but were forced out by state and local officials who viewed them as a cult.

By 1844, the population of Nauvoo had swelled to more than 12,000, making it one of the largest cities in Illinois. In addition to

Reconstruction of the Mormon Temple in Nauvoo that was
originally built, but not completed, in the mid-1840s

building some 2,000 homes, church members began constructing the Nauvoo Temple, an impressive five-story Greek Revival–style building with a zinc-domed bell tower. While never completed, the temple measured 128 feet by 88 feet and is said to have cost about $1 million.

Just as had happened in Ohio and Missouri, the Mormons faced religious persecution in Illinois (largely related to the church's growing political power as well as its practice of polygamy). Following the murder of Joseph Smith in 1844 in Carthage, a majority of church members, led by Brigham Young, made plans to relocate to Utah. In 1846, after most of the Mormons departed Nauvoo, the temple was vacated. In 1848, an arsonist set fire to the temple and three years later it was leveled by a tornado.

In 1937, the Utah-based LDS Church began repurchasing the original temple site and surrounding 3.3-acre block. In 2002, a complete reconstruction of the original Mormon Temple was dedicated. Today, while non-Mormons are not allowed inside the temple, the 54,000-square-foot building has become a magnet for visitors and Nauvoo has become one of the LDS Church's most sacred places. Many of the homes of other early Mormon Church leaders, such as Brigham Young, have also been restored and are open to the public— kind of a Mormon Williamsburg.

A good source of information about the community is the Historic Nauvoo Visitors' Center, Main and Hubbard Streets in Nauvoo, www.historicnauvoo.net.

## Trivia

**In 1929, the Illinois General Assembly designated the crimson-colored cardinal as the state's official bird.**

★ ★ ★ ★ ★ ★ ★ ★ ★ ★ ★ ★ ★ ★ ★ ★ ★ ★ ★ ★ ★ ★ ★ ★ ★ ★ ★ ★ ★ ★ ★ ★ ★ ★ ★

### Enter—and Exit—the Icarians

Nauvoo

There must be something in the water in the Nauvoo area that attracts dreamers. Shortly after the departure of Joseph Smith's followers in 1846, a community of utopians moved into the region. Called the Icarians, the group was founded by a radical French philosopher, Étienne Cabet, who, in 1840, published an influential book, *Voyage en Icarie*, which described an idealistic, communal settlement.

In March 1848, Cabet and his followers decided to try out his theories in the New World and set out for America. After an unsuccessful attempt to establish a utopian colony in Texas, Cabet and several hundred of his disciples relocated in early 1849 to the community of Nauvoo, which had recently been abandoned by the Mormons. In 1851, the Illinois State Legislature approved an Icarian Community charter, which established Nauvoo as the first official Icarian colony. In 1852, settlers from Nauvoo crossed the Mississippi River and established another colony in Corning, Iowa.

Cabet's philosophy was that members of the colony would work together and share all property, which, in turn, would eliminate poverty and achieve a peaceful existence. The concept seemed to work for several years but in 1852, Cabet and his wife returned to France so he could defend himself against charges of fraud by some unhappy former Icarians. Eighteen months later, the two returned to Nauvoo and Cabet—increasingly critical of what he saw as lax morality—imposed new rules on the members, including a ban on smoking and restrictions on talking in workrooms. The actions split colony members who voted in 1855 to expel Cabet and anyone who sided with him.

Cabet responded by establishing a new settlement in the St. Louis area. About 200 members of the original colony remained in Nauvoo while 180 followed Cabet to St. Louis. Cabet's death on November 8, 1856 marked the beginning of the end for both communities. By 1860, the Nauvoo colony had dissolved as a result of financial problems while the St. Louis group folded in 1864. The Corning, Iowa, colony managed to survive until 1898.

Today, descendants of Icarian settlers still own the Baxter Vineyards (2010 E. Parley), one of the oldest wineries in Illinois. Emile Baxter, one of the original colony members, planted the first wine grapes in Nauvoo in the late 1850s. Western Illinois University in Macomb (about 45 miles east of Nauvoo) is also home of the Baxter-Snyder Center for Icarian Studies, a collection of letters, manuscripts, photos, and other information regarding the Icarians.

## What Do You Do with 6,500 Pounds of Pachyderm?
Oquawka

For nearly three decades, Norma Jean had been a circus star. Starting in the 1960s, the 6,500-pound female Asian elephant had performed for the Clark and Walters Wild Animal Circus. While the circus included the usual contingent of clowns, trapeze acts, plate spinners, glass and chair balancers, contortionists, trained dogs, jumping ponies, and monkeys, the most popular performer was Norma Jean.

In mid-July of 1972, the Clark and Wallace Circus was booked to perform in the small Mississippi River town of Oquawka. On the morning of July 17, as the circus was preparing for its performance that day, Norma Jean's trainer, a performer known as "Possum Red," chained the elephant to a large tree on the town's main square.

Unfortunately, that day the skies over Oquawka turned black as a summer thunderstorm rumbled in from the west. Suddenly, it began to rain and there were flashes of lightning, which seemed to be alarmingly close to the community. Concerned about the safety of Norma Jean, "Possum Red" began to uncouple the elephant from the tree. However, before he could unchain her a bolt of lightning slammed into the tree. A surge of wild electricity coursed through its trunk and into the chains, instantaneously electrocuting Norma Jean and tossing her trainer 30 feet away (miraculously, he was uninjured).

The pachyderm's demise presented the circus and the community

★ ★ ★ ★ ★ ★ ★ ★ ★ ★ ★ ★ ★ ★ ★ ★ ★ ★ ★ ★ ★ ★ ★ ★ ★ ★ ★ ★ ★ ★ ★ ★

with a problem—what do you do with a dead, three-plus ton elephant? Town officials decided that since she died in the city park, the best thing to do was to dig a 12-foot-deep pit next to her body and bury her on the spot. So, a few days after the accident, Norma Jean was somewhat unceremoniously pushed into the hole and covered over.

And that's where the story would have ended if not for a local pharmacist, Wade Meloan, who felt the elephant deserved better. He began a fundraising effort and eventually collected enough money to build a 12-foot-high limestone monument atop her grave.

On Memorial Day weekend in 1977, Meloan spearheaded a dedication ceremony for Norma Jean. A curving 8-foot-by-12-foot concrete wall topped with a concrete statue of an elephant was erected on the site and an elephant from a visiting circus was on hand to lay a wreath on the grave. A collection of Norma Jean memorabilia is displayed in a glass case and a plaque on the wall reads: THIS MEMORIAL IS DEDICATED IN MEMORY OF AN ELEPHANT NAMED NORMA JEAN, WHO WAS KILLED BY LIGHTNING AT THIS LOCATION, AND LIES BURIED HERE.

Rest in peace, Norma Jean.

## Arabian Nights on the Mississippi River
Quincy

Without a doubt one of the strangest sights in the historic town of Quincy is a two-story Moroccan-style castle that sits on a bluff overlooking the Mississippi River. Located south of the downtown, the structure known as Villa Kathrine was erected in 1900 by a wealthy local eccentric named George Metz—and it's said to be haunted by a dog.

Metz's fortune was inherited; in fact, he never worked a day in his life. His father, William, was a successful local pharmacist. After his mother died in 1897 (his father had passed away four years earlier), Metz embarked on a two-year tour of the Mediterranean and Africa. When he returned, he decided to construct a private residence that incorporated the architectural style and design of the Mediterranean/Northern African buildings he had admired during his travels.

**Villa Kathrine, an unusual Moroccan-style home built in Quincy**

Metz furnished the house with Mediterranean-Arabic furniture, artifacts, and antiques that he had purchased during his travels. Few photos of the house's interior exist so it's not known how it was originally arranged.

Metz's main companion for many years was a 212-pound bull mastiff, named Bingo. According to reports, Metz bought the dog, said to be the biggest mastiff in the world, in 1900 in Denmark. When Bingo died in 1906, the enormous canine was said to have been buried in Metz's rose garden.

In 1912, Quincy grocer Archibald Behrens and his wife persuaded Metz to sell his home to them. At the time, Metz was sixty-three years old and his family was concerned about him living alone in the two-story house. Behrens and his wife said they loved the house and all of its furnishings and promised to be good stewards.

★ ★ ★ ★ ★ ★ ★ ★ ★ ★ ★ ★ ★ ★ ★ ★ ★ ★ ★ ★ ★ ★ ★ ★ ★ ★ ★

The Behrens, however, were fronting for a local railroad, which wanted to buy the house, tear it down, and use the site for a railroad yard. In return for their role in the purchase, the railroad promised the contents of the house to the Behrens.

Apparently, once Metz moved out of the house vandals descended on it and carted off many of the antiques and furnishings. It's said that the Behrens ended up with only a single rug.

After selling the house, Metz moved into the Hotel Newcomb in downtown Quincy and, later, the nearby Lincoln Douglas Hotel. He died of pneumonia in 1937.

The railroad, however, never proceeded with its plans and in 1955, the Quincy Park District obtained the villa and surrounding property for a neighborhood park. In recent years, the partially restored house has been home of the Quincy Tourist Information Center.

As for those stories of the place being haunted, some believe that the spirit of Bingo still wanders the site. The ghost, however, appears to be housebroken. . . .

To tour the house, visit the Quincy Tourist Information Center at 532 Gardner Expressway in Quincy. For more information, go to seequincy.com.

## Vishnu Springs: A Midwestern Night's Dream
Tennessee

Hidden in the rolling hills of Western Illinois, about 6 miles north of the hamlet of Tennessee (population: 144), is a genuine ghost town known as Vishnu Springs. Established in the 1880s as a health spa, it has been largely abandoned since the early twentieth century. Not surprisingly, it's also said to be haunted.

Vishnu Springs traces its roots to the mid-1800s, when a man named Ebenezer Hicks began purchasing property around Tennessee, including a parcel, called Section 7 of the Tennessee Township, which contained a small natural spring. Sometime in the 1880s, Dr. John Aiken became convinced the spring had medicinal powers and began selling bottles of the spring water as a health tonic.

Apparently Dr. Aiken's health elixir did not make him a wealthy man and he moved on. But Darius Hicks, son of Ebenezer Hicks, thought there was something special about the spring and, in 1889, began developing a resort/health spa on the site. In 1889 and 1890, the younger Hicks erected the three-story Capital Hotel. About the same time, he also married Hattie Rush, a widow from Missouri with three children. Hattie Hicks suffered from a variety of ailments, and it is believed she came to the area to take advantage of the spring's healing qualities. Within a few years, Vishnu Springs had been sufficiently built up that it included the hotel, several stores and homes, a livery stable, a racetrack, and a photography studio.

But Vishnu Springs appeared to be cursed. In the early 1900s, a horse-drawn merry-go-round was installed to amuse the children of spa guests. One day, the clothing of the man who operated the ride became ensnared in the device's mechanism and he was crushed to death. Additionally, in 1886, Hattie Hicks died from a kidney ailment. Hicks quickly remarried—but scandalized the community by wedding his own stepdaughter, Maud, who was twenty-six years his junior. By all accounts the marriage was a happy one, but Maud died in 1903 while giving birth to their third child.

In 1908, Hicks committed suicide after becoming embroiled in a scandal involving Nellie Darrah, whom he had hired as a nanny for his children. Darrah, who became pregnant by Hicks, had sought an illegal abortion but there were complications and she was rushed to a hospital.

By the 1920s, the community was abandoned. However, in 1935, Macomb resident Ira Post, who had visited the spa as a child, purchased the site and restored the old hotel as a family retreat. After his death in 1951, the family closed up the property due to vandalism problems.

In the early 1970s, the hotel was rented out to Western Illinois University students, who held music festivals and raised crops to pay the bills. In 2003, Olga Kay Kennedy, a WIU graduate and the granddaughter of Ira Post, donated Vishnu Springs and 140 acres around the hotel to Western Illinois University for a wildlife sanctuary.

**Just about all that remains of the old resort community of
Vishnu Springs is the Capital Hotel, which is said to be haunted.**

In recent years, the relative mystery surrounding the remote spring
coupled with the tales of strange sightings—said to be the ghost of
Nellie Darrah—have made it an irresistible lure for many, especially
at Halloween time. But be aware that looking for the ghost of Nellie
Darrah brings a curse—unless you're visiting Vishnu Springs as part of
a formal tour, you will be arrested for trespassing.

For more information, contact the Friends of Vishnu Springs,
www.vishnusprings.org.

# Forget the Burning Bush—It's the Jesus Tree, Quincy

It takes a bit of faith to see the so-called Jesus Tree, located in the Roman Catholic Calvary Cemetery in Quincy. Sometime in the late 1980s, a cemetery worker was strolling through the cemetery grounds when he noticed something unusual about an ancient birch tree. The tree had a protruding knot on one side that, to him, resembled a life-size, bearded, longhaired man in a long robe, standing with his arms wrapped around a lamb—the image of Jesus.

Within a short time, thousands of visitors were stopping by daily to view what became known as "The Jesus Tree" or "The Good Shepherd Tree." It's said that the best way to view the image is to stand 15 to 20 feet away from the tree at the northeast corner of the roped off area. From there, you can see the big knot, which, from the right angle and in the right light, does appear to look like a person holding something. If you stare long enough you begin to see eyes and long hair in the bark.

It's either Jesus or Jerry Garcia.

The Calvary Cemetery is located at 1730 North 18th Street in Quincy.

Some believe this birch tree reveals the image of Jesus holding a lamb.

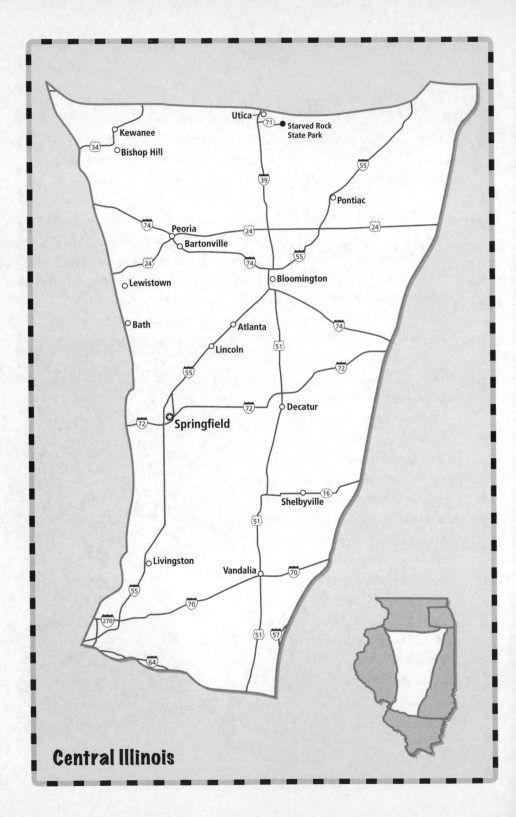

Central Illinois

# 4

# Central Illinois

"You might be from Central Illinois if your idea of a traffic jam is ten cars waiting to pass a tractor on the highway."

—Anonymous

**Central Illinois is** *the epicenter of Abraham Lincoln territory. In Springfield, the state capital and the community where Lincoln became famous, there is a President Abraham Lincoln Hotel, the Abraham Lincoln Capital Airport, the Lincoln Douglas Café, the Lincoln Tower Apartments, the Lincoln Land Community College, the Lincoln Greens Golf Course, Lincoln Yellow Cab, Lincoln Landscaping, Lincoln Limousine, Lincoln Land Alarm Co., Lincoln Land Title, Lincoln Chiropractic Clinic, and the Mr. Lincoln Campground RV Center.*

*Springfield is also home of the Abraham Lincoln Presidential Library and Museum as well as Lincoln's Tomb, where the sixteenth president was put to rest after his 1865 assassination. All this rampant Lincolnmania reflects the fact that in 1837, the twenty-eight-year-old Lincoln arrived in Springfield, which became the state capital that year, to start a law practice. During the next twenty-three years Lincoln resided in the city and for seventeen of those years he lived in a house at 413 South Eighth Street (now restored as a national historic site). It was in Springfield that Lincoln was married (to Mary Todd) and where his four sons were born. While in Springfield, Lincoln was elected to four terms in the Illinois House of Representatives (1834–1842), the U.S. House of*

★ ★ ★ ★ ★ ★ ★ ★ ★ ★ ★ ★ ★ ★ ★ ★ ★ ★ ★ ★ ★ ★ ★ ★ ★ ★ ★ ★ ★ ★

*Representatives for one term (1847–1849), and, ultimately, the U.S. Presidency (1861–1865).*

*Springfield isn't the only place in Central Illinois that canonizes Lincoln. About 20 miles northwest of Springfield is New Salem, the settlement where he lived from 1831 to 1837. Additionally, there are at least a dozen other communities ranging from Beardstown to Bloomington where he argued legal cases, gave political speeches, stayed while visiting friends, and spent the night. In fact, it's impossible to find any town that boasts, "Lincoln did absolutely nothing here," although plenty would no doubt qualify.*

*But perhaps the highest honor ever bestowed on Lincoln occurred, appropriately, at the Illinois State Fair in Springfield in 2009. On the occasion of the bicentennial of Lincoln's birth, sculptor Sharon BuMann carefully carved—out of 1,200 pounds of butter—a life-size likeness of a young Lincoln sitting on the ground reading a book. Next to him is an equally lifelike sculpture of a jersey cow and a half-split log.*

*"I suspect he's supposed to be milking the cow and splitting the wood, but has decided to read instead," BuMann told United Press International. "I wanted to depict him doing what he was most famous for: reading."*

*No doubt Mr. Lincoln would have been honored.*

★ ★ ★ ★ ★ ★ ★ ★ ★ ★ ★ ★ ★ ★ ★ ★ ★ ★ ★ ★ ★ ★ ★ ★ ★ ★ ★ ★ ★ ★ ★ ★ ★

### Real Life Flintstones Homes
Atlanta

During the energy crisis in the 1970s, when the price of oil jumped and people were lined up in gas lines at nearly every service station, Andy Davis had a brainstorm. An electrician and builder, Davis, who lived in the Eastern Illinois hamlet of Armington, started to wonder if there might not be a better way to build houses. Specifically, Davis began mulling the idea of building a house encased in dirt—a cave home.

So in the mid-1970s, Davis, who lived in a conventional rural farmhouse with his wife and nine children, constructed a new house for his family in a hillside with sides and a roof made of thick concrete and encased in several feet of dirt. To heat the place, he installed a Franklin stove. His neighbors thought he was crazy, but the first winter living in the home, 1976-77, the Davis family's heating bill was $2.

By the 1980s, Davis had become a folk hero to back-to-nature advocates and just about anyone else tired of paying astronomically high heating and air conditioning bills. His cave house was featured on the cover of *Money* magazine and *Mother Earth News* (probably the only time those two publications ever agreed on a topic).

Responding to the volume of requests from others wanting to build a cave house, Davis established a company, Davis Caves, to build and sell blueprints for earth-sheltered homes. Davis died in 1995 but the company continues to be run by family members.

In a 1979 interview with the Associated Press, Davis noted, "We're 15 feet underground and there's 5½ feet of earth on top of the specially constructed concrete roofing. The temperature varies very little. It's a natural constant 57 or 58 degrees, regardless of what it is outside, and that can easily be raised to the desired comfort level.

"We're storm proof, fire proof and quiet," he added. "We might have to mow the roof now and then."

The company offers tours of a cave model home located at 1584 US 136 outside of Atlanta, Illinois, on the first Sunday of every month from 2 p.m. to 4 p.m. For more information, go to www.daviscaves.com.

★ ★ ★ ★ ★ ★ ★ ★ ★ ★ ★ ★ ★ ★ ★ ★ ★ ★ ★ ★ ★ ★ ★ ★ ★ ★ ★ ★ ★ ★ ★

## An Industrial Park to Die For

Bartonville

Progress and history can make strange bedfellows. That's certainly the case with the former site of the Illinois Asylum for the Incurably Insane in Bartonville, which is a curious blend of a modern industrial park surrounding an imposing and historic but slowly decaying main administrative building and semi-neglected graveyards.

The Bartonville compound was a state-of-the-art mental health facility for its time. Under the direction of its first superintendent, Dr. George A. Zeller, the hospital tried to break from the traditional ways of dealing with the insane—namely locking them up in cells—and utilize a more humane, campus-like approach.

The cemetery is the focus of the most unusual stories surrounding Bartonville. In fact, in the 1920s Dr. Zeller, who served as superintendent from 1902 to 1913 and from 1921 to 1935, penned a book about the hospital in which he recounts several unusual experiences he had at the facility including one involving one of the gravediggers, a patient known as "Old Book."

Dr. Zeller wrote that normally the process of burying a patient was an informal matter since many of the deceased had no families. However, at his first internment, Old Book removed his cap, wiped tears from his eyes, and then leaned on an ancient elm tree in the middle of the cemetery (which became known as the "Graveyard Elm") and began wailing loudly. The doctor said that Old Book repeated this same display at every subsequent burial.

Years later, Old Book passed away and several hundred staff members and patients gathered for a small graveside service. In his book, Dr. Zeller wrote that when the coffin was lowered, all in attendance suddenly heard a "wailing voice" and saw Old Book standing next to the elm tree, "weeping and moaning with an earnestness that outrivaled anything he had ever shown before."

Dr. Zeller said he immediately had the casket opened to see if Old Book was inside and when the lid was lifted the wailing suddenly

Cemetery at the former Illinois Asylum
for the Incurably Insane in Bartonville

Illinois has 76,000 farms covering more than twenty-eight million acres, which is nearly 80 percent of the state's total land area.

stopped and the figure by the tree disappeared. To everyone's surprise, Book was in the coffin, still dead.

These days, a handful of the old Bartonville buildings remain standing including the Bowen Building, erected in 1903, which has been boarded up and abandoned since the hospital closed in 1972.

The site of the Bowen Building is on Constitution Drive off US 24 (via Pfeiffer Road) in Bartonville. The cemeteries are located south of the building, off Enterprise Drive. For more information, visit http://peoria-asylum.com/.

## The Redneck Fishing Derby
Bath

In the mid-1990s, Illinois River boaters and anglers began noticing an unusual fish in the water. This particular fish wasn't like the usual species such as channel catfish and largemouth bass. This fish was more aggressive. In fact, when startled by engine vibrations, this fish leaped out of the water and almost seemed to attack the boat.

It turned out the fish was an Asian carp and its arrival in the Illinois River was bad news. The carp were accidentally introduced into the river in the mid-1990s after being transported to Louisiana by catfish farmers who wanted them to clean up their pens (the Asian carp are voracious eaters so the hope was that they would remove algae and suspended matter in farm ponds). Unfortunately, flooding in the early 1990s released the carp into the Mississippi River basin and they've been steadily making their way upriver ever since.

Participants compete to catch the most Asian carp with fishing nets at the Redneck Fishing Tournament in Bath.

Asian carp literally out-eat and out-procreate native species of fish. The fear of fish and game experts was that the carp might proceed up the Illinois and reach the Great Lakes, destroying their multi-million dollar sports fishing industry.

State and federal agencies responded by trying to poison the carp as well as by installing electrified barriers on the river just south of Chicago. The barriers appeared to stall their advance for a few years but in December 2009, Asian carp were detected within a few miles of Lake Michigan.

In 2004, after learning firsthand about the dangers of Asian carp, Betty DeFord, manager of the Boat Tavern in the tiny Illinois River town of Bath, decided to organize the "Original Redneck Fishing Tournament." DeFord said she got the idea after being attacked by carp while on a boat ride with her husband and daughter.

The rules were pretty basic—cruise around on the Illinois River in a motorboat, catch the agitated, leaping fish with a net, and avoid getting hit in the head. The winner is the person collecting the most fish. The first year five boats competed and captured about 200 carp in an hour's time. The fish were donated to a local processing plant to be made into fishmeal and fish oil.

Since then the contest has taken off. In 2009, more than one hundred boats competed for cash prizes. Many contestants arrived wearing colorful costumes and showed off their moves while netting the fish. In the end, 1,539 fish were netted. The winner, Brent Martin of Warrensburg, Missouri, snagged an amazing 112 fish in a two-hour heat.

For more information, check out the Boat Tavern at 218 East 1st Street in Bath or go to www.redneckfishingtournament.com.

### The Swedish Meatball Capital of America
Bishop Hill

Bishop Hill is one of the few places in Illinois (outside of an IKEA store) where you can order your *köttbullar* with lingonberries and find authentic *skorpor* to dip in your coffee. It's no exaggeration to say that the tiny community of 125 residents is a slice of the old country (if you're from Sweden) tucked into the cornfields of Illinois.

So how does a Swedish village end up in the middle of the American Midwest? Bishop Hill traces its beginnings to 1846, when Eric Jansson, a controversial Swedish religious figure, fled his homeland with several hundred of his followers to escape religious persecution. Later that year, one of his followers purchased 480 acres (which eventually grew to include more than 12,000 acres) in Central Illinois. Upon arriving, Jansson named the new community Bishop Hill, an Americanization of Jansson's birthplace, Biskopskulla Parish.

**Main Street in the historic Swedish
community of Bishop Hill**

Unfortunately, life was difficult for the Janssonists, who encountered bitter cold during their first winter in Illinois. The initial dwellings were little more than crude caves built into the side of a ravine and covered with timber facades. Nearly a quarter (ninety-six) of the estimated 400 members of the colony died in the first year. Within a few years, the residents, who worked in a communal system under Jansson's guidance, had erected about twenty large commercial buildings, including a ninety-six-room, four-story dormitory known as the "Big Brick."

★ ★ ★ ★ ★ ★ ★ ★ ★ ★ ★ ★ ★ ★ ★ ★ ★ ★ ★ ★ ★ ★ ★ ★ ★ ★ ★ ★ ★ ★ ★ ★ ★

In 1850, the colony was dealt a serious blow when Jansson was shot to death by John Root, the husband of one of his cousins, in a dispute over Root's desire to leave the community with his family. Following his death, control of the colony was given to a seven-member board of trustees, which established democratic rule. For the next half-decade, Bishop Hill continued to be prosperous. However, a national financial downturn in the late 1850s seriously affected the profitability of the colony, which voted to dissolve in 1861.

Today, while only a handful of the descendants of the original Janssonists still live in Bishop Hill, the town has embraced its Swedish roots. As a result nearly two dozen historic buildings have been preserved and remain in use. Additionally, the town has a couple of local eateries devoted to authentic Swedish cuisine. The Bishop Hill Colony Bakery offers a variety of Swedish breads and pastries prepared from scratch, including *limpa* (rye bread with ground anise and orange peel), *rusks* (a dry biscuit also known as *skorpor*), and orange lingonberry muffins. The Red Oak Comfort Food and Pie Company offers menu items based on classic Swedish cooking including *köttbullar* (Swedish meatballs) and *kåldomar* (beef cabbage roll covered in tomato sauce).

*Skål!*

Bishop Hill is located about three hours southwest of Chicago via I-55 and I-80, and IL 5, 4, and 39. For more information, go to www
.bishophill.com.

## Trivia

**The geographic center of Illinois is located in Logan County, about 28 miles northeast of Springfield.**

# Fooling the Devil

It's said that farmers who didn't want to give Satan a corner in which to hide invented the round-shaped barn. If that's true then Illinois must be pretty near the gateway to hell. The state is home to dozens of oval barns (most built between 1900 and 1935), including one of the largest in the country. Called Ryan's Round Barn, it is more than 80 feet tall and about 85 feet in diameter. The big domed barn has three interior levels and includes a 16-foot-high silo in the center.

The barn's builder, however, wasn't a superstitious farmer but rather a prominent Chicago brain surgeon, Dr. Laurence Ryan. The good doctor completed the giant round building in 1910 to house his prized Black Angus cattle. He wasn't trying to trick Satan but rather he believed a round barn would be less likely to be damaged by a tornado. As a firm believer in the scientific approach to agriculture, he also believed the shape would result in a more efficient operation.

Today, Ryan's Barn is part of the Johnson-Sauk Trail State Park, which is located 5 miles north of Kewanee, via IL 78. For more information, go to http://dnr.state.il.us/lands/landmgt/parks/r1/johnson.htm.

The Ryan Round Barn, one of the biggest round barns in the world.

★ ★ ★ ★ ★ ★ ★ ★ ★ ★ ★ ★ ★ ★ ★ ★ ★ ★ ★ ★ ★ ★ ★ ★ ★ ★ ★ ★ ★ ★ ★

### What's in a Name?
Bloomington

Anyone who has ever spent much time in a bar has no doubt consumed some of those sodium-saturated snack foods sold in nearly every
drinking establishment—primarily because salty stuff makes one thirsty.

These beloved tavern foods include beef jerky, Red Hot Sausages,
pickled eggs, and, of course, the aptly named BEER NUTS (trade-
marked with all capital letters). The Shirk family has made the latter
in Bloomington since the late 1930s. Often called the quintessential
American bar food, BEER NUTS are actually Virginia Extra Large and
Jumbo Runner peanuts that are shelled and cleaned but retain their
red skins. The nuts are roasted and glazed in oil, corn syrup, and salt
(but no beer). The exact steps involved in the latter process are considered a company trade secret (factory tours are not allowed) and are
said to be what makes BEER NUTS different from your run-of-the-mill
honey-roasted peanut.

BEER NUTS didn't start out as a tavern treat. The confection was
actually invented in the early 1930s in a Bloomington candy store known
as the Caramel Crisp Store. At the time, the shop's bestsellers were popcorn balls and handmade candy. Originally called "Redskins," the salty-
sweet peanuts were sold by the scoop to entice thirsty customers to buy
the shop's orange soda drink. In 1937, Russell Shirk convinced his father
to purchase the candy store, where he had been working after school.
Over time, the focus of the business shifted from candy to the tasty
nuts, which were packaged in bags and called "Shirk's Glazed Peanuts."
In 1953, a local potato chip distributor, Eldridge Brewster, convinced
the Shirks to allow him to sell them to bars and taverns throughout the
region. He also coined a new name, "BEER NUTS."

The nuts were an immediate hit with the adult beverage crowd
and by 1960 BEER NUTS were available in every state. A decade later,
the company was producing ten million pounds per year. In 1973, the
company moved into the 100,000-square-foot facility in Bloomington,

The BEER NUTS factory in Bloomington

in which it is located today. While the peanut version continues to be the top seller—about 85 percent of the business—the company has added other glazed nuts including cashews and almonds.

The BEER NUTS plant is located at 103 North Robinson Street. Tours of the plant are not available, but the facility has a well-stocked gift shop that sells hats, shirts, golf balls, and, of course, packages of those sweet but salty legumes.

# Big, Smelly, Dirty, and Shy

During the past century, rural Central and Eastern Illinois has been the location of an extraordinary number of sightings of the elusive creature known as "Bigfoot." The earliest accounts appeared in the late nineteenth and early twentieth century, with reports of a "wild man," described as being large and hairy, glimpsed in the woods around Effingham. In the 1940s, a large gorilla or monkey-like creature was allegedly spotted near Mount Vernon.

But it wasn't until the 1960s that these sightings began to increase in frequency. In 1963 two men reported seeing a tall, hairy hominid-like creature near a river north of Decatur. They were close enough to report that the dirty, gray creature smelled terrible. Three years later, four teens parked on a remote "lover's lane" in Montezuma Hills near Decatur were startled by a large, black ape-like animal that smelled badly. In the early 1970s, there were dozens of sightings in the vicinity of Farmer City and Clinton, both located north of Decatur.

Since then, the sightings have tailed off although some cryptozoologists (people who study legendary animals such as Bigfoot) believe they still occur but just aren't reported in the mainstream media. Yeah, blame it on the media.

## Fred Francis's House of Wonders

Woodland Palace
Kewanee

Frederick Francis was a man far ahead of his time. He was born on his family's farm about 4 miles east of the future town of Kewanee on January 21, 1856. His father, Sullivan Francis, was a farmer and, in the winter months, a schoolteacher, who tutored his son. In 1874, Francis entered the Illinois Industrial University in Urbana (the first person from the Kewanee area to attend the college), which later became the University of Illinois. During his years at the school, he earned a degree in mechanical engineering.

While in school, Francis began to exhibit the traits that would define his life—a natural curiosity, a gift for designing things, and an ability to build his designs. In 1878, Francis went to work with the Elgin Watch Company. While there, he obtained several patents including one for an unbreakable watch spring. About a decade later, Francis married a widow named Jeanette Crowfoot and the two relocated to his family property in Kewanee (his parents had passed away by then). He continued to receive royalties from his watch patents, which became his primary source of income for the rest of his life.

In 1889, Francis began work on the home that would become his legacy. He designed and built nearly every part of the house and its furnishings. The distinctive brick exterior of the home was achieved after Francis purchased a pile of secondary quality bricks from a nearby brickyard. Using a hammer and chisel, Francis chipped each brick to remove soft spots and flaws. He also incorporated a silver dome on top of a white limestone tower, which gives the place its palace-like appearance.

Other unique features of the home included an elaborate heating and cooling system powered by a windmill and an early version of indoor plumbing, including a crude shower and a flush toilet. And he did all this without having any electricity in the house and without ever owning a vehicle (he rode his bicycle everywhere).

A devotee of the "Physical Cultural" movement of the late nineteenth and early twentieth centuries, Francis strongly believed in being physically active, including doing daily exercise. As part of his beliefs, he maintained a strict vegetarian diet and rarely wore shoes or socks, believing that valuable minerals could be absorbed from the earth through the feet. Additionally, he often walked around his property nude (known as "air bathing").

As he grew older, Francis developed a special signal with his mailman. If the flag of the mailbox was not up, the mailman should check to see if he was all right. On December 22, 1926, the mailman saw the flag was not up and found Francis dead of a self-inflicted gunshot wound. He left a note saying that he could no longer live with the pain from a hernia. In his will, Francis left his entire estate to the City of Kewanee.

**Woodland Palace, the handmade home of inventor Frederick Francis.**

# Haunted America Midwest Conference, Decatur (most years)

Every June for two days, many of the world's paranormal aficionados flock to the annual Haunted America Midwest Conference, a celebration of things that go bump in the night. Established in 1997 by Troy Taylor, a Chicago author and self-described "supernatural historian," the event attracts about 250 true believers and other interested parties who listen to seminars on topics like "Ghosts on Video," "What You Need to Know about Demons," and "Paranormal Forensics."

While held in the haunted Lincoln Theater in Decatur—called the most haunted small city in the Midwest—for its first fourteen years, the Haunted America Midwest Conference has moved around to other Illinois communities in recent years, including Jacksonville. The Decatur Haunted America event was the first of its type in the country and has apparently proven so successful that Taylor's company, American Spookshows, has branched into other parts of the country with the Haunted America East Coast Conference (Massachusetts) and the Haunted America West Coast Conference (California).

Who would have known that ghost stories could be so lucrative? For more information, go to www.americanspookshows.com.

Now known as Francis Park, the site includes a sixty-space RV park, walking trails, and picnic areas, and is open daily May through September. Tours of Woodland Palace are offered daily during the season. The park is located 4 miles east of Kewanee, off US 34. For more information, go to www.cityofkewanee.com/francis.php.

# Here's Something You Otter See

Step into the Union Federal Savings and Loan in Kewanee, and you'll find something besides the usual loan officers and bank tellers— a river otter named Andy. Since 1991, Andy (and a companion otter named Oscar, who died in 2008) has lived in a special, climate-controlled pool in the center of the bank. According to bank officials, the two were captured in the wild in Louisiana and relocated to the bank by a previous bank president who wanted to educate people about river otters, which at the time were an endangered species in Illinois. Union Federal Savings and Loan is located at 104 North Tremont in Kewanee.

Andy the River Otter, who lives inside the Union Federal Savings and Loan in Kewanee

★ ★ ★ ★ ★ ★ ★ ★ ★ ★ ★ ★ ★ ★ ★ ★ ★ ★ ★ ★ ★ ★ ★ ★ ★ ★ ★ ★ ★ ★

### Trivia

In 1978, then–Illinois governor James Thompson declared that Morton was the official **Pumpkin Capital of the World** because 85 percent of the world's canned pumpkin is processed in the community.

## America's Pyramids

Dickson Mounds
Lewistown

When you think about those big, prehistoric monoliths, you usually picture Egypt's pyramids, Greece's temples, or Incan structures in South America. You don't think of North America's native people. But nearly camouflaged across the wide expanses of the American Midwest and South are hundreds of earthen mounds, some quite large, that, in their own way, are as impressive as any stone structure built in Athens or Machu Picchu.

Archaeologists believe that the mounds were built over a long period of time, between about 3000 BC and AD 1200. The mounds served as burial places for the Native Americans as well as the foundations for ceremonial temples and homes of prominent individuals and families.

One of the best examples of a Native American burial mound is Dickson Mounds in Central Illinois. The Dickson Mounds Museum, located at the site, is devoted to telling the story of the region's earliest inhabitants.

In 1833, William Dickson purchased the bluff and, in 1866, while clearing trees to plant an orchard, he discovered an ancient Indian burial ground. A few years later, his son, Thomas, destroyed a section of a burial mound while building a house. In 1927, Thomas Dickson's son, Dr. Don F. Dickson, began carefully excavating a portion of the mound. Dr. Dickson, who was a chiropractor, recognized the

**Entrance to the Dickson Mounds Museum near Lewistown**

importance of preserving the site so he dug around the buried bodies, leaving them undisturbed.

His work attracted University of Chicago archaeologists, who joined Dickson to excavate the area. The digs uncovered the remains of nearly 250 Native Americans, which were protected, first, under a tent and later enclosed in a museum building. From the 1930s to 1992, the bones and hundreds of artifacts unearthed by Dr. Dickson were displayed to the general public in the private Dickson Mound Museum. Visitors could actually wander through tunnels in the mounds, walking among the ancient skeletons.

In 1945, Dr. Dickson, who died in 1964, sold the site to the state of Illinois. In 1972, a new museum structure was built on the site, which was designed to resemble the low, squared shape of the original mounds.

★ ★ ★ ★ ★ ★ ★ ★ ★ ★ ★ ★ ★ ★ ★ ★ ★ ★ ★ ★ ★ ★ ★ ★ ★ ★ ★ ★ ★ ★ ★

**Since 1949 the town of Kewanee (population 13,000) has been known as the Hog Capital of the World because it leads the nation in hog production.**

In the early 1990s, Illinois state officials responded to repeated requests from Native American groups to properly respect the Indian remains by agreeing to re-cover the burial site and rebuild the museum so that it did not expose the remains to the public. The result is that the remains are no longer available for public viewing. The revamped facility opened in 1994 with a new focus on the history of the various people who have lived in the Illinois River Valley region.

Located 5 miles southeast of Lewistown, the museum is open daily from 8:30 a.m. to 5 p.m. For more information, go to www.museum .state.il.us/ismsites/dickson/geninfo.html.

## Grave Remarks

Oak Hill Cemetery
Lewistown

In 1915, Chicago lawyer Edgar Lee Masters, a partner of the legendary barrister Clarence Darrow, published a collection of brief, free-form poems known as *Spoon River Anthology*. The pieces described a fictional small town, Spoon River, which was named after an actual river of that name that flowed near his hometown of Lewistown in Central Illinois.

Each poem serves as an epitaph for a deceased resident of this mythical small town and is delivered by the dead person. Since they're dead, many of the characters—and there are more than 200 different voices—feel free to speak candidly and frankly about their hopes, dreams, secrets, petty complaints, and shames. The result is a work

★ ★ ★ ★ ★ ★ ★ ★ ★ ★ ★ ★ ★ ★ ★ ★ ★ ★ ★ ★ ★ ★ ★ ★ ★ ★ ★ ★ ★ ★

**Trivia**

**The Chicago Bears professional football team was established in Decatur in 1920 and was originally known as the Decatur Staleys. A year later, the team moved to Chicago and became Da Bears.**

that has been hailed by critics and gone on to become one of the best selling books of poetry in American history.

The setting for the poems is the Oak Hill Cemetery in Lewistown, which Masters simply calls "The Hill," and many of his characters were based on real people that he knew or knew of in Lewistown and nearby Petersburg, where he also grew up. Local legend says that Masters never moved back to Lewistown or Petersburg because some of his poems cast those folks in a less than flattering light. It's been reported that a copy of *Spoon River Anthology* wasn't even available at the Lewistown Library until after 1972. Masters died in Pennsylvania in 1950 but, fittingly, was buried in Petersburg.

Time has a way of healing things and these days Masters has finally become accepted in Lewistown and Petersburg. In fact, in October the communities along the Spoon River host the Annual Spoon River Drive Fall Festival. As part of the event, Oak Hill Cemetery hosts readings from *Spoon River Anthology*.

It seems like Masters had the last word, even from beyond the grave.

The Oak Hill Cemetery is located at 1022 North Main Street in Lewistown.

## Lincoln's Lincoln
Lincoln

Abe Lincoln is big stuff in his namesake community of Lincoln. Really big stuff. In fact, the town boasts a giant fiberglass statue of the sixteenth president, reading a law book, while sitting in what the

★ ★ ★ ★ ★ ★ ★ ★ ★ ★ ★ ★ ★ ★ ★ ★ ★ ★ ★ ★ ★ ★ ★ ★ ★ ★ ★ ★ ★ ★ ★ ★ ★

**Lincoln, home of the world's largest covered wagon**

*Guinness Book of World Records* has called the world's largest covered wagon. Known as the Railsplitter Covered Wagon, the massive construct boasts a 12-foot, 350-pound likeness of the former president as well as a covered wagon that weighs five tons and measures 24 feet tall, 12 feet wide, and 40 feet long.

The wagon was hand built of oak in a six-month period in 2001 by former Illinois policeman David Bentley of Pawnee, who wanted to create something inspirational and memorable while recovering from heart disease. Originally, Bentley parked the big wagon in his yard adjacent to historic Route 66. In late 2006, however, he decided he wanted to sell his creation and offered it to Lincoln because of the town's connection to the former president (it is the only community in the United States to have been named for Lincoln prior to his being elected president) and also because the town is located on Route 66. When the asking price of $10,000 plus $2,000 for moving the wagon seemed a bit out of reach for the community, in stepped Larry Van Bibber, a local philanthropist, who donated the full amount.

In January 2007, the Railsplitter Wagon was moved to a site adjacent to an auto supply store on the corner of Woodlawn Road and Route 66 in Lincoln. Two years later, the peripatetic wagon was moved again to a patch of open space in front of the Best Western Lincoln Inn at 1750 5th Street in Lincoln. This time, community leaders announced it would be the wagon's last move. "This is really a great location," Logan County Board chairman Larry Carlton told the *Lincoln Courier.* "Right on Route 66. I think it just fits." Additionally, the town received a federal grant to erect a snazzy, chrome Route 66 interpretive exhibit adjacent to the wagon. Of course, if they wanted to do a real mash-up of Abe and Route 66, they might have put him in a classic '65 Lincoln Continental parked in the town. In other words: Lincoln in a Lincoln in Lincoln.

## Trivia

According to local historians, the phrase "Will It Play in Peoria?" most likely originated in the 1920s. Vaudeville producers believed that if a production did well in Peoria—seen as a typical, average American city—it would succeed anywhere.

# Freaks, Geeks, and Antiques

The Pink Elephant Antiques Mall is a throwback to the days of classic roadside attractions. Housed in the former Livingston High School building, the antiques store's owners have accumulated an eclectic collection of fiberglass statues as well as a renovated Twistee Treat ice cream cone–shaped building and a flying saucer structure that are all parked in front in an effort to draw attention to the site.

Perhaps the most bizarre and visually striking icon anchored to the front of the business is the 24-foot-high "Beach Guy," a fiberglass image of a man garbed only in swim trunks with one hand at his waist and the other outstretched as if holding something (it's said that he originally held a soda can). Apparently, "Beach Guy" was manufactured by a fiberglass firm in Sparta, Wisconsin, and then was posed in front of a different antiques shop in Benld, Illinois. Some say that he used to stand in front of a gay bar in St. Louis. He was relocated to Pink Elephant in about 2006.

Pink Elephant Antiques is located at 908 Veterans Memorial Drive in Livingston. To get there, take exit 37 off I-55. The shop is open daily from 9:30 a.m. to 5:30 p.m. For more information, call (618) 637-2366.

Bizarre sights abound at Pink Elephant Antiques Mall in Livingston.

★ ★ ★ ★ ★ ★ ★ ★ ★ ★ ★ ★ ★ ★ ★ ★ ★ ★ ★ ★ ★ ★ ★ ★ ★ ★ ★ ★ ★ ★ ★ ★ ★ ★

### Getting Your Kicks on Route 66
Route 66 Hall of Fame & Museum
Pontiac

Over the years Route 66, the nation-spanning highway that once ran from Chicago to Los Angeles (2,448 miles), has taken on nigh mythical status. There's a National Historic Route 66 Federation with chapters in nearly a dozen states, several dozen guidebooks about the road, and even a video game ("King of Route 66" for Playstation 2).

**This giant mural depicting the classic Route 66 is painted on the back of the Route 66 Hall of Fame & Museum in Pontiac.**

It's often referred to as the "Mother Road" or as the "Main Street of America." The road, which was established in 1926, was immortalized in a 1946 hit song performed by Nat King Cole ("Get Your Kicks on Route 66") as well as a popular television show (called, naturally, *Route 66*) that ran from 1960 to 1964.

But if all that's not enough, there is also the Route 66 Hall of Fame & Museum, which has been housed in the historic former Pontiac Old City Firehouse since 2003. The HOF&M celebrates the famed road, particularly as it swept through Illinois. Inside are displays describing the history of the road and more than 1,000 Route 66–related artifacts including old road signs, a restored gas station pump, maps, photos, and other memorabilia. On the south side of the fire station is a giant wall mural of the famous Route 66 road sign in front of which visitors can park their cars for snapshots.

The Route 66 Hall of Fame & Museum is located at 110 West Howard Street in Pontiac. For more information, go to www.il66assoc.org /attraction/route-66-association-hall-fame-museum. And tell them Tod and Buz sent you.

### Mobile Marrying Man
Shelbyville

Shelbyville wedding minister Darrell Best knows how to make an entrance. When he's performing a marriage, he doesn't just bring a Bible—he shows up with the whole darn chapel.

(Continued on page 199)

# Peoria's St. Louis Arch

St. Louis, Missouri isn't the only Midwestern city with a big arch. In fact, Peoria boasts its own version of the famed Gateway Arch. The Peoria arch is exactly the same as the one in St. Louis.

Except it's much smaller. And you can't go inside. And it stands in front of a used auto parts store in an industrial district. And it has a full-sized Buick automobile perched on a crossbeam that spans the center of the arch. And it pretty much serves to promote the auto parts store rather than commemorate the gateway to westward expansion. But other than those things, it's nearly the same.

Peoria's miniature St. Louis Arch has its own Buick automobile.

(Continued from page 197)

Best is the owner of Best Wedding Chapel—housed in an historic former Catholic Church building—as well as the "Best Man," a souped-up 1942 American La France fire truck that has been converted into a wedding chapel on wheels. While it was Best's idea to buy a vintage fire truck and use it for mobile weddings, the conversion of the truck into the "Best Man" was the work of the CMT television show, *Trick My Truck*, which, in 2008, transformed it from an aging red fire engine into a gleaming white vehicular chapel complete with a working organ, bell tower, and two rows of pews.

The TV show selected Best's wagon for a makeover after his wife, Lisa, and three sons had written to the producers and pitched the

**"Best Man," a former fire engine, has been transformed into a mobile wedding chapel.**

idea. They told the show that Best already had the fire truck but lacked the ability and the financial means to transform it into something that would make his dream of being able to perform drive-up nuptials a reality. Over several months and an estimated 2,000 man-hours of work, the *Trick My Truck* crew reconstructed the vehicle, at no cost to Best. His main expense has been building an enlarged garage at the rear of the church in which to house the vehicle.

Best, who was a credit union president in the St. Louis region before deciding to open his wedding chapel business in 1999, said he formally unveiled the "Best Man" at the Illinois State Fair in Springfield in 2009, performing about eight weddings and renewal ceremonies. "I like driving it in parades," he said. "People really respond to seeing it."

Best Wedding Chapel is located at 159 North Washington in Shelbyville. For more information, go to www.BestWeddingChapel.com.

## Welcome to Abe World

Abraham Lincoln Presidential Library and Museum
Springfield

One has to wonder what old Abe Lincoln would think about the official Presidential Library and Museum created in his honor. If the sixteenth president were alive he would no doubt be amazed and a bit overwhelmed by the place, which is a splashy blend of twenty-first century high-tech flash with nineteenth century history (perhaps to be expected since many of the displays were designed by a former Disney "imagineer").

Opened in 2005, the 100,000-square-foot museum, which cost $145 million, tells Lincoln's life story and important place in American history using state-of-the-art exhibits; life-size wax figures of Lincoln and his friends, family, and associates; and touch screens, TV monitors, holograms, and other devices. Additionally, the museum contains

(Continued on page 203)

# Spaced Out

Pluto is in a furniture store in Kewanee, Saturn is in a Kroger's grocery store in East Peoria, Neptune is in an auto dealership in Roanoke, while Uranus sits on a brick pedestal in a Pekin park. All odd places to find planetary bodies but all part of an unusual re-creation of the solar system found in Central and Western Illinois. Described as the world's largest scale model of the solar system, the celestial replica stretches across more than 2,000 square miles.

The sun is represented by the east wing of Peoria's Lakeview Museum, which is painted with a large yellow orb. Using a scale of 43 feet for every million miles, the closest planet is Mercury, a quarter of a mile away from the museum in a camera shop. Venus (a half mile away) is tucked inside a print shop while Earth (three-quarters of a mile away) can be found in a gas station. The farthest spot in the solar system is the dwarf planet, Eris, located in the science building on the Western Illinois University campus (62 miles west of the museum).

The Lakeview Museum is located at 1125 West Lake Avenue in Peoria. For more information, go to www.lakeview-museum.org.

Lakeview Museum is host of the world's largest scale model of the universe.

Lifelike mannequins of President Abraham Lincoln
and his family greet visitors at the Abraham Lincoln
Presidential Library and Museum in Springfield.

(Continued from page 200)
the "Treasures Gallery," filled with historic Lincoln memorabilia such as letters, documents, personal items, and clothing, including one of his famous stovepipe hats and the bloodstained gloves he carried on the night he was assassinated in 1865.

While the marriage of theme-park technology and history works in many cases, some critics have questioned a few of the exhibits, particularly one devoted to the 1860 election that is presented as if the contest had been covered by contemporary television news organizations. With veteran newsman Tim Russert (who died in 2008) providing the commentary, the presentation even includes faux television commercials that might have been created had television existed back then.

On the other hand, the two 4-D theaters, particularly one called "Ghosts of the Library," offer a fascinating explanation about why historians study stuff like what is contained in the Lincoln Library. The cool holographic special effects enhance the message and help make a potentially boring subject more interesting.

The actual Lincoln Library is a separate part of the complex that is generally only visited by Lincoln scholars and researchers, although it's open to anyone. It contains more than 10,000 Lincoln-related books, almost 1,500 letters written and/or signed by Lincoln, more than 1,000 photographs of Lincoln and other related subjects, and more than 250 artifacts directly related to the former president and his family. Incorporated into the facility is a 3,500-square-foot gift shop selling everything from Lincoln busts and books to replicas of his famous stovepipe hat and Lincoln Log sets.

The Abraham Lincoln Presidential Library and Museum is located at 212 North Sixth Street in downtown Springfield. It is open daily from 9 a.m. to 5 p.m. For more information, go to www.PresidentLincoln.org.

★ ★ ★ ★ ★ ★ ★ ★ ★ ★ ★ ★ ★ ★ ★ ★ ★ ★ ★ ★ ★ ★ ★ ★ ★ ★ ★ ★ ★

### Unrest in Peace
Lincoln's Tomb
Springfield

Strange as it sounds, the remains of President Abraham Lincoln were moved seventeen times between his funeral in Springfield in 1865 and 1901, when his casket was embedded in two tons of solid concrete. Many of the moves were the result of delays and unexpected problems encountered while building his elaborate tomb in the Oak Ridge Cemetery and later having to repair it. However, at least one move was a direct result of a bizarre body-snatching attempt that occurred in 1876.

Following Lincoln's assassination on April 14, 1865, his body was brought to Oak Ridge and placed in a receiving vault in a nearby hillside until his supporters could raise enough money for a proper monument. In 1874, an impressive stone memorial was finally completed and Lincoln's body was interred in a marble sarcophagus inside the structure (alongside his three dead sons). The multilevel structure included a 117-foot-high obelisk surrounded by life-size bronze sculptures of soldiers representing the four Civil War services (infantry, artillery, cavalry, and navy).

Two years later, a pair of Midwestern counterfeiters concocted a scheme to steal Lincoln's body and trade it for cash and the release of one of their associates who was in jail. Authorities were cagey enough to have placed an inside man in the operation, but as a result of their clumsiness failed to arrest those involved on the night of the body-snatching attempt. The two were arrested in Chicago about ten days later and found guilty.

According to several accounts, a group of Lincoln's Springfield friends were so concerned others might try to abscond with the president's remains that a few weeks later they secretly removed Lincoln's coffin and hid it beneath a pile of old lumber and later buried it between the walls of the tomb. In 1900, the tomb was beginning to crumble because it had been built on unstable ground. During the

Lincoln's Tomb in Springfield

★ ★ ★ ★ ★ ★ ★ ★ ★ ★ ★ ★ ★ ★ ★ ★ ★ ★ ★ ★ ★ ★ ★ ★ ★ ★ ★ ★ ★ ★ ★ ★ ★ ★

reconstruction of the tomb's foundations and walls, Lincoln's body and those of his wife (she had died in 1882) and children were moved to yet another secret location. Finally, on September 26, 1901, Lincoln's coffin was placed inside a steel cage and embedded in concrete in a chamber located 10 feet beneath the tomb floor. The granite sarcophagus that visitors file by inside the tomb is empty—the sixteenth president is located beneath it.

Abraham Lincoln's Tomb is located in the Oak Ridge Cemetery at 1441 Monument Avenue in Springfield. At the entrance of the tomb is a striking bronze bust of the sixteenth president created by sculptor Gutzon Borglum, who also carved Mount Rushmore. Visitors often rub the nose of the bust for good luck. In fact, it's been rubbed so much that it's shiny compared to the rest of the bust.

### All Hail the Butter Cow
Illinois State Fair
Springfield

The Illinois State Fair in Springfield, held nearly every year since 1853, is one of those old time agricultural celebrations with parades, a carnival, horse races, tractor pulls, hog-calling, beef, sheep and poultry shows—and the butter cow. The latter, introduced to the fair in 1922, is exactly what it sounds like, a life-size (or larger) representation of a cow sculpted from hundreds of pounds of unsalted butter.

The butter cow is the unofficial mascot for the state fair and is such a popular element that the state fair web page has a "Butter Cow Cam," where viewers can watch the unveiling of the sculpture on the first day of the fair and see it throughout the fair's ten-day run in mid to late August.

Of course, over the years the butter cows have become more and more elaborate, as the sculptors introduce themes and other elements. For example, in 2007, butter artist Sharon BuMann sculpted a virtual diorama in butter that included a surprisingly realistic depiction of a young girl reading a book to her dog, which is looking up at an owl perched in a tree. In the foreground, a cow and a colt are kicking their legs up in celebration (the theme that year was "Celebrate and Educate"). In honor of Abraham Lincoln's 200th birthday in 2009, the scene included a grazing cow standing beside a young Lincoln who is reading a butter book.

The butter cow scenes are presented inside a special refrigerated rotating display case. To make each scene, BuMann, who has crafted them since 2004, uses about 1,200 pounds of butter and works in 34- to 36-degree temperatures for as many as one hundred hours over about a week and a half. To support the butter statues, BuMann first builds a metal armature, which she covers with the butter.

Since butter permeates the skin—in the past some butter sculptors have had health-related problems from absorbing butter—she wears rubber gloves and dresses in a raincoat and galoshes. Because of the cold, she takes a break every two hours. BuMann, who also creates butter cows for two or three other state fairs each year, estimates there are perhaps only three or four other people in the country who are proficient at butter sculpting.

As to what happens to all that butter after the fair is over—Springfield holds the world's largest buttered popcorn festival about a week later.

Not really.

The butter is actually removed from the metal frame, packed into buckets, and stored in a freezer in Decatur for use the following year.

## Central Illinois–style Haute Cuisine
Springfield

What would you call a sandwich that consists of two toasted slices of thick bread placed side-by-side and topped with either ham slices or a large hamburger patty, then covered with a creamy cheese beer sauce and a mound of french fries? A heart attack on a plate? Jenny Craig's worst nightmare? Nope, it's a Horseshoe sandwich and it was invented in Springfield.

**The Horseshoe sandwich was invented in Springfield.**

According to most epicurean historians (they do exist!), Chef Joe Schweska invented the Horseshoe in 1928 at the once-prestigious Leland Hotel in downtown Springfield (the hotel is now an office building). Chef Schweska's wife, Elizabeth, is said to have suggested the sandwich when he came home one day and said he needed a new item for the hotel lunch menu.

After reading a recipe for a Welsh rarebit sauce, she is said to have come up with the idea of some type of open-faced sandwich covered with the cheese sauce. Chef Schweska was inspired and concocted his own sauce—made with melted cheddar cheese, beer, flour, butter, Worcestershire sauce, and pinches of dry mustard and cayenne pepper—as well as figuring out the rest of the ingredients.

Originally, the sandwich meat was ham cut from a bone, which came out in the shape of a horseshoe—hence the name (the potatoes are called the Horseshoe's "nails"). While many restaurants later slathered the entire sandwich, including the fries, with the cheese sauce, the original Horseshoe had the cheese sauce poured over the ham and toast with potato wedges (not french fries) placed on top.

After it was introduced at the Leland, the Horseshoe was an instant hit. In the 1940s, Schweska moved on and one of his former protégés, Steve Tomko, became the hotel's chef and the main architect of the Horseshoe. As Tomko moved around to various other restaurants in Springfield in subsequent years, including Wayne's Red Coach Inn and Norb Andy's Tabarin, he served the popular Horseshoe. In later years, several writers credited Tomko with inventing the sandwich.

Today, at least one other Springfield eatery claims to be the home of the original Horseshoe—Norb Andy's Tabarin—and more than a half dozen joints in Springfield serve their own variations of the legendary sandwich. More often than not, however, the newcomers will serve it with turkey or hamburger patties or deep fried pork tenderloin or a chicken patty—and put the cheese on top of the fries and the sandwich. And that's not a real Horseshoe.

## Corn Dog on a Stick Was Invented in—Springfield?

Cozy Dog
Springfield

The corn dog—dipping a hot dog on a stick into batter and quickly frying it to a crispy delicacy—is said to have made its commercial debut in Springfield in 1946. Called a Cozy Dog, this edible concoction was the creation of Ed Waldmire Jr., who apparently began tinkering with the concept during World War II, when he was in the Air Force and stationed in Texas.

Waldmire later wrote he got the idea for the Cozy Dog after seeing a hot dog baked in cornbread in Oklahoma. However, he thought

Cozy Dog in Springfield is said to be where the corn dog on a stick was invented.

the dish took too long to prepare. He later mentioned his desire to develop a quicker cooking batter to a friend, Don Strand. A few years later Strand told him he had come up with a mix that could stick to a hot dog while it was deep-fried.

"Using cocktail forks for sticks, the U.S.O. kitchen in which to experiment, we made a very tasty hot dog on a stick that we called a crusty cur," he continued. "They became very popular both at the U.S.O. in town and at the P.X. on the airfield."

After Waldmire was discharged in 1946, he returned to his hometown of Springfield, where he and his wife decided to sell the cornmeal-covered franks on a stick. His wife, however, didn't care for the name crusty cur, so after trying out a handful of names they settled on the friendlier sounding Cozy Dog. That year, he began selling them at the Lake Springfield Beach House and at the Illinois State Fair. Within a short time, he opened the first Cozy Dog House stand on South Grand between Fifth and Sixth Streets (in front of his house) and in 1949 added the first Cozy Dog Drive In on South Sixth Street, which was part of Route 66.

Interestingly, Waldmire, who died in 1993, never claimed he invented the corn dog and, in fact, would only take credit for having come up with a better way to make one. Despite his modesty, food critic Michael Stern notes, "you don't have to be a street food connoisseur to savvy the difference between a cozy dog and an ordinary corn dog. Dipped in batter and deep-fried when ordered, the cozy's batter jacket has a vivid crunch and the dog within is plump with juice."

These days Cozy Dog is run by Sue Waldmire, Ed's ex-daughter-in-law, who continues to use the original batter recipe. In 1996, the Cozy Dog Drive In relocated next door to its original location and is now located at 2935 South Sixth Street in Springfield.

In 1989, the Illinois General Assembly designated Big Bluestem as the official state prairie grass. Presumably John Deere, headquartered in Moline, manufactures the official state lawn mower.

### The Chilli Capital of the World
*Springfield*

Of all the culinary inventions associated with Springfield, few generate as much heat—figuratively and literally—as the simple dish known as chili. The folks in Springfield are proprietary about their chili—in fact, they don't even spell it the same as everyone else: in Springfield it's chilli (with two "l's").

According to local historians, the different spelling can be traced to the community's first chili joint, the Dew Chilli Parlor, which opened in 1909. It's said that the restaurant's owner, Dew Brockman, purposely spelled the spicy dish with two "l's" because it was shown both ways in his dictionary. Others insist that the strange spelling was because he wanted to play off the first four letters in the word, Illinois (maybe he should have called it Chillinois).

Springfield eventually boasted more than a dozen chilli parlors and hosted an annual chili (or chilli) cook-off with local restaurants, taverns, and cooks. Most of those businesses have closed in recent decades, including the original Dew Chilli Parlor, which shut down in 1995. However, in 1997, Marianne McKay, the daughter of Joe Rogers, owner of the original Den Chili Parlor, opened Joe Rogers' Original Recipe Chili Parlor, which continues the tradition of Springfield-style chilli (her father's original joint, which his widow sold in 1985, closed in 1998).

So what's so unique about Springfield's chili? For one thing, it's not to everyone's liking. It's not thick and chunky like some national brand canned chilis but has a thinner consistency. It contains lots of spicy, seasoned ground beef and/or beans swimming in a tomato-based broth that is topped with a thin layer of hot chili oil. The result is something that is hot (Joe Rogers offers five grades of "heat"), tasty, and definitely not low calorie.

"The oil is where the heat resides," notes restaurant critic Michael Stern. "Matters of style aside, Springfield chili, as made at Joe Rogers, is pretty wild stuff, definitely not for the fastidious epicure."

In 1993, the Illinois Legislature unanimously passed a resolution proclaiming Springfield as the Chilli Capital of the Civilized World, formally adopting the Springfield way of spelling the dish.

**Joe Rogers' Chili still serves hot and tangy Springfield-style chili (or chilli, as some call it).**

★ ★ ★ ★ ★ ★ ★ ★ ★ ★ ★ ★ ★ ★ ★ ★ ★ ★ ★ ★ ★ ★ ★ ★ ★ ★ ★ ★ ★ ★ ★

Springfield Chilli can still be found at a handful of local eateries including Joe Rogers' Original Recipe Chili Parlor at 820 South 9th Street, D'Arcy's Pint at 661 West Stanford Avenue, Cook's Spice Rack and Chilli Parlor at 910 North Grand Avenue West, Joe's Chili Bowl at 2401 South MacArthur Boulevard, and Big Mike's Prize Winning Chili at 101 South 4th Street.

## Without a Leg to Stand On

Springfield

Housed in a nineteenth century commissary that looks like a stone castle, the Illinois State Military Museum in Springfield is a repository of traditional military memorabilia including vintage military uniforms, historic photos and maps, a wide variety of weaponry—and a wooden leg. The latter once belonged to the infamous Mexican General Antonio Lopez de Santa Anna, the man who defeated Davy Crockett, Jim Bowie, and a ragtag army of Texans at the Alamo in 1836.

So what's the artificial leg of one of the most vilified Mexican historical figures (at least if you're a Texan) doing in a museum in Illinois? It turns out that at the Battle of Cerro Gordo during the Mexican War, a group of soldiers from the Fourth Regiment Illinois Volunteers managed to sneak behind enemy lines and surprised Santa Anna while he was dining on roasted chicken. Santa Anna escaped but left behind some $18,000 in gold, his fake leg, and his lunch. After turning the gold over to the U.S. Army, the soldiers kept the leg as a souvenir (not sure what happened to the chicken, however). Following the war, they displayed their war trophy at Illinois county fairs, charging folks for a look at the famous general's prosthetic limb. In 1882, the Mexican War Veterans Association donated it to the state of Illinois.

Since the early 1920s, the Illinois National Guard has served as the custodian of the leg, which is tucked into a brown leather boot. Over the years the Mexican government has made several unsuccessful requests for the return of the limb. In 1998, the animated television

Mexican general Antonio Lopez de Santa Anna's
wooden leg is displayed in the Illinois State
Military Museum in Springfield.

★ ★ ★ ★ ★ ★ ★ ★ ★ ★ ★ ★ ★ ★ ★ ★ ★ ★ ★ ★ ★ ★ ★ ★ ★ ★ ★ ★ ★

comedy, *King of the Hill*, aired an episode during which two characters liberated the leg from the museum and returned it to Mexico.

These days, Santa Anna's fake leg is housed in an elaborate exhibit that re-creates the moment of its capture. The leg is displayed in a carriage while two mannequins dressed as period Illinois infantry soldiers look on. Nearby is an open chest filled with gold coins and atop another chest, a replica of the chicken meal abandoned by the general during his escape.

The Illinois State Military Museum is located at 1301 North MacArthur Boulevard, Springfield. The museum is open Tuesday through Saturday, 1 p.m. to 4:30 p.m. For more information, go to www.il.ngb.army.mil/Museum/default.htm.

### The Last Word Accordion to Roy Bertelli

Oak Ridge Cemetery
Springfield

Roy Bertelli really wanted to be buried in the historic Oak Ridge Cemetery, the same place where Abraham Lincoln was laid to rest. An accomplished accordion player, arranger, and composer from Springfield—he wrote more than 5,000 arrangements and had performed with Lawrence Welk—one day he stopped by the cemetery office to check on plots and was surprised to discover that a small, triangular plot located at the entrance to the road leading to Lincoln's Tomb was available. Amazed at his good fortune, the man who billed himself as "Mr. Accordion," immediately bought the lot.

Unfortunately for Bertelli, however, the cemetery had mistakenly sold the land to him, so a few weeks later it sent him a letter informing him of the error. Shortly after receiving that letter, he was sent another telling him that the cemetery intended to reclaim the plot and threatening to sue him.

The cemetery's actions angered the feisty musician, who was a World War II veteran and not one to back down from a fight. He not only decided to fight to keep the plot—successfully, it turned

The grave of Roy Bertelli, "Mr. Accordion," located near Lincoln's Tomb

out—but he built his future burial crypt above ground, making sure it couldn't be missed, and erected a giant polished granite tablet adjacent to the crypt on which he had the image of an accordion and musical notes as well as his name and the words, MR. ACCORDION, engraved. It's estimated he spent more than $30,000 on his final resting place.

For several years afterward, Bertelli would periodically visit his grave, climb atop his crypt with his accordion, and play for cemetery visitors. He died in 2003 at the age of 92. Mr. Accordion's grave is located in Oak Ridge Cemetery on Monument Avenue, just south of Lincoln's Tomb.

★ ★ ★ ★ ★ ★ ★ ★ ★ ★ ★ ★ ★ ★ ★ ★ ★ ★ ★ ★ ★ ★ ★ ★ ★ ★ ★ ★ ★ ★

### Great Tragedy Amid Great Beauty
Starved Rock State Park
Utica

Starved Rock State Park is one of the most scenic spots in Illinois and, unfortunately, also the site of one of the state's most brutal murders. On Monday, March 14, 1960, three upper-middle-class Chicago women, Frances Murphy, forty-seven; Mildred Lindquist, fifty; and Lillian Oetting, fifty; traveled to the park for a three-day getaway. They checked into the rustic Starved Rock Lodge and after lunch decided to hike into the nearby St. Louis Canyon. It was the last time anyone saw the three alive.

That night, Oetting's husband attempted to telephone his wife at the lodge but couldn't reach her. During the next two days, he tried several times to reach her but was told by staff that the three women were simply out of the lodge. Finally, on Wednesday, he called the hotel and insisted the staff check their rooms. They found the women's beds had not been slept in and their bags had not been unpacked. Additionally, a look in the parking lot revealed that Murphy's car, in which they had driven to the park, had not moved since their arrival on Monday.

Oetting contacted the authorities and within a short time state and regional police agencies began an intensive search for the women. Later that day, their bodies were discovered in the canyon lying side-by-side on their backs. Each had been badly beaten about the head and appeared to have been sexually assaulted. Two were tied together with heavy white twine. Investigators found a bloody tree limb that was the murder weapon.

The viciousness of the murders attracted state and national attention. Initially, investigators had no suspects, but in September they traced the twine to the lodge's kitchen, where it was used for wrapping food. One of the lodge's former dishwashers, Chester Otto Wegner, failed a polygraph test and police made him their prime suspect. Eventually, Wegner confessed to the murders. Despite later recanting

**French Canyon at Starved Rock State Park**

his confession on the grounds it was coerced, Wegner was convicted on March 4, 1961 and sentenced to life in prison, where he remains to this day.

Starved Rock derived its unusual name from a Native American legend about an equally tragic occurrence. In the 1760s, a band of Illiniwek warriors, fighting against their enemies, the Potawatomi, was driven to a large eroded butte overlooking the Illinois River. There, the Illiniwek held off the Potawatomi for weeks until dying of starvation.

Despite the unfortunate events associated with Starved Rock, it remains one of Illinois's most popular state parks with an estimated one million visitors per year (it's located about ninety minutes west of Chicago). Visitors can enjoy scenic canyons, many with seasonal waterfalls as well as camping, picnicking, and bird watching. For more information about Starved Rock State Park, go to www.dnr.state.il.us.

★ ★ ★ ★ ★ ★ ★ ★ ★ ★ ★ ★ ★ ★ ★ ★ ★ ★ ★ ★ ★ ★ ★ ★ ★ ★ ★ ★ ★ ★ ★

### Dragon Spoken Here
Vandalia

One of the last things you'd expect to see in the town of Vandalia—which is mostly known for being the site of the third capital of the state of Illinois—is a 30-foot-tall, 40-foot-long gleaming metal, moving, fire-breathing dragon. Known as the Kaskaskia Dragon or the Vandalia Dragon, the imposing creature has been turning heads since he first appeared in 1999.

According to the *Decatur Herald-Review*, the dragon was the brainchild of Walt Barenfanger, owner of an adjacent True Value

**The fire-breathing mechanical dragon of Vandalia**

hardware store and ESC Construction Company. Barenfanger said that in the late 1990s, when things at the construction company were particularly quiet, one of his welders, Paul Schaub, suggested building a dragon from scrap metal. "There wasn't much forethought, there wasn't much afterthought, there wasn't much thought at all," Barenfanger told the newspaper. "He just started welding and out it came."

To make the four-ton, winged metal monster more realistic, its eyes glow bright red and it breathes flames. The latter is produced using a propane tank in his stomach that feeds gas through his mouth, where it is ignited electronically. The results are impressive, particularly at night.

Visitors can make the dragon breathe fire by purchasing a special token for $1 at either the True Value hardware store or LoMac's Liquor Store, across the street. Pop the token into a coin box near the dragon and then stand back as the creature suddenly snorts out several short puffs of fire. It doesn't last very long but it's pretty cool.

Vandalia's dragon is located at 2024 Progress West Drive, adjacent to Old US 40. For more information, go to www.kaskaskiadragon.com/.

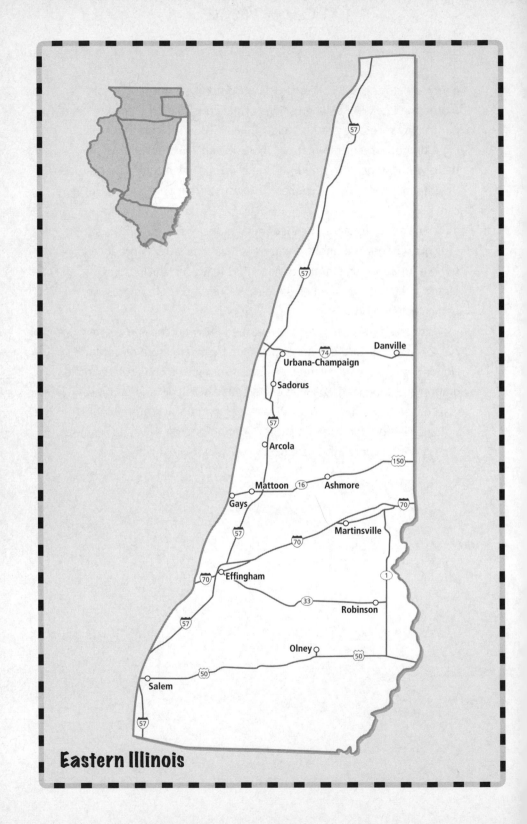

**Eastern Illinois**

# 4

## Eastern Illinois

"ENERGY EFFICIENT VEHICLE.
RUNS ON GRASS AND OATS.
CAUTION: AVOID EXHAUST!"

—Sign behind an Amish buggy

**Eastern Illinois, the** *part of the state that is above I-64 and more or less sandwiched between I-57 and the Indiana border, is home to the University of Illinois at Urbana-Champaign (as well as Eastern Illinois University in Charleston), the state's only two-story outhouse, the log cabin where Abraham Lincoln's parents lived, and the original Jimmy John's subway sandwich shop. Like Central and Western Illinois, it's mostly farming country with miles and miles of corn and soy. In fact, the region's rich farmland is what attracted the area's most unique residents, the Amish, in the mid-nineteenth century.*

*About 4,500 Amish live in the Arthur-Arcola area, making it the heart of Illinois Amish Country. The Amish religion dates to the sixteenth century, with the birth of the Anabaptist movement in Europe (Anabaptists believed baptism should be reserved for adults). The Amish are a branch of the Swiss Anabaptists that follow the teachings of Jakob Ammann, who preached a message of discipline, pacifism, simple living, and a rejection of material things.*

*The Amish in Eastern Illinois, most of whom are Old Order Amish, are easy to spot, dressed in plain nineteenth century clothing; women wear*

long dresses, dark stockings, and black bonnets while married men have long beards (unmarried men shave) and wear dark vests and pants, suspenders, homemade white shirts, and wide-brimmed hats. They generally shun modern conveniences, such as cars and tractors, choosing to drive horse-drawn black buggies and work their fields with six- to eight-horse hitches. In their homes and in conversations between each other, the Amish often speak a dialect known as Pennsylvania Dutch, which is a hodgepodge of German and English words.

Of course, that's not to say the Amish avoid contact with outsiders—although they don't pose for photographs for religious reasons and ask visitors to be respectful and not try to take pictures of their faces. Many open their homes and businesses to outsiders. In the Arthur-Arcola Amish Country, it's possible to share a meal in an Amish home, tour an Amish dairy farm, or buy fresh fruits and vegetables from an Amish produce stand. The area is home to more than 200 Amish businesses ranging from quilt shops to bakeries to woodworking shops. There's even a company, ACM Tours, which offers custom tours of the Amish Country.

So don't be surprised if you're in Eastern Illinois and you find you have to share the road with a horse-drawn Amish carriage or startled when you stop into some furniture store in Arthur and hear the employees speaking an unfamiliar tongue. In other words, it's nothing to get "ferhoodled" (confused) about.

✦ ✦ ✦ ✦ ✦ ✦ ✦ ✦ ✦ ✦ ✦ ✦ ✦ ✦ ✦ ✦ ✦ ✦ ✦ ✦ ✦ ✦ ✦ ✦ ✦ ✦ ✦ ✦ ✦ ✦ ✦ ✦ ✦ ✦

## Having Fun the Amish Way

Rockome Gardens and the Illinois Amish Interpretive Center
Arcola

So what do people who eschew modern conveniences and dress like they're off the set of *Little House on the Prairie* do for a good time? They head to Rockome Gardens, which is often described as the world's only Amish theme park.

The gardens were started in the late 1930s by a non-Amish couple, Arthur and Elizabeth Martin, who wanted to develop the largest flower garden in the county. With that in mind, they purchased a 208-acre farm near Arcola and devoted seven acres of the farm for gardens, rock decorations, and a small cottage.

Since it was during the Great Depression, Arthur Martin, who owned a local factory, would sometimes have his employees work on the gardens when things were slow at the factory. In addition to planting sunken gardens, the workers built an elaborate series of rock walls and sculptures. The rockwork was constructed using metal frames that were covered by thick concrete in which the rocks were embedded. Over the years, the garden grew more beautiful and more rock sculptures were added.

The fabulous garden with its rock walls, archways, and formations began to attract attention and the Martins were more than happy to share it with any visitors. People started referring to the place as Martin's Rock Home, which Arthur Martin shortened to "Rockome Gardens."

In 1952, the Martins deeded the farm, including the gardens, to the Mennonite Board of Missions and Charities of Elkhart, Indiana. The board converted the property to a retirement village. In 1958, the Mennonites sold it to Elvan Yoder, a Mennonite raised in the Amish faith who originally intended to farm the property. Yoder, however, soon saw the potential of the place as an attraction.

In subsequent years, Yoder began developing a kind of Amish theme park around the rock gardens. Visitors could enjoy buggy rides,

An Amish worker whisks by one of the unique rock formations found at Rockome Gardens near Arcola.

tour an Amish home, or buy homemade gifts. By the late 1960s, Rockome included a tree house, lookout tower, antiques museum, haunted barn attraction (now called the Enchanted Cave), rock shop, restaurant, and a piano-playing chicken (since replaced by one that plays Tic Tac Toe).

In 2006, the Yoders sold the theme park to local businessmen Bob McElwee and Brent Bolen, who spiffed up the attractions and renovated the restaurant, which now serves Amish-influenced family-style meals. In 2010, the Rockome Garden Food Store opened, which sells Amish cheeses, baked goods, handmade soaps, homemade candy, and a variety of bulk foods.

Wandering the gardens, it's not uncommon to see Amish employees cleaning up restrooms or planting and weeding in one of the half dozen gardens—which have some 36,000 annual and perennial flowers—or behind the counter in the food store. It's a quieter, gentler nineteenth century version of a theme park.

However, I think that damned Tic Tac Toe–playing chicken cheats . . .

Rockome Gardens, which is also home of the Illinois Amish Interpretive Center (it contains exhibits explaining the Amish religion and culture in Illinois), is located 5 miles west of Arcola on 125 North County Road 425 E. For more information, go to www.rockome.com.

## Trivia

In 2008, the Goldrush Apple, a cross of Golden Delicious and an experimental disease-resistant apple known as Co-op 17 that was developed by the University of Illinois, was named Illinois's official state fruit.

★ ★ ★ ★ ★ ★ ★ ★ ★ ★ ★ ★ ★ ★ ★ ★ ★ ★ ★ ★ ★ ★ ★ ★ ★ ★ ★ ★ ★ ★ ★ ★ ★ ★ ★

### The World's One & Only Official Hippie Memorial
Arcola

Arcola artist and sign maker Bob Moomaw, who also served as a railroad clerk and tax assessor, had a quirky sense of humor. In the early 1990s, Moomaw created a memorial to the free-spirited hippies of the 1960s using iron rods and scrap metal. The result was an unusual 62-foot-long metal structure that contains objects and other things that represent various important points in his life, which he called the "webs of his life."

Interestingly, Moomaw, who died in 1998 at the age of sixty-three, didn't consider himself a hippie. At his funeral, his wife Sharron said he had a beard and a ponytail while attending Eastern Illinois University but was no hippie. "He was there at the same time and place as the hippies were, but he was raising his children then to use the freedom of their minds to search for knowledge in education as he did. As he said, to his shame, he was no hippie!"

"Hippies, he said, gave us room to breathe; and that is what aspect of their lives he was honoring."

Moomaw began building his sculpture in 1991. It was originally tucked behind a fence at his sign shop. When he died, Moomaw bequeathed his memorial to a friend, Gus Kelsey, an Arcola native who lives in Michigan, who worked with the city to permanently install the monument on city-leased land adjacent to the railroad tracks that run through the center of the town. Kelsey spent about $8,000 refurbishing the piece of folk art.

The monument is essentially a timeline of Moomaw's life. To the left of the center, the piece is short, narrow, and more sparsely decorated because, according to Moomaw's widow, it represents the first twenty-six years of his life, including the Great Depression, World War II, the McCarthy era, and the repressed 1950s. To the right of center, the sculpture's spare look reflects the President Ronald Reagan years, when America slipped back into a period of small-mindedness.

**The World's Only Official Hippie Memorial in Arcola**

"The memorial rises to 6 feet (in the center) representing the 1960s to the 1980s when the hippies hit and raised the ceiling off everything," Sharron Moomaw said. "Everyone got to stand up against oppression and repression . . . The metal shapes are brightly colored showing love and a peace symbol and—individuality."

Right on.

The One & Only Hippie Memorial is located at 135 North Oak Street in downtown Arcola.

★ ★ ★ ★ ★ ★ ★ ★ ★ ★ ★ ★ ★ ★ ★ ★ ★ ★ ★ ★ ★ ★ ★ ★ ★ ★ ★ ★ ★ ★ ★ ★ ★ ★ ★ ★

## Lawn Rangers of Arcola

In 1980, a group of thirteen Arcola men wanted to participate in some way in their town's annual Broom Corn Festival parade. That year, actor Clayton Moore, who played the Lone Ranger on TV and in films, was the parade's grand marshal. The group decided that the only skill they really possessed was mowing lawns. Thus was born the World Famous Arcola Lawn Rangers (a play on words on Clayton Moore's most famous role), a precision lawn mower drill team that marches in formation and performs tongue-in-cheek maneuvers with a corn broom and a lawn mower. Since then, the rangers have appeared in every subsequent Broom Corn Festival—in the late nineteenth century Arcola was the largest corn broom producer in the world—and in parades around the country, including the NFL Hall of Fame Game in Canton, Ohio, and President Barack Obama's 2009 Inaugural Parade in Washington, D.C. In recent years, the team has included more than one hundred rangers, all of whom must complete a rigorous training program—about ten minutes worth of instruction.

### This Lincoln Rises Above the Rest
Ashmore

To figure out why the tiny hamlet of Ashmore is the site of the world's tallest statue of Abraham Lincoln, you have to play the game of six degrees of Abe Lincoln. It goes something like this: The tallest president, at 6 feet, 4 inches, was Abraham Lincoln. Lincoln was from Illinois. Illinois—specifically a small town called Lerna—was also home of Lincoln's father and stepmother. The largest community near Lerna

Tallest statue in the world of President Abraham Lincoln

★ ★ ★ ★ ★ ★ ★ ★ ★ ★ ★ ★ ★ ★ ★ ★ ★ ★ ★ ★ ★ ★ ★ ★ ★ ★ ★ ★ ★ ★ ★ ★

is Charleston. Charleston was the site of one of the Lincoln-Douglas debates and is only 3 miles from Ashmore. Ashmore is home of the world's tallest statue of Abe Lincoln.

While that really doesn't answer the question of why, it is true that there is a 62-foot representation of the sixteenth president in a grotto adjacent to a resort near Ashmore. The six-story statue was crafted in 1968 by the Gordon Display Company to commemorate the 110th anniversary of a debate in Charleston between Lincoln and Stephen A. Douglas for a U.S. Senate seat in 1858. The statue depicts a standing Lincoln, one hand holding a document and the other outstretched with a pointed finger. According to news accounts, the monster Abe originally stood off East Harrison Avenue, just outside of Charleston. But apparently the statue arrived too late for the anniversary and a proposed park that was to be developed around it never happened. The enormous Abe stood abandoned in a field for several years and became a popular shooting target for vandals.

In 1978, Honest Abe was moved 3 miles east and set up in a clearing in some woods adjacent to a private campground. Unfortunately, in the mid-1990s the campground went bust and the jinxed giant once again fell into disrepair—at one point it was described on a web page as the world's ugliest Lincoln. Even his upraised digit was knocked off.

In 2002, however, the Lincoln Springs Resort Company purchased the defunct campground and developed it into a popular barbecue restaurant, miniature golf course, and game center. The company also repaired and repainted the Lincoln statue—reattaching his

*Trivia*

**Drummer silty clay loam is the official state soil of Illinois. Apparently all the cool dirts were taken.**

## Ebertfest Gets Two Thumbs Up, Champaign

Film festivals are a dime a dozen. So when *Chicago Sun-Times* film critic Roger Ebert launched his own in 1999, he wanted something different from the rest. So he decided to have one that focused on movies that never got the attention he felt they deserved. Thus was born the Overlooked Film Festival, held each April in Ebert's hometown of Urbana-Champaign. The event, the name of which was shortened to simply "Ebertfest" in 2008, is a celebration of great films that few people paid much attention to when they were released.

The event is organized by the College of Media at the University of Illinois, Ebert's alma mater, but the critic is the only one involved in deciding what films will be shown. During the festival, twelve to fourteen films, including a silent movie, are shown between Wednesday and Sunday in the historic Virginia Theatre (203 West Park) in Champaign. Ebert has attended the festival nearly every year despite a battle with cancer in 2006 that left him no longer able to talk. The official website, which lists dates, times, and admission information, is www.ebertfest.com.

finger—and created a new, free attraction called "Abe's Garden." Visitors can park and walk around the massive president and view several peacocks in enclosures as well as a dozen rough-hewn Lincoln sculptures created by Charleston chainsaw artist Bill Monken. The statues depict the president at various ages and stages of his life.

The Godzilla-size Lincoln statue is located at 9699 North County Road 2000 East in Ashmore. For more information, go to www.lincoln springresort.com.

# The Mother of All Soaps Hailed from U of I

Irna Phillips, who graduated from the University of Illinois in 1923, is credited with inventing the soap opera genre, which first became popular on radio and, later, on television. Phillips earned a degree in drama at the University of Illinois at Urbana-Champaign and later a master's degree in journalism at the University of Wisconsin–Madison. After working as a schoolteacher in Ohio for several years, she relocated to Chicago where she began working for radio station WGN. There she convinced her superiors to air a daytime serial specifically targeted at women. The show, *Painted Dreams*, is considered the first daytime soap opera (so-called because most of the sponsors sold products aimed at housewives, such as soap). Phillips went on to create a number of hit daytime radio and television shows including *The Guiding Light, The Road of Life, As The World Turns,* and *The Edge of Night*. She died in 1973 and was the first inductee into the Soap Opera Hall of Fame in 1994. Now we know whom to blame for Anthony Geary.

## Even God Can't Miss It
Effingham

The folks behind the world's largest cross, a 198-foot tall and 113-foot wide white "T" made out of 180 tons of steel anchored in 33 tons of steel footings and a sea of concrete, weren't trying to be subtle. Called the "Cross at the Crossroads," the big icon, dedicated in 2001, cost more than $1 million according to some estimates and took about five years to complete. The cross consists of four separate

The world's largest freestanding cross is
located in Effingham.

pieces, each covered with a steel skin. It was designed to withstand winds of more than 145 miles per hour.

The world's biggest cross was the brainchild of the late John H. Schultz, a retired seed company owner from Effingham, who saw a nineteen-story white cross alongside I-40 near Groom, Texas. He was inspired to wonder why an even larger one couldn't be built in his hometown. Working with local civic and religious groups, Schultz helped to raise the funds for the cross, which is a few feet taller than the one in Texas, making it the world's largest. An interesting side note: Apparently, the cross isn't any taller because if it exceeded 200 feet, it would come under Federal Aviation Administration rules.

The location of the cross was purposely selected because it's near the intersection of Interstates 57 and 70, so an estimated 50,000 motorists see it every day. In addition to hosting the big cross, the site has a small visitor center, which shows a video on the construction of the cross. Also, on the grounds around the cross are monuments devoted to each of the Ten Commandments (each accompanied by music and audio inspirational messages). The visitor center and the cross are administered by the nonprofit Cross Foundation, which is dedicated to building faith and family on an ecumenical basis.

The world's biggest cross is located on West Knagge Road in Effingham. From I-57, take exit 159 and drive east toward Effingham. Turn right on Raney Street and continue south for 1 mile before taking a right on Pike Avenue. Don't worry—you won't be able to miss it.

### Trivia

**Illinois is forty-ninth among states in percentage of land still containing its original vegetation.**

# Danville's Annual Les Nessman Turkey Drop

In a classic episode of the '80s TV sitcom, *WKRP in Cincinnati*, one of the characters, news director Les Nessman, offers dramatic on-the-scene reporting of a radio promotion gone awry. His station had decided to release live turkeys from an airplane without realizing the birds can't fly. His play-by-play account of the turkeys landing like "sacks of concrete" into a parking lot was one of the show's most memorable moments. In 1996, hot air balloon enthusiasts in Danville decided to honor the episode by creating the annual Les Nessman Memorial Turkey Drop, held on the morning of Thanksgiving Day. The event attracts about a dozen balloonists each year, who compete to drop a turkey—actually rubber chickens dressed up in often bizarre ways—on a target. For more information, contact dean@heritagedevelop.com or phone (217) 446-2365.

## Double-Decker Crapper
### Gays

Nearly everyone who sees the two-story outhouse in Gays for the first time asks the same question—who in the world would ever want to use the bottom stall?

But the unusual commode isn't a joke. It turns out that in 1869, a man named Samuel Gammill built a two-story building on the site. The first floor contained his general store but the top story housed several apartments. To provide bathroom facilities for his businesses, Gammill erected a two-story outhouse, which was attached to the back of his building. The top stall was for apartment dwellers while

The tiny town of Gays boasts something few can—a two-story outhouse.

the bottom one was reserved for his employees and customers. Each level had two holes—one for men and one for women, which was customary at the time.

Flash-forward more than a century and Gammill's building was in bad shape. In 1984, the structure was taken down for safety reasons but the exterior outhouses, still in good condition, remained. Gene Goodwin, who was mayor of Gays at the time, had an idea: Why not restore the old outhouse as an attraction and turn the surrounding land into a small park? With the help of his son, Goodwin replaced worn out boards, repainted, and reroofed the structure.

In recent years, the Gays outhouse has, indeed, become a roadside attraction. On any given day, cars or trucks can be seen parked adjacent to the shady park, people snapping photos of the unique double-dump water closet.

As for the mystery of how a two-story outhouse works, according to a 1998 Associated Press story, the holes on the top level were set farther back than the ones on the lower level, with a false wall separating the bottom folks from what came down from above. Still, you have to wonder how well that worked out for them.

The two-story outhouse is located at 1022 Pine Street in Gays, a tiny hamlet of about 250 people that is 7 miles west of Mattoon via IL 16.

### Home of the Legendary Moonshine Burger
Martinsville

When you talk to folks out in Eastern Illinois and ask them what's so special about their area, invariably someone will bring up the Moonshine Burger. Served only at the Moonshine Store, a tiny general store located near the hamlet of Martinsville (30 miles southeast of Charleston), the Moonshine Burger isn't made with imported Kobe beef or anything fancy. It's a basic hamburger (also available with cheese) with no seasonings and do-it-yourself condiments. Or, as Moonshine Store co-owner and chief cook Helen Tuttle told the *Daily Eastern*

★ ★ ★ ★ ★ ★ ★ ★ ★ ★ ★ ★ ★ ★ ★ ★ ★ ★ ★ ★ ★ ★ ★ ★ ★ ★ ★ ★

*News*: "There is no recipe for this. I get the best meat and make it with love, no different than what you would at home."

Helen and Roy Lee Tuttle have owned the Moonshine Store since 1982. William St. Martz established the business in 1889 as a combination general store/local gathering spot/restaurant. It's said the place derived its name from the reflection of the moon in a water puddle in front of the store. Some years ago, a previous owner, Enid Misner, created a lunch menu, which included hamburgers and cold cut sandwiches. The Tuttles expanded the offerings to include grilled chicken, barbecue pork, Polish sausages, hot dogs, and other items, but it's the Moonshine Burger that draws crowds. The Tuttles regularly update their website to list their personal record for how many hamburgers they have served in a single day—it's currently 1,908 Moonburgers sold on April 10, 2010.

Of course, the most amazing thing about the success of the Moonshine Burgers—besides the fact they taste delicious—is Helen Tuttle only operates her two gas grills between 6 a.m. and 12:30 p.m. While the restaurant stays open for another half hour, she turns off the grill promptly at 12:30 p.m. in order to clean up. After that, customers can order cold-cut sandwiches but nothing from the grill.

Perhaps it's that exclusivity, along with the place's old-time country store atmosphere, that contributes to the burger's popularity. The store maintains a guest book signed by visitors from all fifty states and a dozen other countries. In keeping with the overall ambience, after a customer finishes a meal and heads to the cash register to pay, he or she pays on the honor system. There's no written guest check—the person just says what was ordered and pays the amount. Helen Tuttle says that sometimes folks forget to pay and have mailed personal checks to her later.

The Moonshine Store is located at 6017 E. 300th Road near Martinsville. The store's website is www.themoonshinestore.com.

### Swooning in Mattoon

Mattoon

While Illinois certainly has plenty of curiosities—need I mention Rod Blagojevich again?—perhaps the state's most curious story involves what became known as the Mad Gasser of Mattoon. The story began on August 31, 1944, when Urban Raef and his wife, who resided in a house at 1817 Grant Avenue in a middle class neighborhood in Mattoon, smelled a strange odor in the early morning.

Raef thought there might be something wrong with the gas-powered kitchen stove and because he was feeling sick asked his wife to check the pilot light. However, when she tried to get out of bed

Former Kearney home at 1408 Marshall, site of one of the Mad Gasser of Mattoon's first attacks

★ ★ ★ ★ ★ ★ ★ ★ ★ ★ ★ ★ ★ ★ ★ ★ ★ ★ ★ ★ ★ ★ ★ ★ ★ ★ ★ ★

she found she couldn't move. While the paralysis soon faded, the smell caused them to both vomit.

The following evening Mrs. Aline Kearney and her three-year-old daughter were getting ready for bed. As she closed the windows on her home at 1408 Marshall Avenue, she smelled a strong, sweet odor and began to feel her lips burn and her throat becoming very dry. She also noticed she was losing feeling in her legs.

It was only after the alleged attack on the Kearney family appeared in the local newspaper that other affected parties came forward. Scott Maruna, author of a 2003 book about the events titled, *The Mad Gasser of Mattoon*, noted, "within forty-eight hours, the gasser had attacked four residences, all within eight blocks of each other."

Despite increased police patrols and the presence of state and federal law enforcement, there were seven more reports of gas-related incidents on September 6 followed by additional reports during the next four nights.

The final incident occurred on September 11, when a widow, Bertha Bence, reported that her bedroom suddenly filled with a strong but sweet smell that made her nearly faint. Her sons ran outside and saw a dark-clad figure running away and found footprints in the flowerbed outside her window.

With that, the Mattoon Gasser disappeared and was never seen—or smelled—again.

Within days, law enforcement authorities concluded there had been no attacks and a year later, the prestigious *Journal of Abnormal and Social Psychology* published a study that cited the Mattoon case as a nearly perfect example of the phenomena called "mass hysteria."

Many Mattoon residents, however, believed something—or someone—else had been responsible. A half century after the attacks, Maruna, a former Mattoon resident, interviewed dozens of Mattoon residents familiar with the case and uncovered evidence implicating a man named Farley Llewellyn.

Maruna said the story had been hushed up for decades because Llewellyn's father was a well-respected local figure. He said that the younger Llewellyn had a chemistry degree and maintained a well-equipped laboratory in a trailer in his family's backyard. He was also said to have had a tenuous grip on his sanity.

On September 11, shortly after the last attack, Llewellyn's family quietly committed him to a state mental institution, where he remained for the rest of his life.

So what do you think—Mad Gasser or mass hysteria?

## The White Squirrels of Olney

Olney

It's difficult not to smile the first time you spot one of Olney's albino gray squirrels. The little creatures are unexpectedly cute—for a member of the rodent family with snow white fur and pink eyes—and seem downright soft and cuddly from afar.

A colony of more than one hundred white squirrels lives in the community, many in the shaded Olney City Park in the middle of the town. As with most of Illinois oddities, there is more than one explanation for how they ended up in Olney. Version one is that in about 1902, local farmer William Yates Stroup found a pair of pure white baby squirrels in a nest after shooting their mother. He took them home and his two sons, George and Era, raised them by hand. Later, he brought them into town and presented them to a local saloon, which put them on display. After a state law was passed prohibiting keeping wild animals in confinement, the squirrels were taken to the woods and released.

Version two involves a different farmer, George W. Ridgely, who found a cream-colored and a white squirrel playing on his farm near Sumner (12 miles east of Olney). After several attempts, Ridgely and a neighbor trapped the two squirrels, which they decided to breed. In 1902, they sold a white male and a white female to an Olney saloon (same one as in the other story). The two animals were placed on display in the bar until passage of the state law prohibiting wild animals in captivity. After that, they were released into the woods.

243

One of Olney's white squirrels hides in a tree.

Olney's white squirrel population probably reached its peak in the 1940s, when an estimated 800 of the creatures lived in the park. Since the mid-1970s, a formal squirrel count is conducted each fall. In recent decades, the albino population has gradually decreased. Those studying the animals contributed the decline to an increasing population of cats, a natural enemy. Since 1997, Olney has prohibited both dogs and cats from running at large in the community in an effort to protect the squirrels.

## Trivia

**The white-tailed deer was designated the official state animal of Illinois in 1982.**

Local ordinances grant the squirrels the legal right-of-way on every street and sidewalk and there are big fines for anyone trying to capture one. If you absolutely feel compelled to take a white squirrel home and don't want to go to jail, the Chamber of Commerce (201 East Chestnut Street) sells souvenir stuffed animal toy versions.

While the squirrels can be found in several places, the best place to spot one is the city park, located at 584 North Highway 130 in Olney. Happy hunting (just kidding).

### Heath Bar City USA

Robinson

Don't stop in the Eastern Illinois town of Robinson if you're on a diet. Or diabetic. Or don't like toffee or chocolate. That's because Robinson, a town of about 6,800 people, is where all the world's Heath Bars are made.

In fact, Robinson, located near the Illinois-Indiana border, was the birthplace of the popular toffee and milk chocolate confection, which was invented there in 1928 by L. S. Heath and his two sons, Bayard and Everett. The elder Heath, a schoolteacher, had mortgaged his house in 1914 to buy a local candy shop because he wanted to give his sons a trade.

During the first decade, the candy store primarily served as a local soda fountain and dairy outlet. However, a visiting salesman from Champaign stopped in the shop one day and shared the recipe for a candy he called "trail toffee." The Heaths, who had acquired candy-making equipment when they bought the shop, tinkered with the concoction for several months, refining it into a tasty toffee made with sugar, butter, and almonds that was covered with milk chocolate—and the Heath English Toffee Bar was born (later shortened to Heath Bar).

The bars were handmade until 1942, when the Heaths decided to streamline the process and moved into a larger, more modern candy-making factory in the community. In the 1950s, the family began making Heath Toffee Ice Cream bars and in later years began making crushed Heath Bar mix-ins for Dairy Queen and other ice cream vendors (Dairy Queen uses them in their popular "Blizzard").

The Heath family sold out to a Finnish candy company, Leaf, in 1989. A few years later, Heath was acquired by candy giant Hershey. But despite ownership changes, the Heath Bar manufacturing facility has remained in Robinson, where about 10 percent of the town's population work at the plant.

Not surprisingly, the Heath Bar is a big deal in Robinson, which is also home of the Heath Bar Museum and Confectionary. Opened in 2007, the museum is housed inside the original Heath Brothers Confectionary building, where the candy was first made. The museum is filled with Heath Bar memorabilia, such as the old copper kettles in which the toffee was once mixed.

Additionally, the museum has an old-time soda fountain serving ice cream, sundaes, and other treats. And perhaps the coolest thing is that the museum sells fresh-from-the-factory Heath Bar products by the pound. There goes the diet.

The Heath Bar Museum is located at 125 Court Street in Robinson. For more information, call (618) 544-5309.

# The World's Largest Bagel Nosh is in . . . Mattoon?

The Eastern Illinois town of Mattoon, population about 18,000, seems an unlikely place to be the center of American bagel-dom. But there, in the heart of the Midwest and far from more bagel-centric cities such as New York, is not only the world's largest bagel factory, owned by the national brand, Lender's Bagels, but also the world's biggest free bagel breakfast, held—naturally—during the annual weeklong Bagelfest in mid-July. Some 70,000 bagels with cream cheese and jelly are given away on a Saturday morning during the festival, courtesy of Lender's.

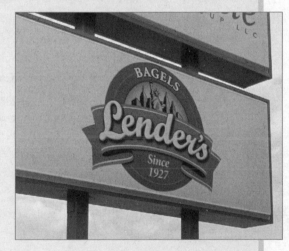

Sign in front of the Lender's Bagel factory in Charleston, largest bagel bakery in the world

Mattoon became the bagel capital as a result of the Lender's Company, which started in New York in 1928, opening a bagel manufacturing plant in the town in 1962. Over the years, the plant grew and now produces more than a billion bagels per year. In 1986, the company decided to create the annual Bagelfest, which attracts an estimated 40,000 people. At the event in 1998, Lenders baked the world's largest blueberry bagel, a 714-pounder (the record has since been eclipsed) that was 59 inches in diameter with a 15-inch diameter center hole. Does that come with a schmear or not?

For updates on the annual Mattoon Bagelfest, go to www.mattoon bagelfest.com.

# Birthplace of the Solar (Power) System?

One of the state's more obscure claims to fame is that Olney was the birthplace of solar power. The town even has a brass plaque that states that John Boyle Jr. and H. E. Willsie built an experimental solar-power collector in the town in 1902. According to a 1994 article in the *St. Louis Post-Dispatch*, the two built a "prototype hot-box collector" that utilized sunlight to heat water in the box enough to vaporize sulfur dioxide, which, in turn, powered a low-temperature engine. In the article, Timothy Jones of Collinsville, who had researched the two men's experiments, said it was likely that Boyle and Willsie, who weren't from Olney, selected the town because it was remote and they could keep their work secret—and they succeeded far too well.

### The Landlubbers Sea Museum
Sadorus

The big sign over the old brick building declares: NATIONAL MUSEUM OF SHIP MODELS AND SEA HISTORY. In the large plate glass windows in the front of the building are intricate models of sailing ships and schooners and brigades. In dry dock at the rear of the building is a large yacht under a tarp. The only thing missing is water.

The National Museum of Ship Models and Sea History is a repository of maritime exhibits and models housed in a 132-year-old building in the tiny farming town of Sadorus, population about 425. Wandering through the two-story, 9,000-square-foot museum offers a chance to view more than 250 carefully crafted, almost delicate model ships including the 11-foot-long Roman barge used in the 1963 blockbuster, *Cleopatra*, a 27-foot-long scale model of the *Queen Mary* constructed using more than a million toothpicks, and a submarine model that was used in the 1990 movie, *Hunt for Red October*.

How a nautical museum ended up in a landlocked agricultural community in Eastern Illinois is quite a story. The captain of this collection is Charles Lozar, an architect with a doctorate in urban planning. Lozar once taught at the nearby University of Illinois at Urbana-Champaign so he was familiar with the area. For more than fifty years, Lozar had traveled around the world collecting ship models. In the 1990s, while living in California he decided to open a maritime museum devoted to displaying his collection. However, after discovering that the state already had more than three dozen museums of that type, he began casting about for a different site.

According to Lozar, when he learned that a historic building with tall ceilings could be obtained inexpensively in Sadorus, he knew he had

**Front of the National Museum of Ship Models and Sea History in landlocked Sadorus**

found a home for his proposed museum. In 1999, he bought the building, which was originally constructed in about 1878, and spent the next three years renovating the structure. The museum opened in 2001.

The National Museum of Ship Models and Sea History is located 12 miles south of Champaign. From May 1 through November 30, the museum is open Saturday from 11 a.m. to 4:30 p.m. and by appointment. During the rest of the year, it is open by appointment only. To arrange a visit call (217) 398-1998. For more information, go to www.lincolnshireprop.com.

## The Man Who Invented Miracle Whip
Salem

In an age when people like Heidi Montag and Paris Hilton can be celebrities for no apparent reason, it doesn't seem fair that the man who gave the world Miracle Whip is largely forgotten. Of course, part of that could be because Kraft Foods, the company that produces the Whip, doesn't acknowledge his role in the creation of the sweet fake mayonnaise substitute. According to Kraft historians, the company's researchers created the popular sandwich spread in the early 1930s as a cheap substitute for mayonnaise. Kraft formally unveiled the creamy white spread at the Chicago World's Fair in 1933. During the event, visitors could watch vats of the thick sauce being made in a glass-enclosed kitchen. The name, "Miracle Whip," is said to have been derived from the special whirling, "emulsifying" machine that a Kraft engineer named Charles Chapman developed to blend the twenty different spices and ingredients that go into the stuff.

Or at least that's what Kraft says.

Another version of the story, which is told in the Eastern Illinois town of Salem, is that Miracle Whip was invented by a local restaurant owner, Max Crossett, who owned a cafe in the city's downtown where he served a popular salad dressing and sandwich spread that he created, called "Max Crossett's X-tra Fine Salad Dressing."

★ ★ ★ ★ ★ ★ ★ ★ ★ ★ ★ ★ ★ ★ ★ ★ ★ ★ ★ ★ ★ ★ ★ ★ ★ ★ ★ ★ ★

**The former location of Max Crossett's Café, where Miracle Whip quite possibly was invented.**

In this version of the story, Crossett sold his special recipe for $300 to Kraft in 1931, which in turn re-branded it as "Miracle Whip." Kraft admits that it did buy a number of salad dressing recipes at that time but disputes the claim that Crossett invented Miracle Whip.

While Crossett is no longer around to resolve the matter, the building that housed his original cafe remains standing at 100 North Washington Street (it's now the offices of the *Marion County Observer* newspaper). There's no plaque on the brick building noting its role in the invention of Miracle Whip. In fact, there are no signs anywhere in Salem that make note of the fact. There are, however, several signs pointing out that Salem is the birthplace of a three-time losing presidential candidate, William Jennings Bryan (his birth home at 408 South Broadway is now a museum), and even a statue of Bryan in a local park named after him.

Max just doesn't get any respect.

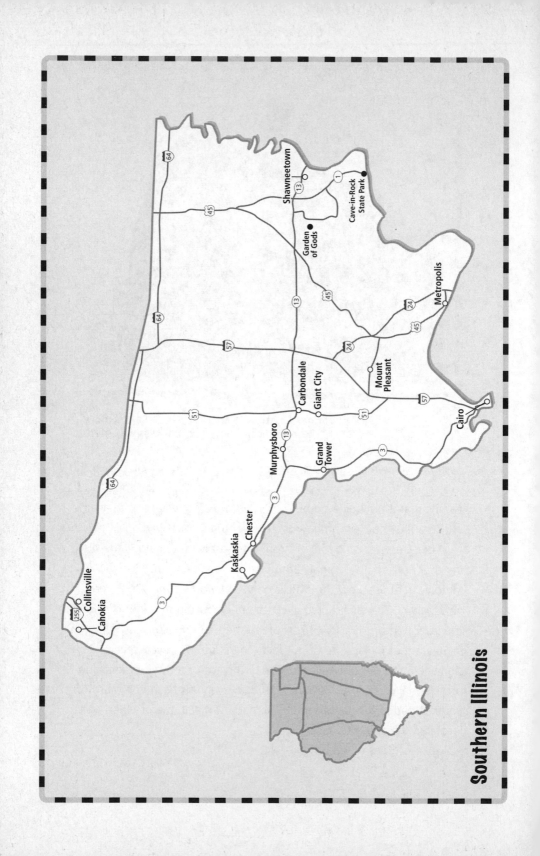

Southern Illinois

# 6

## Southern Illinois

"Off to the south of the big-time Illinois and considerably older is another Illinois not well known even to Illinoisans."

—*The Other Illinois*, Baker Brownell, 1958

**Southern Illinois isn't** *quite like the rest of the state. That's partly because many of the region's early settlers were first and second generation Southerners. As a result, linguists note that in pockets of the region, people speak with a kind of Southern accent and use different words for some things. For example, a can of Coke in most of the state is called "pop." In Southern Illinois, it's "soda." Likewise, the word creek is pronounced with a long "e" sound in most of the state but in the south it's referred to as a "crick."*

*Southern Illinois is often called "Little Egypt" and several cities have Egyptian names, such as Cairo (but pronounced "Kare-row" in Southern Illinois), Karnak, and Thebes. The origin of the term is clouded in the mists of the past, but supposedly sometime in the nineteenth century the northern part of the state experienced a severe drought while rain fell on the southern part and produced plenty of crops. Allegedly, people from the north came down to the south seeking corn and wheat, and these trips were referred to as "going down to Egypt."*

*Geographically, Southern Illinois is a natural playground with the state's largest national forest—the 280,000-acre Shawnee National Forest—as well as the state's largest manmade lake—26,000-acre Carlyle*

★ ★ ★ ★ ★ ★ ★ ★ ★ ★ ★ ★ ★ ★ ★ ★ ★ ★ ★ ★ ★ ★ ★ ★ ★ ★ ★ ★ ★ ★ ★ ★

*Lake—and what has been described as the state's only "true" southern swamps, at the Cache River State Natural Area.*

*And while many folks will rave about Chicago's Italian beef and deep-dish pizzas, Southern Illinois is home to some of the best barbecue found outside of Austin, Memphis, or Kansas City. In places such as the 17th Street Bar and Grill in Murphysboro (featured on the Food Network), Triple E Bar-B-Q in Marion, and Johnson's Southern Style Bar-B-Q in Harrisburg, smoked meats, dry rubs, and savory sauces have been made into high art.*

*Now if you don't mind, I'm gonna grab me a soda and go sit by the crick.*

★ ★ ★ ★ ★ ★ ★ ★ ★ ★ ★ ★ ★ ★ ★ ★ ★ ★ ★ ★ ★ ★ ★ ★ ★ ★ ★ ★

## Almost as Old as Original Sin

Holy Family Log Church
Cahokia

Here's how old the Holy Family Log Church in Cahokia is—when it was rebuilt in 1799, the United States of America had only existed for twenty-three years, Abraham Lincoln wouldn't be born for another ten years, and Rod Blagojevich wouldn't be impeached for another 210 years. The land on which the wooden building sits is the site of two earlier Catholic churches: a log church built in about 1699 (destroyed by fire in the 1730s) and a second log church erected shortly after, which burned in 1783.

The current (third) church is considered typical of the French Creole architectural style of its time. It utilizes a *poteaux-sur-solle* (post-on-sill) construction, meaning it was built with vertical walnut logs placed upright on a horizontal base. The entire structure, which seats one hundred, is held together with wooden pegs rather than nails. Over the years, the church's original appearance was changed when white clapboarding was slapped on the exterior. In 1949, in honor of the parish's 250th anniversary, the building was returned to its original rough-hewn appearance.

The church is one of a handful of reminders of Cahokia's founding in 1699 by French priests of the Seminary of Foreign Missions at Quebec, who arrived in the area to convert the local Indians. By the 1740s, Cahokia, named after a local tribe that was a sub-tribe of the Illinois tribe, had grown to become an important trading center between the French, who controlled most of the area that became the state of Illinois, and local tribes. Following the French and Indian War in 1763, France ceded its holdings in present-day Illinois to England, including Cahokia, and many of the French settlers moved away to avoid living under British control. In 1778, Cahokia was taken without resistance by troops of the Continental Congress of the United States and residents swore allegiance to their new country.

★ ★ ★ ★ ★ ★ ★ ★ ★ ★ ★ ★ ★ ★ ★ ★ ★ ★ ★ ★ ★ ★ ★ ★ ★ ★ ★ ★

**The oldest church in Illinois is the Holy Family Log
Church in Cahokia, built in 1799.**

Of course, today just about the only link to the community's
French roots is the fact that you can find french fries in most local
restaurants.

The Holy Family Parish Log Church is located at 116 Church Street
in Cahokia. A newer, larger main Catholic church was built in the late
twentieth century for regular services, but the old log church is open
for tours from Memorial Day weekend through Labor Day from 10
a.m. to 4 p.m. (except on Sunday when it opens at 11 a.m.). Church
services in Latin are held in the log church on Sunday at 9 a.m. For
more information, go to http://holyfamily1699.org.

**The hottest temperature ever recorded in Illinois was 117 degrees Fahrenheit, recorded on July 14, 1954, in East St. Louis.**

## The Oldest Wooden Building in Illinois
Cahokia

The Cahokia Courthouse, built in 1737 by Captain Jean Baptiste Saucier, the builder of Fort de Chartes, the main French military outpost in the region at the time, is considered the oldest wooden structure and oldest courthouse in the state. In 1793, the Common Pleas Court of the United States Northwest Territory purchased the building from Saucier's son to use as a territorial courthouse and public meeting place. In 1814, the county seat was relocated to Belleville and the 35-foot by 43-foot building was used as a saloon, storehouse, public hall, and even as a home during the next decades.

In 1904, the building was uprooted and moved to St. Louis to be exhibited at the Louisiana Purchase Exposition. Two years later, the Chicago Historical Society purchased the log structure and moved it to Jackson Park as part of an historic display. In 1938, Illinois state archaeologists excavated the original site of the courthouse in Cahokia and uncovered a number of artifacts and objects related to the building. A year later, as a federal Works Progress Administration (WPA) project, the building was completely reconstructed using as much of the original materials as available (unfortunately each time it was moved the building lost some of its original pieces) and re-erected at its original Cahokia location.

Architecturally, the courthouse is considered one of the best remaining examples of the same *poteaux-sur-solle* construction used to build the Holy Family Log Church. Structurally, it is a vertical log

**Built in 1737, the Cahokia Courthouse is the oldest wooden building in Illinois.**

building with a double-pitch roof of cedar shingles. The interior is divided into four rooms. It contains two large limestone fireplaces, shuttered casement windows, and French-style doors.

Today, the building, located at 107 Elm Street in Cahokia, is open for regular public tours. Rooms contain exhibits describing the history of the courthouse and a re-creation of a 1790s courtroom. For more information, go to www.illinoishistory.gov/hs/cahokia_courthouse.htm.

# Cairo—Where the Civil War Was Fought for Another Century

Few places in Illinois have as turbulent a history as the town of Cairo (pronounced Kare-row). Situated at the southernmost tip of Illinois, bordered on two sides by Kentucky and Missouri, Cairo is the most Southern-influenced community in the Northern state of Illinois. During the Civil War, Cairo, which sits where the Ohio and Mississippi Rivers join, became a key military camp and naval base for the Union forces. Following the war, the troops left and the town became the most racially segregated community in Illinois in spite of state and federal laws against discrimination. In the late 1960s, it experienced racial violence and rioting as well as a decade-long boycott of white-owned businesses (many closed rather than hire black workers). As a result the town, once an important shipping center, has declined. Today, the town's population of 3,000 is about one-fifth of what it once was at its peak in the 1920s, and many streets contain abandoned buildings.

### Illinois Notorious Pirate Cove
Cave-in-Rock State Park

As soon as you see Cave-in-Rock, you know why there are so many stories and legends associated with the place. Located on the edge of the Ohio River, it's a 55-foot-wide opening carved out of a limestone cliff by erosion. The mouth of the cave is slightly smaller (about 20 to 25 feet high) and narrower than the big main chamber and there's an opening in the cave ceiling that allows in a decent amount of light. Standing in the middle of the cave, it's easy to imagine it serving as a perfect location for a tavern or a trading post—or a hideout for outlaws and river pirates.

The first non–Native American to see the cave was M. de Lery of France who, in 1729, explored its inky depths and named it "caverne dans Le Roc," meaning cave in the rock. In the late eighteenth century, a man named Jim Wilson discovered the cave and converted it into a tavern known as "Wilson's Liquor Vault and House of Entertainment." Wilson quickly realized that the cave was a perfect hiding place for brigands, who could prey on passing boats.

After Wilson was killed by his own men, the cave was taken over by Samuel Mason, who gave it its official name, "Cave-in-Rock," and began inventing even more diabolical schemes to attract passing boats. Mason is said to have intentionally devised ways to make passing ships run aground so he and his crew could rob them.

Among the most notorious outlaws associated with the cave were Micajah (called "Big Harpe") and Wiley Harpe ("Little Harpe"), who have been described as America's first serial killers. The two cousins hailed from Tennessee and had escaped from prison in that state after being convicted of several murders. It's been said they didn't kill for profit like most thieves but because they enjoyed it. They joined up with Samuel Mason but were soon told to leave because their violence appalled even Mason's pirate gang.

In 1799, a posse tracked down Micajah and killed him. Wiley escaped and, along with another pirate, was responsible for killing Samuel Mason for the reward money. When the two tried to collect, however, Wiley was recognized and arrested. He was hanged in 1804. It's estimated that the two Harpes killed more than forty people.

By the late 1830s, Cave-in-Rock was cleaned out of its undesirable element and the area became more known for being a local landmark and, occasionally, a temporary shelter for pioneers heading west. In 1929, the state of Illinois acquired the cave and about sixty-four acres

Cave-in-Rock was once a notorious pirates' hangout.

of surrounding land for a park (the size has since increased to 204 acres). These days Cave-in-Rock State Park is a popular hiking, picnicking, and camping area. Additionally, the park has a lodge with four guesthouses for rent and a restaurant.

But no pirates.

For more information, go to dnr.state.il.us/lands/landmgt/parks/r5 /caverock.htm.

★ ★ ★ ★ ★ ★ ★ ★ ★ ★ ★ ★ ★ ★ ★ ★ ★ ★ ★ ★ ★ ★ ★ ★ ★ ★ ★ ★ ★ ★ ★

## Trivia

The state of Illinois is home to the second largest aviation system in the United States with 137 airports (eighty-three public and fifty-four private), 270 heliports, and more than 840 aviation facilities.

### Ode to a Spinach-Eating Sailorman
Chester

Popeye is a big deal in Chester. The town is the birthplace of Elzie Crisler Segar, the cartoonist who created the famed spinach-noshing, abnormally strong sailor. Over the years, it has become a shrine to the beloved comic strip character and his cartoon mates, including Olive Oyl, Wimpy, Bluto, and Swee' Pea. While Segar died in 1938 and is buried in California, in 1977 the community decided to remember him by erecting a 6-foot-tall bronze statue of his greatest creation in a park named in Segar's honor. In 1980, it also started the annual Popeye Picnic, a weekend-long event that celebrates his creations.

Popeye first appeared in Segar's popular "Thimble Theatre" newspaper comic strip on January 17, 1929. Within a short time, the pugnacious sailor with one eye and huge forearms had become the star of the strip, which had started in 1919. Over the years, Popeye has appeared in hundreds of cartoons, comic books, and, in 1980, a musical starring Robin Williams.

Part of the reason Chester is so proud of Segar, who was born there in 1894, is that the cartoonist based many of the characters in his strip on local residents. For instance, it's said Popeye was inspired by Frank "Rocky" Fiegle, a small, wiry man said to have been exceptionally strong as well as fast with his fists. Likewise J. Wellington Wimpy was physically similar to the rotund J. William Schuchert, the

Chester, birthplace of Popeye creator Elzie Segar,
commemorates that tie with statues of characters
from the popular comic strip and cartoons.

local opera house manager, for whom Segar once worked. It's said Schuchert, like Wimpy, had a fondness for hamburgers. Olive Oyl was loosely based on Dora Paskel, a tall, lanky woman who owned a general store in Chester. It's said she wore her hair in a bun, like Olive, and dressed similarly to how Segar drew the character, including wearing button-up shoes.

Starting in 2006, Chester has erected statues of additional characters from the comic strip throughout the community. For instance, a (more or less) life-size statue of Wimpy, holding a hamburger, was placed at the Chester Gazebo Square, while another depicting Olive Oyl, Swee' Pea, and Eugene the Jeep was installed near the county courthouse. A statue of Popeye's frequent adversary, Bluto, was erected in a bank parking lot, and one of Castor Oyl (Olive's brother) and the Whiffle Hen, was installed in front of the local hospital. The town plans to unveil a new statue each year until 2019, which will be Segar's 125th birthday. For more information, go to www.popeyethesailor.com.

## Ancient City of the Americas
Cahokia Mounds
Collinsville

The oldest known archaeological site in North America is Cahokia Mounds State Historic Site, located about 12 miles east of St. Louis, Missouri, near Collinsville, Illinois. Scientists say Native Americans (known as Late Woodland Indians) first settled the area in about AD 700. Over the next 400 years, a richly complex civilization developed that hunted, fished, and gathered as well as grew corn, squash, and seed-bearing plants. Despite that diet, the culture found the energy to construct large earthen mounds, apparently as burial mounds and temple mounds.

In Cahokia, an estimated 120 mounds of various sizes were built from "borrow pits" using stone and wood tools, with the dirt transported in baskets on people's backs. More than fifty million cubic feet of earth was moved to create the Cahokia Mounds. The biggest

Cahokia Mounds were the location of the largest prehistoric civilization north of Mexico.

of the Cahokia dirt hills is Monks Mound, which contains about twenty-two million cubic feet of earth. The rectangular mound is about fourteen acres at its base and rises to more than 100 feet high. Archaeologists have uncovered evidence of a large building that once stood on its summit, where the main chief is believed to have lived, performed religious ceremonies, and conducted business.

Cahokia's peak period was from AD 1050 to AD 1200, when the community is believed to have spread over 6 square miles and had a population of between 10,000 and 20,000 (it was the largest community north of Mexico). No one knows why such an apparently thriving civilization declined but by the late 1300s it was largely abandoned.

Interestingly, when the mounds were first recognized as something special in the nineteenth century, most scientists believed they were the work of the Toltec civilization of Mexico or some mysterious lost culture. Few believed that ancestors of the Native Americans could have designed and built such massive and complex earthen projects. It wasn't until 1894, after the Smithsonian Institute sent a team of archaeologists to study the site, that scientists established a direct link between the mound builders and Native Americans.

Today visitors can climb Monks Mound, named after French monks who lived in the area from 1809 to 1813 and farmed the terraces of the mound, and view reconstructions of an ancient stockade wall and "Woodhenge," a circle of wooden posts around a larger central post that uses sunlight to determine the season and time of the year. The 2,200-acre site preserves about seventy of the original mounds. A modern interpretive center is open daily 9 a.m. to 5 p.m. between May 1 and October 31 (it has reduced hours in the winter months). Guided tours of the site are available in the summer months.

Cahokia Mounds, located at 30 Ramey Street in Collinsville, is a National Historic Landmark as well as a World Heritage Site. Go to www.cahokiamounds.org for more information.

### A Colossal Condiment
Collinsville

When the G. S. Suppiger catsup bottling plant, which bottled Brooks Catsup, decided to build a water tower near its Collinsville facility in 1949, it didn't just erect one of those boring round balls or big cylindrical tanks on stilts. It went for something more creative—it put up the world's largest catsup bottle.

Nearly 70 feet tall atop a 100-foot steel base, the big steel catsup bottle, which looks just like a Brooks catsup (that's how the company spelled ketchup back in the day) bottle, was designed by the

This giant replica of a Brooks Catsup bottle (actually a water tower) is considered the world's largest ketchup bottle.

★ ★ ★ ★ ★ ★ ★ ★ ★ ★ ★ ★ ★ ★ ★ ★ ★ ★ ★ ★ ★ ★ ★ ★ ★ ★ ★ ★ ★ ★ ★ ★

W. E. Caldwell Tank Company of Louisville, Kentucky, which also constructed a 120-foot water tower shaped like a Louisville Slugger bat in its hometown. The Brooks Catsup water tower, which originally cost about $24,000, is said to be big enough to hold 100,000 gallons of water—or about twenty-five million servings of catsup.

By the 1970s, however, the Collinsville landmark had fallen on hard times. Brooks Catsup was no longer produced at the nearby plant. The bright red and white paint on the iconic water tower had faded and begun to peel. The world's largest catsup bottle had begun to look more like the world's biggest eyesore.

Fortunately, a group of local volunteers decided to try to save the big bottle. In 1993, the Catsup Bottle Preservation Group was founded to work with the water tower's owners to restore it to its original splendor. Over the following two years, the volunteer group raised enough money to repaint and repair the tower. In 1998, the Brooks Largest Catsup Bottle Festival was started as an annual event to celebrate the successful restoration of the bottle. The event, held every July since then, includes a hot dog eating contest, Hula Hoop contest, a catsup tasting contest, and a car show. In 2009, the tower was again repainted, this time by its owner, Bethel-Eckert Enterprises, a company that supplies dried, chilled, and frozen grocery foods to the U.S. military (but, surprisingly, not catsup!).

The world's largest catsup bottle is located at 800 South Morrison Avenue in Collinsville, just south of the downtown area.

*Trivia*

**Illinois has only about 2,300 acres of high quality prairie land remaining, compared to more than twenty-two million acres in 1820.**

★ ★ ★ ★ ★ ★ ★ ★ ★ ★ ★ ★ ★ ★ ★ ★ ★ ★ ★ ★ ★ ★ ★ ★ ★ ★ ★ ★ ★ ★

## Sculpted by the Almighty
Garden of the Gods

Few places in Illinois are as naturally beautiful as the appropriately named Garden of the Gods Wilderness Area. Located 59 miles southeast of Carbondale, the 3,300-acre wilderness area is tucked inside the Shawnee National Forest.

A large part of what makes this hunk of land especially scenic is that it is so different from the rest of Illinois. The wilderness area includes several thousand acres of old growth forests (meaning they've never been cut down) as well as unexpectedly beautiful

**Rock formations at Garden of the Gods**

★ ★ ★ ★ ★ ★ ★ ★ ★ ★ ★ ★ ★ ★ ★ ★ ★ ★ ★ ★ ★ ★ ★ ★ ★ ★ ★ ★ ★ ★ ★ ★ ★ ★

sandstone cliffs and unusual rock formations. According to scientists, the Garden of the Gods area was formed about 320 million years ago when a thick bed of grayish sandstone covered Southern Illinois. This layer of rock was later uplifted, and then carved by erosion to create the hoodoos (tall, thin spires of rock), giant rounded boulders, and other rock formations found in the garden. Interestingly, the region was never covered by glaciers, like much of the rest of Illinois, so there is no evidence of glacial scarring.

The result is a place that just doesn't resemble any other place in Illinois. Visitors who take the short but fairly steep quarter-mile Observation Trail through the garden are treated to a plethora of magnificent sights. In addition to the 100-foot-high bluffs, the garden includes unusual formations with names such as Camel Rock (it looks like a big dromedary with a single hump), Anvil Rock (looks just like an old anvil), and Table Rock (yup, it's flat like a table top). There is also a two-legged formation called Big H Rock (shaped like the eighth letter of the alphabet) and Devil's Smokestack (a stand-alone rock pillar).

Garden of the Gods Wilderness Area is located off IL 34 and Karbers Ridge Road. For more information, go to www.shawneeforest.com /Hiking/GardenoftheGods.apx.

*Trivia*

The coldest recorded temperature in Illinois was -36 degrees Fahrenheit on January 5, 1999 in Congerville (located 24 miles south of Peoria).

# Land of the Giants, Giant City State Park

Another spectacular natural spot found in the Shawnee National Forest is the Giant City State Park, a collection of picturesque sandstone bluffs and canyons that served as rock shelters for Native Americans as far back as 10,000 years ago. The 4,000-acre park, created in 1927, was named in the nineteenth century by early visitors who thought its tall, narrow bluffs, which can rise to 80 feet, reminded them of the narrow streets of a city, which because of the size of the walls would have been inhabited by giants. The bluffs and rock formations were created more than 20,000 years ago by the melting water of a Pleistocene glacier. The area wasn't developed for public use until the early 1930s, when Civilian Conservation Corps (CCC) had three work camps in the park to build trails as well as stone picnic shelters and the impressive Giant City Lodge.

The park, located 12 miles south of Carbondale via East Walnut Street and North Giant City Road, has a visitor center that includes exhibits on the park and its natural history and a gift shop. For more information, go to dnr.state.il.us/lands/landmgt/parks/r5/gc.htm.

### A Visit to Satan's Spiny Ridge

Devil's Backbone and Bake Oven
Grand Tower

Perhaps the most amazing thing about visiting the Devil's Backbone and Devil's Bake Oven is how pretty and scenic they are in spite of their demonic names. In fact, after reading all the scary literature on the Internet about both—they're supposedly among the more haunted spots in Illinois—one would have expected to find them to be a misty, dark place with strange noises, weird shadows, and unexpected cold spots. But instead, there's actually a nice little campground and picnic area called Devil's Backbone Park adjacent to the two landmarks. And since both the spine and the oven are covered with trees and thick green foliage, they appear downright pastoral rather than frightening.

The tales about Devil's Backbone and Bake Oven date to the eighteenth century, when river travelers first reported the presence of deadly rapids at the base of nearby Tower Rock, a steep hunk of land that juts out of the Mississippi near the town of Grand Tower. Supposedly the Native Americans had long been aware of this water hazard and, in an attempt to warn away others, told stories of evil spirits living in this stretch of the river. Against this backdrop, the rocky ridge adjacent to Tower Rock became known as the Devil's Backbone and a larger rock mound at the end of the ridge became the Devil's Bake Oven.

In the early 1800s, Devil's Backbone and Bake Oven became known as hiding places for hostile Native Americans and river pirates, who preyed on passing steamboats. The boats would slow to navigate the rapids and sometimes crew would disembark from the vessel in order to use ropes to tow it through the rapids—making the ship an easy target. In the mid-nineteenth century, a small iron manufacturing industry cropped up in the area; two iron furnaces operated on the west side of the Backbone until about 1870. Additionally, several houses were built around the Bake Oven, including the foundry superintendent's home on top of the Bake Oven.

The latter site, where you can still find the stone foundations, is allegedly one of the region's most haunted locations. According to local legend, the ghost of the beautiful daughter (are there any other kind in ghost stories?) of the former superintendent still wanders the site. It's said that her father was excessively protective and wouldn't allow her to accept suitors. One day, however, she fell in love with a

**Devil's Bake Oven and ruins of an old foundry near Grand Tower**

particularly handsome young man who tried to call on her. When the father turned away the young man, the daughter began slipping out of the house to meet him secretly at night. The father discovered her deceit and persuaded or paid the young man to move on. The daughter became so distraught that she wept for weeks and soon died, either of grief or some illness. Since then, folks have reported seeing a strange, ghostly shape resembling a young woman, which supposedly wanders the former site of the superintendent's house. There have also been claims of crying and moaning at night, supposedly the ghost still kvetching about her lost love.

★ ★ ★ ★ ★ ★ ★ ★ ★ ★ ★ ★ ★ ★ ★ ★ ★ ★ ★ ★ ★ ★ ★ ★ ★ ★ ★ ★ ★ ★ ★

It is perhaps appropriate the final words about Devil's Backbone and Devil's Bake Oven should come from writer Mark Twain, who satirized the region's plethora of satanic-sounding names in his 1883 memoir, *Life on the Mississippi*. Twain, who once piloted riverboats through the area, wrote that near Grand Tower is "the Devil's Bake Oven—so called, perhaps, because it does not powerfully resemble anybody else's bake oven; and the Devil's Tea-table . . . away down the river we have the Devil's Elbow and the Devil's Race-course, and lots of other property of his which I cannot now call to mind."

Devil's Backbone and Bake Oven are located off IL 3, adjacent to the tiny hamlet of Grand Tower. Follow the signs to Devil's Backbone Park; the Backbone and the Oven are located directly north of the park, just past an elevated natural gas pipe bridge.

# Illinois's Cursed First Capital

In 1809 when Illinois became a U.S. territory, the settlement of Kaskaskia, which had been established by the French in 1703, was designated the territorial capital. At the time, Kaskaskia, located about 18 miles west of Chester, was an important trading post and one of the largest communities in the region. Kaskaskia lost the capital in 1818, when Illinois gained statehood, and the new state capital was shifted to Vandalia (which, in turn, lost the capital to Springfield in 1837). As for Kaskaskia, about twenty-five years later most of the town was wiped away when the Mississippi River shifted out of its channel.

# Birthplace of Memorial Day— Maybe, Carbondale

On April 29, 1866, a group of Civil War veterans marched through the town of Carbondale and gathered at Woodlawn Cemetery to commemorate their fallen comrades. General John A. Logan, a Civil War hero and native of nearby Murphysboro, spoke at the service, which attracted a good-size crowd. According to Carbondale boosters, that event marked the first ever Memorial Day (originally called Decoration Day) observation. Two years later, General Logan, then serving as National Commander of the Grand Army of the Republic, issued a formal proclamation creating a national Memorial Day. Of course, like all such matters, not everyone buys Carbondale's role in the creation of the Memorial Day holiday. In fact, some two dozen communities claim to be the holiday's birthplace. In 1966, President Lyndon Johnson declared that Waterloo, New York, was the official birthplace, which seemed to settle the issue. Or not. Carbondale, as well as several of the other contenders, continues to maintain it was first. "It was here," insisted Carbondale mayor Brad Cole in a 2007 *Chicago Tribune* story.

### It's a Bird, It's a Plane, It's a Statue
Metropolis

Superman began regularly appearing in Metropolis when Jim Hambrick—not Clark Kent—moved into the community.

While Hambrick can't fly and doesn't have X-ray vision, he does have more than 100,000 Superman-related collectibles ranging from the bright green kryptonite crystal used to create the "Fortress of Solitude"

in the 1978 Christopher Reeve movie to the brown and gray costume
(for black and white filming) worn by actor George Reeves in the 1950s
TV show. Hambrick operates the Superman Museum and Superstore
gift shop, which displays about 20,000 items from his massive Man of
Steel collection (he continually rotates stuff in and out of the museum).
He is a lifelong Superman memorabilia collector and dealer, who
moved his collection of all things super to Metropolis in 1993.

Superman's formal involvement with Metropolis—besides the fact
Metropolis is his home base in his comic book adventures—began in
the early 1970s when Robert Westerfield, now deceased, relocated to
Metropolis from Kentucky and wondered why there wasn't some type
of association with the world-famous superhero character. Through
his efforts, the town gained official recognition as Superman's hometown via a proclamation of the Illinois Legislature and formal recognition from DC Comics, publishers of the *Superman* comic books
in 1972. Additionally, the local newspaper changed its name to the
*Metropolis Planet* (the *Daily Planet* is the name of the fictional newspaper in Superman's hometown).

In 1973, the Amazing World of Superman Museum opened and
plans for a $50 million Amazing World of Superman theme park in
Metropolis were unveiled. Funding for the park, however, fell through
and a year later the museum closed. In 1978, with the release of a
new *Superman* movie, the town tried once again to capitalize on its
Superman connection by creating the annual Superman Celebration
(held each June) and, in 1986, erecting a 7-foot, fiberglass statue of

*Trivia*

The state of Illinois measures about 400 miles from its northern border to its southernmost tip.

**Statue of Superman in the center of Metropolis**

the Man from Krypton in the center of the town. When that statue—
now owned by Hambrick—proved to be less than invulnerable to
vandals, the community raised more than $100,000 and, in 1993,
replaced it with a more striking 15-foot bronze Superman statue that
stands in front of the courthouse.

These days, Metropolis is a super place with plenty of super things
to remind you you're in Superman's town. Outside of Hambrick's
Superman Museum is a phone booth in which visitors can pretend to
be changing into Superman. The annual Superman Celebration draws
more than 30,000 super fans, attracted by the presence of Superman-
related celebrities. In recent years, guests have included stars from
the *Smallville* TV show and the various Superman movies. In 2010,
the community erected a second statue, a life-size bronze image of
actress Noel Neill, garbed as Lois Lane, Superman's girlfriend (Neill
played the character in the 1950s TV show and showed up for the
dedication of the statue).

It's all quite super, man.

The Superman statue, which is a popular location for photos (President Barack Obama posed in front of it during his 2008 campaign)
stands in front of the Massac County Courthouse at 1 Superman
Square in downtown Metropolis. The Lois Lane statue is on the corner
of Eighth and Market Streets. Hambrick's Superman Museum and
Superstore is down the street at 611 Market Street.

## *Trivia*

**Kaskaskia Island is the only part of Illinois that is located west of the
Mississippi River.**

# The Birdman's Final Nesting Place

One of Alcatraz's most famous prisoners, Robert Stroud, aka the Birdman of Alcatraz, is buried in Metropolis. So what's the connection between the Birdman and Superman's town? It turns out that Stroud's mother grew up in Metropolis and was buried there. When he died, his family put him in a grave next to her. Ironically, Stroud didn't have many ties to the community. He was born in Seattle, Washington, arrested for murder in Alaska, killed a prison guard, and spent the rest of his life in federal penitentiaries in Leavenworth, Kansas, and Alcatraz in California. While in prison he gained fame for raising canaries and developing methods for helping them to combat diseases. He died of natural causes in a federal prison hospital in Springfield, Missouri, on November 21, 1963 (the day before President Kennedy was assassinated). His grave is marked with a simple headstone, and someone has placed a small ceramic canary beside his final resting place.

## Some Pig!

Grave of King Neptune
Mount Pleasant

King Neptune may just have been the most expensive piece of pork in history. During World War II, the 700-pound pig raised more than $19 million in war bonds—or about $27,143 per pound.

The story of King Neptune began in the early 1940s, when he was donated by a West Frankfort farmer to a Navy recruiter to be eaten during a fundraising pig roast. The recruiter, Don Lingle, however, came up with an alternative idea. He decided to auction the pig to

★ ★ ★ ★ ★ ★ ★ ★ ★ ★ ★ ★ ★ ★ ★ ★ ★ ★ ★ ★ ★ ★ ★ ★ ★ ★ ★ ★

**Grave of the famous pig, King Neptune**

raise money for war bonds. At the end of the auction, the winner would return the pig to be auctioned again later. In this way, King Neptune could be sold over and over, each time raising money for the war effort.

After the war, King Neptune was scheduled to be sent to the Chicago Stockyards to be slaughtered, but Lingle gained ownership and placed him on a farm in the Mount Pleasant area where the animal spent the remainder of his days—as happy, you might say, as a pig in slop. After Neptune died in 1950, Lingle had him buried with full military honors on land about 6 miles east of the town of Anna, off IL 146. A headstone was placed on the grave that read: BURIED HERE—KING

NEPTUNE, FAMOUS NAVY MASCOT PIG AUCTIONED FOR $19,000,000 IN WAR BONDS 1942–1946 TO HELP MAKE A FREE WORLD.

In 1957, the state of Illinois relocated King Neptune's grave during the construction of I-57. His tombstone was moved to a new site about a mile east of the intersection of IL 146 and I-57. By the late 1980s, that stone had been heavily vandalized so the state refurbished it and moved it to a new location near exit 31 on I-57, where it can still be found. Some pig indeed.

## It Came from the Muck

Murphysboro

Murphysboro is a quiet agricultural town of about 13,000 residents located 8 miles northwest of Carbondale. It's a modest town built along the Big Muddy River and surrounded by dense woods. It's the kind of place that has one of those official blue Tourist Attraction signs indicating the location of the "Big Top Bait Shop."

Over the past half century, however, residents have been visited on several occasions by a strange creature usually described as being 7 to 8 feet tall, having mud-caked white or gray fur, weighing more than 300 pounds, and smelling terrible. Known as the Big Muddy Monster or the Murphysboro Mud Monster, he (or she) was initially spotted in the vicinity of the Big Muddy River, hence the name, and has shown up in other parts of the community over the years.

The earliest reports appeared in the 1950s, but the most publicized sightings occurred between June and July of 1973. The first was shortly after midnight on June 25, when Randy Needham and Judy Johnson were parked in a car near a boat ramp at the southwestern edge of Riverside Park on the edge of the Big Muddy. As the *New York Times* reported later that year, "the couple heard a loud cry from the woods next to the car . . . Needham looked up from the front seat. There, lumbering toward the open window was a light-colored, hairy, seven-foot creature matted with mud."

**Riverside Park, where the Murphysboro Mud Monster was first seen in 1973**

The story said that Needham drove to the police station and filed an "unknown creature" report. The police took Needham and Johnson's claim seriously because Johnson was married—but not to Needham—so coming forward was potentially scandalous.

The following day police investigators studied the scene of the sighting and found "peculiar" footprints in the mud. One of the officers, Jimmie Nash, told the *Times*, "I was leaning over when there was the most incredible shriek I've ever heard . . . It was in those bushes. That was no bobcat or screech owl and we hightailed it out of there."

A day later, residents of a farmhouse outside of town, but near the river, heard similar shrieking sounds and four-year-old Christian

Baril told his father he had seen a "big ghost out back." Later that same night, two teenagers, Randy Creath and Cheryl Ray, were on the porch of her parents' home when they heard something in the brush. When they turned on the lights, they suddenly encountered a towering creature resembling a white gorilla covered with mud. They reported that it had the foul odor of river slime.

There would be two other reports of the creature later that summer, and then it was all over. Despite a department wide "creature-hunt," the local police came up empty-handed. Since then many have unsuccessfully sought to catch a glimpse of the big, hairy, monster that seems to live around the Big Muddy River. If you decide to give it a try, the best advice is to just follow your nose.

## The Old Slave House

Shawneetown

One of the creepiest places in Illinois—which is saying a lot in a state that is home to John Wayne Gacy and H. H. Holmes—is the Crenshaw House, also known as the Old Slave House or Hickory Hill near Shawneetown. The three-story mansion, which overlooks the Saline Valley, was built in 1834 by John Hart Crenshaw, a wealthy local salt mine operator. According to many historians, Crenshaw used slave labor in his mines, despite the fact that slavery was illegal in Illinois. Apparently, there was an exemption in the law that allowed Crenshaw and other mine operators to lease slaves from owners in slave territories.

However, Crenshaw is believed to have gone beyond simply leasing a few slaves to work in the salt mines. It is said that he became actively involved in kidnapping free blacks and runaway slaves and making them work in his mines (or selling them off). Proof of his unsavory activities can be found in the mansion's attic, which consists of about a dozen cell-like rooms with barred windows, chains, and small wooden bunks.

Crenshaw's illegal operations came to a halt after 1842, when he was indicted for kidnapping a free black woman and her children.

While he was acquitted of the crime, rumors began to swirl about his activities. One of his salt works mysteriously burned down and, while it was rebuilt, it marked the start of a decline in his business. By the early 1860s, Crenshaw had sold the mansion and moved to a small farm near, ironically, a town named Equality. He died on December 4, 1871.

As for his slave house, it was purchased in 1906 by the Sisk family, which turned it into a roadside attraction in the 1920s. Visitors could tour the old house and hear some of the legends and stories associated with it. That's also when there began to be reports about strange moaning noises and other weird sounds. According to Troy Taylor, author of *Weird Illinois*, and the www.prairieghosts.com website, "a number of people told of uncomfortable feelings in the slave quarters like sensations of intense fear, sadness and of being watched. They also told of cold chills, being touched by invisible hands and feeling unseen figures brush by them."

In 1996, the aging mansion, the floors of which had begun to sag, was closed to the public. A few years later, it was purchased by the state of Illinois, which announced plans to renovate it and reopen it as a state historic site. The state, however, has not had the funding to proceed so there's no timetable for when that might occur.

The Old Slave House is located about 5 miles south of the intersection of IL 45 and Route 13.

# index

## A

Abingdon, 136–38
Abraham Lincoln Presidential Library and Museum, 200, 202–3
accordion player, 216–17
Adler Planetarium, 61
African Americans, 3
Alsip, 3–4
Alton, 138–44
Amboy, 107–9
Amish, 223–24, 225–27
antiques, 195
apples, 227
arch, 198
archaeological site, 264–66
architecture, 29–31, 40–43, 45–47, 51–53, 67–68, 80, 100–101, 102, 103, 129–31, 164–66, 181, 185–87, 195, 257–58
Arcola, 225–27, 228–29, 230
Art Institute of Chicago, 47–49
Ashmore, 230–33
Atlanta, 173
Aurora, 5–6
aviation system, 262

## B

Bachelor's Grove Cemetery, 94–96
bagels, 247
Baha'i House of Worship, 100–101, 103

Balaji Temple, 5–6
Balbo Monument, 55–56
BAPS Shri Swaminarayan Mandir, 8–10
barbecue, 254
barbed wire, 109–11
barn, round, 181
Barrington, 6–8
Bartlett, 8–10
Bartonville, 174–76
baseball, 13–14, 53–55
Bath, 176–78
Beach Guy, 195
BEER NUTS, 182–84
Belushi, John, 12, 91
Benville, 145–47
Bertelli, Roy, 216–17
Berwyn, 10–11
big bluestem, 212
Bigfoot, 184
Big Muddy Monster, 281–83
Billy Goat Tavern, 12–14
Biograph Theater, 71–73
Birdman of Alcatraz, 279
birds, 152–53, 161
Bishop Hill, 178–80
Bloomington, 182–84
bluegill, 118
blues music, 64–67
bridges, 158–59
Bryan, William Jennings, 251
Buckingham Fountain, 39–40
burial mounds, 189–91, 264–66

Burnham Park, 55–56

Burr Oak Cemetery, 3–4

butter cow, 206–7

Byron, 108

## C

Cabet, Étienne, 162–63

Cahokia, 255–58

Cahokia Mounds, 264–66

Cairo, 259

Calvary Cemetery, 169

Capone, Al, 16–18

Carbondale, 275

cardinal, 161

carp, 176–78

Carthage, 147–49

castle, 164–66

catsup bottle, world's largest, 266–68

cave home, 173

Cave-in-Rock State Park, 259–61

cemeteries, 3–4, 6–8, 84–86, 92–96, 169, 174–76, 191–92, 204–6, 216–17

chainsaw art, 107–9

Charles Mound, 125

Cheap Trick, 125

Chess Records, 64–67

Chester, 262–64

chest measurement, largest, 147

Chicago, 12–81

Chicago area, 1–103

Chicago Bears, 192

Chicago Cubs, 13–14, 53–55

Chicago Cultural Center, 67–68

Chicago River, 14, 38

chilli, 212–14

Choo-Choo Restaurant, 89

churches. *See* houses of worship

Collinsville, 264–66, 266–68

corn brooms, 230

corn dogs, 209–11

costumes, 128

covered wagon, world's largest, 193–94

cow made of butter, 206–7

crime, 3–4, 16–18, 71–76, 90–91, 218–19, 259–61

cross, world's largest, 234–36

Crown Fountain, 20

Cry Baby bridge, 158–59

## D

Dairy Queen, 86–88

Danville, 237

Decatur, 187, 192

Deere, John, 114, 212

DeKalb, 109–11

Des Plaines, 81, 83–84, 89

Devil's Backbone and Bake Oven, 271–74

Dickson Mounds, 189–91

Dillinger, John, 71–73

dinosaurs, 33

Dixon, 105–6, 111–13

dog poop, 62–64

dragon, 220–21

Drummer silty clay loam, 232

Dutch Days Festival, 115–16

**E**

Earp, Wyatt, 155–58
Ebert, Roger, 233
Effingham, 234–36
elephants, 84–86, 163–64
Excalibur nightclub, 69–71

**F**

factory
 world's largest bagel, 247
 world's largest cookie and
  cracker, 39
farm equipment, 114
farms, 176
fascism, 55–56
Ferris Wheel, 75
Field Museum, 24–26, 33
Fighting Leathernecks, 157
films, 233
fire, 37, 154–55
fish, 176–78
fluorite, 35
flying saucer, 195
food, 12–14, 21–24, 27, 28, 39,
 43–45, 81, 83–84, 86–88, 89,
 182–84, 189, 207-14, 239–40,
 245–46, 250–51, 254
football, 192
Forest Park, 84–86
Forgottonia, 134–35
fountain, 20, 39–40
Francis, Frederick, 185–87

Fulton, 115–16
funeral homes, 98–99
 drive-up viewing, 81

**G**

Galena, 119
Galesburg, 149–51
Garden of the Gods, 269–70
gardens, 225–27
Gateway Arch, 198
Gatling's Chapel, 81
Gays, 237–39
ghosts. *See* haunted places
Giant City State Park, 271
Gold Coast neighborhood, 78–80
gold-plated object, world's larg-
 est, 129
Grand Tower, 271–74
Grant, Ulysses S., 119
Griggsville, 152–53
Groundhog Day, 130

**H**

Hambrick, Jim, 275–78
hamburgers, 239–40
haunted places, 6–8, 35–36,
 69–71, 92–96, 120–21,
 142–44, 158–59, 164–68, 187,
 272–73, 283–84
Heath Bars, 245–46
heaviest man, 145–47
Hefner, Hugh, 78–80
Hemingway, Ernest, 96–98
highest point, 125

# index

hippies, 228–29

historic places, 90–91, 96–98, 111–13, 114, 119, 149–51, 155–58, 189–91, 251, 255–56, 257–58, 283–84

hitchhikers, 92–94

hogs, 191

Holmes, H. H., 73–76

Holy Family Log Church, 255–56

Horseshoe sandwich, 207–9

hot air balloons, 237

hot dogs, 27

houses of worship, 5–6, 8–10, 100–101, 103, 255–56

Hughes, Robert Earl, 145–47

Hull House, 34–36

Huntley, 108

## I

Icarians, 162–63

ice cream cone–shaped building, 195

Illinois

central, 170–221

eastern, 222–51

geographic center of, 180

government, 144

highest natural point, 125

northern, 104–31

southern, 252–84

state animal, 245

state bird, 161

state dance, 29

state fish, 118

state flower, 111

state fossil, 34

state fruit, 227

state insect, 113

state mineral, 35

state motto, 129

state prairie grass, 212

state snack food, 12

state soil, 232

state tree, 111

western, 132–69

Illinois State Fair, 206–7

Indian statue, 82, 116–18

International Museum of Surgical Science, 66

Italian beef sandwiches, 28

## J

James R. Thompson Center, 45–47

Jesus Tree, 169

Johnson-Sauk Trail State Park, 181

Joliet, 86–88, 90–91

Justice, 92–94

## K

Kaskaskia, 274, 278

Kenar, Jerzy S., 62–64

ketchup bottle, world's largest, 266–68

Kewanee, 181, 185–87, 188, 191

King Neptune, 279–81

# index

## L

lake, manmade, 253–54
Lakeview Museum, 201
laundromat, world's largest, 10–11
Lawn Rangers, 230
leaning tower, 102
Lewistown, 189–92
libraries, 67–68, 200, 202–3
Lincoln, 192–94
Lincoln, Abraham, 171–72, 192–94, 200, 202–6, 230–33
Lincoln Park Zoo, 49–51
Lincoln's Tomb, 204–6
lions, 24–26
Livingston, 195
lungfish, 58–60

## M

Macomb, 154–55
Mad Gasser of Mattoon, 241–43
man, heaviest, 145–47
man, tallest, 140–42
Manhattan Project, 31–32
Marine Corps, U. S., 157
maritime museum, 248–50
Martinsville, 239–40
mascot attire, 128
mass hysteria, 242
Masters, Edgar Lee, 191–92
Mattoon, 241–43, 247
mausoleum, 49
mayonnaise, 250–51
McDonald's, 81, 83–84

meatpacking, 43–45
Memorial Day, 275
Metropolis, 275–78, 279
Midlothian, 94–96
Military Museum, 214–16
Military Tract of 1812, 136
Millennium Park, 20
Millennium Park Bean, 14–16
Mineral Springs Hotel, 142–44
miniature golf, 98–99
miniature rooms, 47–49
Miracle Whip, 250–51
Moline, 212
monarch butterfly, 113
Monmouth, 155–59
monsters, 281–83
Moomaw, Bob, 228–29
Moonshine Burger, 239–40
Moran, "Bugs," 16–18
Mormons, 147–49, 159–61
Morton, 189
Mount Carroll, 120–21
Mount Pleasant, 279–81
mousetrap, 138
Murder Castle, 73–76
Murphysboro, 281–83
Museum of Science and Industry, 57–58
museums, 24–26, 35, 47–49, 57–61, 66, 76–78, 126–27, 190–91, 196–97, 200, 201, 202–3, 214–16, 245–46, 248–50, 276

music, 64–67

**N**

national forest, 253–54
National Museum of Ship Models and Sea History, 248–50
native peoples, 189–91, 272
Nauvoo, 159–61, 162–63
Navy Pier, 76–78
Niles, 102
nuclear reaction, 31–32

**O**

Oak Hill Cemetery, 191–92
Oak Park, 96–98
Oak Ridge Cemetery, 204–6, 216–17
office building, 45–47, 51–53
Olney, 243–45, 248
Oquawka, 163–64
Oregon, 116–18
Oreo cookies, 39
outhouse, double-decker, 237–39. *See also* restrooms
Overlooked Film Festival, 233

**P**

Palatine, 98–99
parks, 49–51, 102, 187, 259–61, 271
Peoria, 194, 197, 198, 201
Phillips, Irna, 234
Piasa bird, 138–40
pictograph, 138–40

pig, 279–81
Pink Elephant Antiques Mall, 195
pirates, 259–61, 272
pizza, 21–24
planetarium, 61
*Playboy* magazine, 78–80
poems, 191–92
Polish community, 22
Pontiac, 196–97
popcorn, 12
Popeye, 262–64
Port Byron, 122
prairie land, 268
prison, 90–91
pumpkin, canned, 189
purple martins, 152–53
pyramid, 129–31

**Q**

Quincy, 164–66, 169

**R**

Raven's Grin Inn, 120–21
Reagan, Ronald, 105–6, 111–13
Redneck Fishing Tournament, 176–78
Reeves, George, 151
restaurants. *See* food
restrooms, 46, 50–51, 51. *See also* outhouse
Resurrection Mary, 92–94
river otter, 188
Robie House, 29–31
Robinson, 245–46

Rockford, 105, 123–25
rock formations, 269–70
Rockome Gardens, 225–27
Roscoe, 126–27
Route 66, 194, 196–97

**S**

Sadorus, 248–50
Salem, 250–51
Sandburg, Carl, 149–51
sandwiches, 28, 207–9
Savanna, 128
sculpture, 14–16, 55–56, 62–64, 107–9, 116–18, 136–38, 206–7, 220–21, 228–29. *See also* statues
Sears Tower, 51–53
Segar, Elzie Crisler, 262–64
settlement house, 34–36
Shawnee National Forest, 269–70
Shawneetown, 283–84
Shedd Aquarium, 58–60
Shelbyville, 197, 199–200
skyscrapers, 51–53, 80
slave house, 283–84
Smith, Joseph, 147–49, 159–61
Smith Museum of Stained Glass Windows, 76–78
soap operas, 234
sock monkeys, 123–25
solar power, 10, 248
solar system, largest scale model of, 201
*Spoon River Anthology,* 191–92

Springfield, 171–72, 200, 202–17
square dancing, 29
squirrels, albino, 243–45
St. Patrick's Day, 14
stained glass, 67–68, 76–78
Starved Rock State Park, 218–19
statues, 31–32, 82, 84–86, 109, 116–18, 192–94, 195, 230–33, 262–64, 276–78. *See also* sculpture
Stockyards, 43–45
submarine, German, 57–58
Superman, 151, 275–78
surgical sciences, 66
Swedish village, 178–80

**T**

Taft, Lorado, 116–18
tallest man, 140–42
temperature
    coldest, 270
    hottest, 257
temples. *See* houses of worship
Tennessee, 166–68
theme park, 225–27
Thirteenth Amendment, 123
toilets. *See* outhouse; restrooms
totem pole, 136–38
trains, 89
Tribune Tower, 40–43
tug-of-war, 122
turkey drop, 237
turkeys, 108

# index

## U

University of Illinois, 233
Urbana-Champaign, 233
Utica, 218–19
utopia, 162–63

## V

Valentine's Day massacre, 16–18
Vandalia, 220–21
vehicles, historic, 126–27
violet, 111
Vishnu Springs, 166–68

## W

Wadlow, Robert Pershing, 140–42
Wadsworth, 129–31
Walgreen's drugstores, 63, 113
war bonds, 279–81
wedding chapel on wheels, 197,
    199–200

White Cemetery, 6–8
white oak, 111
white-tailed deer, 245
Willey, Wonet, 154–55
Willis Tower, 51–53
Wilmette, 100–101, 103
windmill, 115–16
Windy City, 42
wineries, 163
Winfrey, Oprah, 18–19, 21
wooden building, oldest, 257–58
wooden leg, 214–16
Woodland Palace, 185–87
Woodlawn Cemetery, 84–86, 275
Woodstock, 130
Wrigley Field, 13, 53–55

## Z

zoo, 49–51

# about the author

***

**Richard Moreno is** the author of ten books, including *Nevada Curiosities* and *Mysteries and Legends of Nevada* for GPP. He works as a journalism instructor and is the Director of Student Publications at Western Illinois University. He resides in Macomb, Illinois, with his wife and two children.